The Holy Temple In Jerusalem

מגיד
MAGGID

Rav Yisrael Ariel

The Holy Temple In Jerusalem

Maggid Books

The Holy Temple in Jerusalem
Rav Yisrael Ariel

First English edition, 2018

Maggid Books
An imprint of Koren Publishers Jerusalem Ltd.

POB 8531, New Milford, CT 06776-8531, USA
& POB 4044, Jerusalem 9104001, Israel
www.maggidbooks.com

The publication of this book was made possible through the generous support of *Torah Education in Israel.*

ISBN 978-1-59264-517-6, hardcover

A CIP catalogue record for this title is available from the British Library.

Printed and bound in the United States

In Honor of

The Shraga Family

With Great Appreciation
For Your Dedication and Support

Translation: Rabbi Hillel Fendel

Editing: Rabbi Yonatan Shai Freedman and Dr. Julia Borenstein

Typesetting: Tomi Mager

Cover Design: Eliyahu Misgav

Contents

Foreword

"Better is the sight of the eyes than the wandering of the desire." Thus wrote the wisest of men, King Solomon (Ecclesiastes 6:9)

Demonstration and actualization are basic tools of study, and all the more so when dealing with the Holy Temple and its service.

Moses, Father of the Prophets, was Divinely instructed to build the Tabernacle – and even he could do so only after seeing a picture of it with his own eyes. God told him (Exodus 25:8), "Have them make for Me a sanctuary and I will dwell in their midst; according to all that I show you the pattern of the Tabernacle and all its utensils, so shall you make them."

And in fact, the Midrash (*Bemidbar Rabba* 15:4) teaches that Moshe understood the work of the Menorah only after he saw it with his own eyes:

"He had difficulty understanding what the Menorah should look like, more than any other vessel in the Mishkan – until finally Hashem showed him exactly . . . As is written: 'Like the vision that God showed Moses, so was the Menorah made'" (Numbers 8:4).

When Israel used to make the Festival pilgrimage to Jerusalem, they would never cease to be amazed at the Temple's beauty. The Talmud teaches us that the Sages would take special measures to show off the glory of the Holy Temple to the nation. For instance, in Tractate *Yoma* (54a) we read: "When Israel would arrive for the Festivals, the curtain of the Temple would be rolled back so that they could see the Cherubim . . . and the Sages would say: 'Look at how beloved you are before God, like that of the love between male and female.'" Similarly, they would show them the Golden Menorah and the table of the showbread, as stated in Tractate *Chagiga* (26b): "They would lift it [the table] and show the pilgrims the showbread, and say to them: Look at how beloved you are before God, for the bread's removal is as its placement," i.e., it remains as warm and fresh after several days as the day it was baked and placed on the Table.

This, actually, is one of the purposes of the thrice-annual Festival pilgrimage to Jerusalem: to imbue the pilgrims with the impression of the Holy Temple, not only in its outer beauty, but with its inner spirituality, as represented by the dwelling of the *Shekhina*, the Divine Presence, amidst its walls. As Maimonides writes: "Just as Israel comes to be seen before God, as the Torah commands, so too they come to see the holy glory and the House of the *Shekhina*" (*Chagiga* 2:1).

Throughout the generations, many Torah scholars of all types delved into and attempted to understand the details of the Tabernacle and the Temple. However, they did not have the modern tools that we have – whether in drawing, photography, or models – to truly picture the subject.

How fortunate we are to be able to utilize state-of-the-art tools to actually depict in detail the actual Temple and its vessels. We are able to produce small models to scale, computerized diagrams of the entire structure and each item in it, and more.

Furthermore: In the Temple Institute in Jerusalem, visitors can see the Holy Temple utensils exactly as they were in the Beit HaMikdash, to scale, made of silver and gold by top-notch artisans.

They were specifically made for Holy Temple service, ready to be taken in hand the moment the Temple is ready and the priests ascend to the Mountain of the Lord to perform the holy service – "as in the days of old and in the years of yore" (Malachi 3:4).

The Temple Institute, in partnership with Koren Publishers – Jerusalem, hereby present to the modern readership a veritable treasure of paintings, photos, and other depictions of the Holy Temple and its service. The paintings were done by great artists and craftsmen over the course of decades. The same is true for the Temple vessels, utensils and furnishings, in which much effort and skill – and considerable financial resources – have been invested.

Some of the illustrations and photos have already been published in various publications of the Temple Institute. Many paintings and illustrations have been added, however, as well as explanations and commentary, such that the present work is an important and welcome contribution.

With this Encyclopedia, everyone whether teacher or student, father or son, Torah scholar or beginner, can find his way to study, the subject of the Beit Hamikdash accurately and with great fascination. The entire topic is presented here in a most comprehensive and systematic manner. Even a small child can see with his own eyes and examine the Holy Temple and its service – almost like what Moshe Rabbeinu saw when he was taught it in the Heavens.

The present edition has been supplemented with entirely new chapters, and of course many new paintings and pictures. As a continuation of this Visual Encyclopedia, we plan to publish in the near future an encyclopedia of Holy Temple concepts and topics: a five-volume work with approximately 1,000 entries encompassing Jewish Law, Aggada, concepts, and research into the Beit HaMikdash. It will also contain thousands of pictures and paintings to elucidate the contents and the various details of each entry and concept. This expanded work, another Koren publication, promises to enable all those who are interested in knowledge of the Beit HaMikdash to turn to the appropriate entry for a detailed and thorough analysis.

The pages of this work have been written in preparation for the day when the paintings will actually come to life in Jerusalem, the City of God and the Sanctuary. May they be as gates to the Holy Temple, through which the reader will enter the sacred Sanctuary.

The History of the Holy Temple

The History of the Tabernacle and the Holy Temple

In his opening words to the Laws of the Temple, Maimonides writes that the Holy Temple is a house of God, designated for the service of God during the course of the year and for public gathering on the three Festivals.

In addition to the practical aspects, the Temple also conceals within its depths a very profound concept.

The Sages explain that one of the purposes for which the world was created was the Holy Temple. In Tractate *Pesachim* (54a) it is stated: "Seven things were created prior to the world, and they are: Torah, repentance, the Garden of Eden, Gehinnom, the Throne of Glory, the Holy Temple, and the name of the messiah." That is to say, the Temple is the apex of the process of repairing and uplifting the world, culminating with the arrival of the messiah and complete redemption for the entire world.

As we will see in this chapter, Jewish tradition maintains that the first sacrificial offering in history was brought by Adam, the first man, upon Mt. Moriah, the future site of God's Holy Temple. Noah was next to offer sacrifices to God, followed by the Patriarchs of Israel: Abraham, Isaac and Jacob. Generations later, King David expressed his profound desire to construct a House for the Lord – and his son King Solomon was the one to build it. The altar was thus established on the site that had been designated for it from time immemorial.

Our Sages remind us of the fact that Abraham was twice told, "*Lekh Lekha* – Go for yourself!" The first time was when he was famously instructed to make his way to the Land of Israel. The second occasion was after Abraham passed nine Divine tests and was given instructions for the tenth and most difficult one of all: "Go for yourself to the land of Moriah [for the binding of Isaac on the altar]." The Midrash teaches: "*Lekh Lekha* was stated twice, and we don't know which one is more beloved..." and the Midrash concludes, "The second one is more beloved than the first" (*Bereshit Rabba* 39:9). That is, Abraham's journey to Mt. Moriah to build an altar with his son Isaac, and the declaration at the time of establishing the Holy Temple there – this was even more beloved than the original *Lekh Lekha* to the Land of Israel. This is because the Temple is the pinnacle and heart of the Holy Land.

Centuries passed before the Holy Temple was actually constructed in Jerusalem. First, the nascent Nation of Israel left Egypt and built a Tabernacle – the Mishkan – at the foot of Mt. Sinai. The date of the dedication of the Mishkan, the first of Nisan, is considered a pivotal day in the history of the world. As the Midrash teaches us:

"That very day was adorned with ten crowns: It was the first day of Creation, the first for kings, the first for presidents, the first for priesthood, the first for the Divine Presence – as is written, "they shall make a sanctuary for Me" (Exodus 25:8) – first for blessing, first for Divine service, first for the ban on *bamot* (sacrificial platforms outside the Sanctuary), first for slaughtering on the north side thereof, first for the descent of the holy fire" (*Bereshit Rabba* 3:9).

The Sages explain that this date – the first of Nisan, the day of the Creation of the World – was purposely chosen for the dedication of the Tabernacle, to teach future generations that the Mishkan and the Divine Presence within it mark the completion of Creation.

From Mt. Sinai, the Tabernacle continues its journeys to *Eretz Yisrael*, the Land of Israel, encamping in various locations in the Sinai Desert and in the Holy Land: Gilgal, Shiloh, Nov, Givon... until the Temple itself was built by David and Solomon in its pre-ordained spot atop Mt. Moriah in Jerusalem.

As will be described and recounted in the chapters to follow, the First and Second Temples represent the most glorious chapters in Jewish history. Still, the Temple's primary purpose is to serve as an illumination for the entire world and all who live in it. It is the deepest prayer of the Jewish Nation to see the construction of the Third Holy Temple – may it occur speedily – and that it should stand forever as a center of spirituality for Israel and for the entire world.

And thus the Prophet Isaiah foretold (2:2): "And it shall come to pass at the end of the days, that the mountain of the Lord's house shall be firmly established atop the mountains, raised above the hills, and all the nations shall stream to it. And many peoples shall go and say, 'Come, let us go up to the mountain of the Lord, to the house of the God of Jacob, and He will teach us of His ways, and we will go in His paths' – for from Zion shall the Torah go forth, and the word of the Lord from Jerusalem."

Adam's Offering on Mt. Moriah ››

The illustration depicts Adam and Eve after the sin, on the first Sabbath since the creation. Adam praises and thanks God for having formed all of Creation. Our Sages teach in the Jerusalem Talmud (*Nazir* 7:2) that Adam was created from "dust from the earth" (Genesis 2:7) – alluding to the earth from under the altar on Mt. Moriah. The day after his creation, Adam built an altar at this very site, and offered a sacrifice atop it, as the Sages of the Talmud teach us (*Avoda Zara* 8a). It was opposite this altar that Adam HaRishon stood on the first Sabbath of creation, thanked God for having brought him into the world and for having created everything around him (various creations are seen in the background), and expressed remorse for his sin of eating from the Tree of Knowledge.

As explained by the Sages, Eve – a full partner in the sin – similarly took an active role in the act of repentance. On this dramatic occasion of repentance, Adam first sang Psalm 92, "A song of the Sabbath day," describing the wonders of God's creation.

The Offerings of Cain and Abel on the Altar

Cain and Abel brought their offerings to God on the second *Rosh Hashanah* in the history of the world, atop the altar that their father Adam had erected on Mt. Moriah. Abel offered "from the firstlings of his flock and from their fats" (Genesis 4:4), and it was accepted. Cain, on the other hand, brought "fruit of the ground" (ibid. v. 3) – seeds of flax, the Sages teach – and God rejected his offering.

Cain and Abel are seen here standing near their offerings, among the trees of Eden. Abel lifts his hands in praise and thanksgiving as the flames of his sacrifice ascend heavenward, while Cain is seen with crestfallen face, as the flames of his offering turn to the sides.

Noah and His Sons Offer a Sacrifice Atop the Altar Upon Exiting the Ark

The waters of the Great Flood have receded, and Noah and his sons make their way to Mt. Moriah to bring a special offering to God. They sought to express their thanks to God, as the Torah states: "And Noah built an altar to God, and he took of the pure animals... and offered them as burnt offerings upon the altar" (Genesis 8:20).

According to Rabbinic tradition, this altar was built on Mt. Moriah in the same place where Adam had built his altar (*Pirkei DeRabbi Eliezer HaGadol*, chap. 23). The illustration depicts Noah about to light the fire under the sacrifice, as his three sons prepare the other animal and bird-offerings. The women of the family look on in the background, and pools of water remaining from the Flood can be seen in the distance. (The olive trees seen in the illustration reflect the tradition of our sages that the olive branch brought to the ark by the dove was brought from the 'Mount of Anointment' – that is, the Mount of Olives in the vicinity of Jerusalem – See *Targum Yonatan* on Genesis 8:11).

Z. SMEKHOV

Isaac's prayer at Mt. Moriah

Isaac is seen here raising his hands in prayer, facing the site on which the Holy Temple is destined to be built. From afar we can see the caravan of camels bringing Eliezer and Isaac's future wife Rebecca.

In the passage describing the first meeting between Isaac and Rebecca, we read: "Isaac went out to meditate in the field towards evening" (Genesis 24:63); the Talmud explains that Isaac thus instituted the afternoon Mincha prayer, for "meditation is none other than prayer" (*Berakhot* 26b).

Elsewhere in the Talmud (*Pesachim* 88a), the Sages teach us that Isaac's prayer took place on Mt. Moriah, which is called a "field." Abraham called the site a "mountain," Isaac called it a "field," and Jacob referred to it as a "house."

See Rashi's commentary (*Chullin* 91b), where he states: "The site of the Temple is Mt. Moriah where Abraham prayed, and it is the field in which Isaac prayed, as is written, ". . . to meditate in the field" (Genesis 24:63).

Abraham Declares the Establishment of the Holy Temple in Israel

Following the binding of Isaac on Mt. Moriah, Abraham and Isaac lift their eyes to the site designated for the future construction of the Holy Temple. On this occasion Abraham proclaims, "*Ado-nai Yir'eh* – God will see!" – declaring that this hilltop, where Isaac was bound and nearly offered to God, will be the site of a permanent altar on which will be brought offerings to God. Abraham also prayed that the merit of the binding and Isaac's willingness to give his life will stand the future generations of Israel in good stead in times of tribulation, as and Rashi explains (Genesis 22:14): "The Lord will choose and see for Himself this place, to cause His Divine Presence to rest therein and for offering sacrifices here. . . The Midrash Aggada expounds further: The Lord will see this binding to forgive Israel every year and to save them from retribution [as if] Isaac's ashes shall be seen, heaped up for atonement on the altar" (*Bereshit Rabba* 56:9).

In the illustration Abraham is seen as he is being told, "Do not cast your hand at the boy!" Both father and son gaze towards the west, to the site of the future Holy Temple. It was at this time, according to Maimonides (*Guide* 3:45) that Abraham instituted the rule that the Divine Presence dwells in the west, i.e., the site of the Divine Presence in the Temple will be in the western part of the structure, in the Holy of Holies.

The Sanctity of the Encampments in the Desert

This painting portrays the sanctity of Israel's encampment in the desert, and the three principal degrees of holiness thereof: The highest level was that of the Camp of the Divine Presence, that is, the Tabernacle and its courtyard [red in the center]. The second level was that of the Camp of the Levites, where the Tribe of Levi dwelled on the three sides of the Tabernacle (orange). Finally, the sanctity of the general Camp of Israel is of the lowest level; it is here that the other Tribes of Israel camp, on the outside perimeter (light brown).

Jacob's dream at Mt. Moriah

The illustration portrays Jacob's famous dream of the ladder as it is explained by the Sages of the Midrash. The ladder seen by Jacob is actually the ramp leading up to the altar of the Holy Temple, and the angels ascending and descending it are the priests, dressed in their white garments of the Temple service. The priests are as the angels on high, performing the Divine service before God.

According to Rabbinic tradition, the location in which Jacob lay down to sleep – Beit El – does not refer to the place named Beit El, but rather to the site of the Holy Temple, literally "the House of God." The Midrash states that the place in which Jacob prayed was none other than the Holy Temple (*Bereshit Rabba* 68:9). The Midrash further teaches (69:7): Rabbi Shimon bar Yochai said: This teaches that God showed Jacob the Holy Temple.

The Midrash (68:12) continues to describe Jacob's dream as referring to the Holy Temple: "'Behold, there was a ladder' – this was the ramp. 'Rooted in the ground' – this was the altar. 'And its top reached the Heavens' – these were the offerings, whose pleasing fragrance reaches the sky. 'Behold, there were angels of God' –these were the High Priests. 'Ascending and descending it' – going up and down the ramp."

In this light, the meaning of Jacob's vow when he poured oil atop the altar and declared, "This rock that I have placed as a monument will be the House of God" (Genesis 28:22), becomes clear.

Fashioning the Menorah of One Piece in the Desert

Constructing the candelabrum under the harsh conditions of the desert was no easy task. Yet Bezalel indeed fashioned a menorah 'of one piece of pure gold' and set it in the Tabernacle. This illustration depicts the artisans creating the 'beaten' menorah utilizing hammers. A supervisor appointed by Bezalel stands by to ensure that the Menorah is fashioned in accordance with the exact plan given to Moses at Mt. Sinai.

Casting the Golden Menorah

Various Rabbinic sources indicate that the candelabrum was fashioned via the method of casting, a technique considered complex even with the advent of modern technology. This is especially so in the case of the menorah, which was required to be cast at a height of eighteen handbreadths. One of several casting options is pictured here, taking into account the particular conditions of the Sinai desert in which the Children of Israel built the Tabernacle and its vessels. The gold was melted in a special oven, heated to a very high temperature, some 1,000 degrees Celsius. The molten gold was then poured into a special vessel, and from there into a mold prepared precisely for the Menorah and its detailed design. Much hammering work still remained for the artisans to finalize the Menorah's various adornments.

The Tabernacle and Moses's Tent ››

The illustration depicts the center of the Israelites' encampment during their 40 years in the desert. Inside the Tabernacle courtyard can be seen the altar, the smoke of its fires rising above it, and the Cloud of Divinity hovering above the Tent of Meeting. The tents around the Tabernacle are those of the Tribe of Levi. The Torah describes in detail how the Levites were arranged around the Mishkan, including the fact that Moses's tent stood opposite its eastern entrance (Numbers 3:38). The tent of Moses was also where the Seventy Elders convened as members of Moses's court. Whoever wished to seek the word of God would come to this place (Exodus 33:8).

Here we see the Mishkan from the east, and opposite its opening (at the left) is Moses's tent, from where the Torah was taught to Israel.

« Dedicating the Altar in the Tabernacle

This painting depicts the Divine fire that descended upon the altar while Aaron the Priest blessed the nation. Also depicted is Aaron's son Nadab (at his right) falling to the ground after bringing a "strange fire that God did not command" (Leviticus 10:1) to the altar.

The dedication took place on the first of the month of Nisan, a year after the Exodus, in the presence of the entire nation, and everyone there had a part in funding or constructing the Mishkan. The Torah states, "Moses and Aaron came before the Tent of Meeting and came out and blessed the nation... A fire emerged from before God and consumed the sacrifice on the altar. The entire congregation saw and celebrated..." (Leviticus 9:23–24). The Sages add that it was regarding this occasion that it was said, "Rejoice, o righteous ones, in God..." (Psalms 93), and note that this Divine fire did not cease from the altar until the times of King Solomon (*Pesikta Zutrata*, *Shemini*) – when new fire descended.

The Tabernacle at the Foot of Mt. Sinai ››

This painting depicts the Tabernacle erected at the foot of Mt. Sinai. Atop is the *Amud HaAnan* (Pillar of Cloud) that hovered perpetually above it between Israel's journeys. Around the Tabernacle is the Tribe of Levi, those who served in the Mishkan and were, together with the priests, responsible for the sacrificial service. The first commandment given to Israel after Moses received the second set of *luchot* (tablets) and descended from Mt. Sinai on *Yom Kippur*, was to construct the Mishkan. The *Seder Olam Rabba* (5:6) provides the chronology of the events:

"In the third month, on the sixth day, Israel was given the Ten Commandments; this was a Sabbath. On the seventh [of the month], after the Ten Commandments, Moses ascended to the mountain . . . and he was there for forty days and forty nights. On the 17th of Tammuz he came down and smashed the *luchot* . . . He ascended on the 18th of Tammuz, and asked for mercy for Israel . . . God then was appeased towards Israel, and told Moses to sculpt new *luchot* and to ascend . . . He went up on the 29th of the month of Av, and he was taught the Torah a second time . . . He came down on the tenth of Tishrei, *Yom Kippur*, and informed Israel that God had accepted his prayers . . . What did he command them? He commanded them to make the Mishkan – and they set about to do so . . . What blessing did he bestow upon them? He told them, 'May it be God's will that the Divine Presence should be found in all your endeavors.' He said: 'How fortunate you are, Israel, in meriting the service of the Mishkan, and just as you have merited this, may you also merit to receive the Holy Temple, and that the Divine Presence should dwell in your midst – as is written, 'They shall make a Sanctuary for Me and I will dwell amongst them'" (Exodus 25:8).

The Levites encamping around the Mishkan have two important functions: They are responsible for the singing as the daily offerings are brought, and for the assembling and dismantling of the Tabernacle in between each journey in the desert. The tents of Moses and Aaron are placed adjacent to the eastern opening of the Mishkan. The seventy elders – the Sanhedrin – gathered in Moses's tent, where they heard and learned the Torah directly from him, and later transmitted it to the Tribes of Israel. Alongside Moses's tent stood another tent in which was placed the coffin of their ancestor Joseph, son of Jacob, which accompanied the Levites in the desert sojourns.

The Levites Build the Tabernacle ››

In this painting, the Israelites have encamped at one of their stops in the Sinai desert. At each stop the Mishkan needed to be built, and this task was divided among the three Levite families: The family of Merari was responsible for the actual building; a planner (far left) is seen consulting the design and instructing the workers. The family of Gershon (left) was entrusted with putting up the tapestries, and the family of Kohath (right) is carrying the Holy Ark, enwrapped in blue cloth, on its way to the Holy of Holies.

« The Partitions and Levels of Sanctity at the Foot of Mt. Sinai

This painting depicts a unique ceremony at Mt. Sinai, related in Exodus 24: "Moses built an altar under the mountain, and twelve pillars for the twelve Tribes of Israel." This was one occasion when Moses was taught the various levels of Temple sanctity, as written in the same passage: "Moses, Aaron, Nadab, Abihu and the 70 elders of Israel ascended," with the rest of the nation standing at the foot of the mountain. Each one was instructed up to what point he could ascend, corresponding to the Temple gradations, as Rashi comments on Exodus 19:24: "You [Moses] [shall be] a partition for yourself, Aaron [shall be] a partition for himself, and they [the priests] – a partition for themselves. Moses went closer than Aaron, and Aaron closer than the priests, but the people shall altogether not break their position to ascend to the Lord."

In the foreground, Moses is seen here atop the mountain [this is not intended to depict the man of God's actual likeness], enveloped in the protective cloud and with the Book of the Covenant in his hand. At the foot of the mountain are large boulders blocking others from climbing the mountain.

Below Moses we see the altar he built, and around it the priests performing the Divine service, the various offerings, the large bowls, and the 12 pillars marking off the site of the *Azara* (equivalent to the Temple court), where the priests stood (24:4–6).

Below them are seen the 70 Elders of Israel, comprising Moses's Court, just as they are positioned in the *Lishkat HaGazit* (Chamber of Hewn Stone) in the Holy Temple.

The setting of these "partitions" at Mt. Sinai also determined the permanent spiritual framework in the Temple: Moses's was that of prophecy, i.e., the Sanctuary and the Holy of Holies; the priestly "partition" is that of the Temple service in the altar in the *Azara*; and the Sanhedrin represents the Torah in the Temple: the Chamber of Hewn Stone, from where Torah law was issued and taught to all of Israel.

The rest of the nation remained furthest away from the mountain, as Moses was instructed: "Set a boundary for the people around the mountain and tell them to take care not to ascend it or even to touch it; anyone who touches it will certainly die" (Exodus 19:12). The entire mountain was sanctified with the holiness of the "Encampment of the Divine Presence."

‘Covered Wagons’ for the Beams of the Tabernacle

A long convoy of Israelites makes its way to a desert encampment. They go forth with wagons donated by the tribal princes for the purpose of carrying the Mishkan’s beams and tapestries, as is written: “They brought their offering before God: six covered wagons and twelve oxen” (Numbers 7:3). Some of the beams have already been unloaded, and the Levites hurry to stand these in place for the Mishkan.

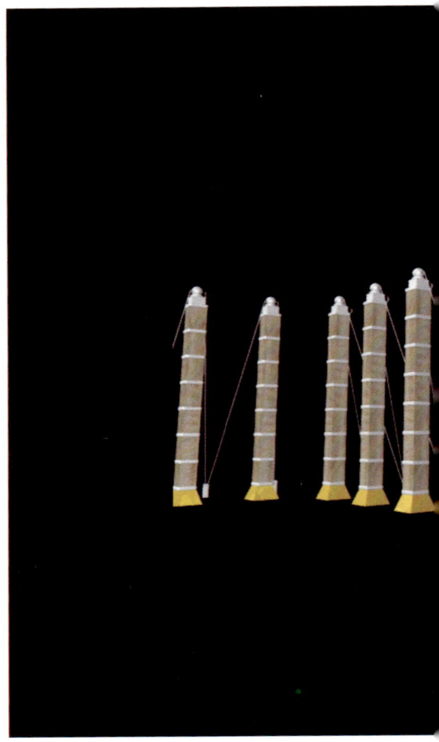

The Height of the Altar in the Desert Tabernacle

The bronze altar in the Tabernacle stands ten cubits high. The Torah notes that it was actually only three cubits tall: "Fashion an altar of acacia wood, five cubits square, and three cubits high" (Exodus 27:1). In practice, though, the altar was elevated to a height of ten cubits, as explained in the Talmud (*Zevachim* 59a) and by Maimonides (*Beit HaBechira* 2:5): "All of the altars – those made by Moses, Solomon, the returning exiles, and the future altar – are ten cubits high; the height of three cubits in the Torah refers only to the actual area where the wood is arranged for the offerings."

Based on this, the ramp leading up to the altar had to be some 30 cubits long. However, the Levites could not have carried such a heavy ramp during their journeys in the desert. Rather, it would seem that whenever Israel arrived at a new encampment site, they would erect a ramp of stones, and then raise the bronze altar atop a structure of stones prepared for this purpose, as shown here.

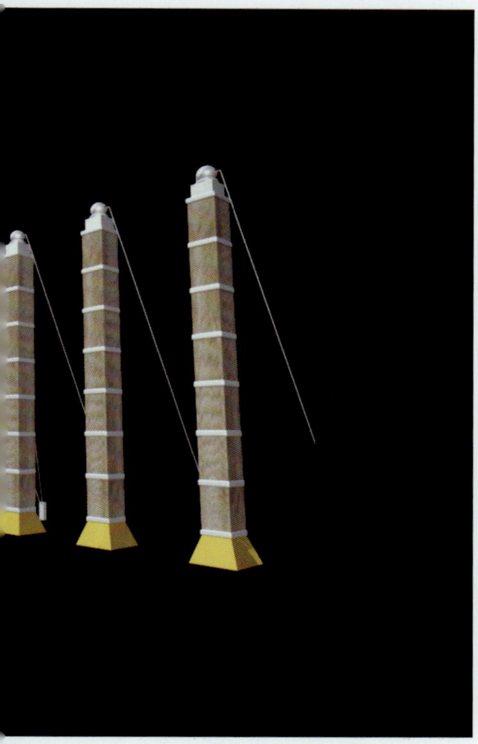

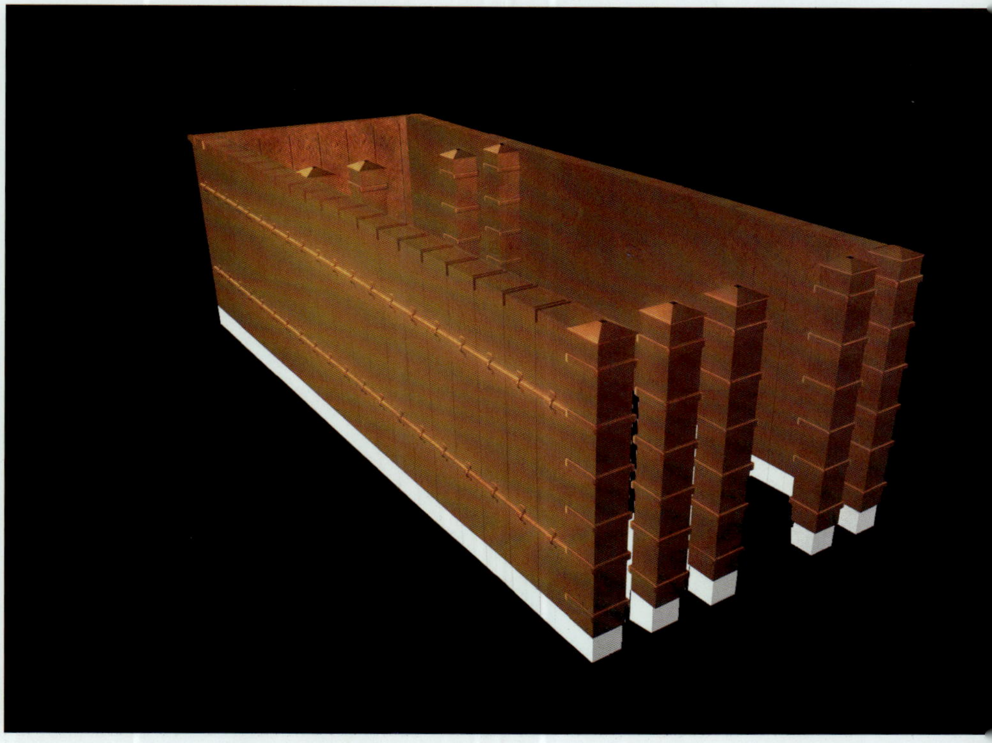

The Components of the Courtyard Beams

The picture depicts nine of the columns on which are hung the curtains that encompass the Tabernacle courtyard. Silver rings on each pillar helped strengthen them, and sockets fashioned of brass at the foot of each helped stabilize them. Atop each pillar were silver hooks from which the tapestries were hung and held taut between the pillars.

The Components of the Tabernacle Beams

Seen here are the 48 wooden beams of the Tabernacle, plated with gold. Each beam stood upon two sockets of silver, fashioned from the silver half-shekels collected from all of Israel. The sockets were quite heavy, and served as a strong foundation for the Tabernacle. Atop the beams were square rings that attached each beam to the one next to it. Alongside the beams can be seen cross-bars that connected the beams and rendered them the Tabernacle walls.

The Tabernacle and its Surrounding Courtyard

The Tabernacle is seen here at the foot of Mt. Sinai, with the *Amud HaAnan* towering above it. The surrounding courtyard is 100 cubits long by 50 cubits wide (50x25 meters). Its fence is made of tapestries of plaited linen stretched across pillars standing on copper sockets, reinforced by silver rings. Outside the courtyard gate stands a screen, 20 cubits long, embroidered of sky-blue, red and crimson wool with twisted linen, standing on four columns. Just outside the Tabernacle are seen the tents of the three Levite families: Gershon, Kohath and Merari. In front of the Tabernacle is a large tent, housing the Sanhedrin of Moses. Nearby it is a small tent in which was placed Joseph's coffin, which accompanied the Levite camp for the forty years of wandering in the desert.

The Copper Laver, Donated by the Women of Israel

The copper laver, with which the priests sanctified their hands and feet before attending to the Divine service, was situated in the Tabernacle courtyard. It was fashioned from the copper mirrors that were donated by the women of Israel. They had flocked to the Tent of Meeting and brought their copper mirrors as a donation for the Tabernacle, and God commanded Moses to accept this donation. Bezalel and his assistants created the copper laver from these mirrors at God's command.

Dividing Up the Land in Shiloh

After standing in Gilgal for 14 years, the Tabernacle was erected in Shiloh, where it stood for 369 years. Shortly after its construction in Shiloh, Joshua and the High Priest divided and allocated the Land to the Twelve Tribes as pictured here. The Talmud (*Bava Batra* 122a) teaches as follows:

The land was divided with the *Urim* and *Tummim*, as is written: "According to the Lots" (Numbers 26:56). How did it work? Elazar the High Priest wore the *Urim* and *Tummim* [on his breastplate]; Joshua and all Israel stood before him. Two urns, one with the tribes' names and one containing the boundaries, were placed before him. Receiving the spirit of Divine Inspiration, he would say: 'Zebulun is coming up and the boundary lines of Acco are coming up with it.' He would then shake the first urn and pull out the name Zebulun, and would then shake the second urn and pull out a slip with the boundary lines of Acco. He would then do the same with Naftali: 'Naftali is coming up and the boundary lines of Ginosar are coming up with it.' He would then shake the first urn and pull out the name Naftali, and would then shake the second urn and pull out the Ginosar boundaries. And so on with each of the other tribes.

The Shiloh Tabernacle: A Station on the Way to the Jerusalem Sanctuary

The Tabernacle in Shiloh served as a temporary Mishkan – between the desert Tabernacle, and the Holy Temple that was later built in Jerusalem. This explains why its walls were of stone, while its ceiling was made of tapestries. Eli the Priest is seen here sitting outside the entrance gate; across from him, next to the altar, stands the mother of the Prophet Samuel, Hannah (in blue), raising her hands in prayer, as was her custom in that very spot. In the center of the courtyard a man is seen cooking the meat of the offering. On the left, a man pulls a large jug of water; in Solomon's Temple, small wheeled-wagons were used for this purpose.

After the nation's entry into the Land of Israel, four different Tabernacles were erected before the Holy Temple was finally built in Jerusalem. As Maimonides explains: "When Israel entered the Land, they established a Tabernacle in Gilgal for 14 years... From there, they went to Shiloh and built a Tabernacle of stone, spreading the tapestries of the Mishkan atop it; it did not have a roof. The [Tabernacle] of Shiloh stood for 369 years. When Eli died, it was destroyed, and they went to Nov and built a [Tabernacle] there. When the Prophet Samuel died, it was destroyed; they then went to Givon and built a [Tabernacle].

From Givon, they came to the eternal structure [in Jerusalem]. The Mishkan stood in Nov and Givon for a total of 57 years" (*Beit HaBechira* 1:2).

The sacrificial service was held in the Shiloh sanctuary on a regular basis, as was the pilgrimage on Festivals. However, the Sages note that the people needed to be reminded and motivated to visit the Tabernacle. The Midrash depicts the situation during the times of Elkanah, father of Samuel, as follows: "Elkanah would go up four times a year – three as commanded in the Torah, and an extra time that he accepted upon himself ... He would ascend [to Shiloh] with all his relatives and household members ... They would take a different route each time; they would pass through a town and lodge in the town center, and people would ask: 'To where are you going?' And they would answer, 'We are going to the House of the Lord in Shiloh, from where the Torah and commandments emanate. Why not come with us and we will go up together?' Tears would immediately come to their eyes, and they would ask, 'Shall we go up with you?' and Elkanah and family would answer, 'Yes!' ... Each time, more and more people would join them, and finally the entire nation once again ascended together..." (*Eliya Rabba* 9).

King Solomon's Temple

« Samuel and David Locate the Site of the Sanctuary

The prophet Samuel is seen here (on the left) with the future King David, preparing for the construction of the Holy Temple. The plans were given to Samuel in the "Scroll of the Holy Temple," originally given to Moses on Mt. Sinai and later passed down from generation to generation until it reached the hands of the prophet Samuel. The meeting took place the night David ran away from King Saul, finding refuge in the home of the prophet (King Saul's soldiers are seen through the window).

The Midrash describes this night as one completely dedicated to Torah study: "The night that David ran from King Saul, he learned from Samuel even more than an accomplished student could learn in 100 years" (*Yalkut Shimoni* to Samuel I, 129). The Talmud teaches (*Zevachim* 54b) that Samuel and David spent the night locating the precise Biblically-mandated spot of the Temple, so that they could transfer the Tabernacle from Shiloh – after Shiloh was destroyed – to its permanent location "in the place that God had chosen."

The verses (Samuel I 19:18–19) recount that David fled from Saul, and then went with Samuel to "Naioth in Ramah." The sages of the Talmud explain this as a play on words; "What connection is there between Naioth and Ramah? Rather, it means that they sat at Ramah and were occupied with that which beautifies [from the Hebrew word *noy*] the world, i.e., the Temple."

The Journey of Ark of the Covenant and 'the Breach of Uzzah'

The painting portrays the journey of the Ark of the Covenant from the home of Avinadav to Jerusalem. The Ark was borne atop a new wagon, with King David and all of Israel dancing before it. Closest to the Ark we see Uzzah, who attempted to catch the Ark as it began to fall – and he himself was then stricken down.

When King David began to prepare the building of the Temple, he arranged to bring the Ark from Kiryat Ye'arim in a grand procession: "David and all the house of Israel played before God on all types of instruments. . . They arrived at Nacon's threshing-floor, and Uzzah cast out [his hand] to the Ark of God and took hold of it, because the oxen stumbled" (Samuel II 6:5–6).

From the verses it is clear that instead of appointing priests and Levites to carry the Ark on their shoulders, as the Torah commanded and as was done in the desert, they placed the Ark in a new wagon, as the Philistines had done when they took the Ark. The Midrash (*Bemidbar Rabba* 21:12) relates that David mistakenly placed the Ark upon the wagon, but that the Ark then suspended itself in the air and the oxen stumbled under it. Uzzah steadied the Ark with his hand, and "God smote him there for his error." That is to say, the punishment was issued because of the mistaken way in which the Ark was transported. As a result, the place was called *Peretz Uzzah* ('the breach of Uzzah'), and the nearby house of Obed-edom was chosen to house the Ark for the ensuing three months.

The Ark of the Covenant and its Journey to Jerusalem

The Holy Ark (seen on the left) arrives in Jerusalem! King David (in the center) joyously "jumped about with all his strength" (verse 14) in honor of the occasion, while the members of the royal household look on from the palace [foreground].

David made the decision to bring the Ark to Jerusalem after he saw that the household of Obed-edom had been blessed as a result of hosting the Ark. The king gathered the nation to accompany the Ark on its way to the Holy Temple with joyous dancing and song: "David went and brought up the Ark of God from the house of Obed-edom into the city of David with joy. . . And David danced with all his might before the Lord, and David and all the house of Israel brought up the Ark of the Lord with shouting and with the sound of [the] shofar. And [as] the Ark of the Lord came [into] the city of David, Michal the daughter of Saul peered through the window, and she saw King David hopping and dancing before the Lord; and she loathed him in her heart. And they brought the Ark of the Lord, and they set it in its place, inside the tent that David had pitched for it." And when it arrived in its place, David offered offerings to God, and distributed the meat to those who participated in the special event.

King David Declares the Altar on Mt. Moriah as the Permanent Sanctuary ››

King David constructs the altar in the midst of the plague that has stricken Israel. He builds it atop Mt. Moriah, precisely where Abraham bound his son at the Divinely-commanded Binding of Isaac. With this, David completes the series of altars built at that site since the days of Adam. David stands and declares: "This is the altar for offerings for Israel!" (Chronicles I 22:1) – designating it as the permanent location for Israel's sacrifices to God, from that time and forever (see Maimonides, *Beit HaBechira* 2:1).

This painting depicts David and the Elders wearing sackcloth as they fall on their faces and implore God to end the plague. We also see a Heavenly fire hovering above the offering, as is written: "[David] called to God, and He answered him with fire from the heavens atop the sacrificial altar" (Chronicles I 21:26).

On the right is seen Ornan the Jebusite and his sons. It was he who sold the site – his threshing-floor – to David for the purpose of the Divine service. The Book of Chronicles I describes how Ornan also sold other items that were needed for the Divine service to David: "The oxen for burnt-offerings, the threshing instruments for wood, and the wheat for meal-offerings" (verse 23).

Z. SMEKHOV

King David Commends the Temple Scroll to Solomon

Moses was given the "Scroll of the Holy Temple" – the construction plans for the Holy Temple – when he ascended Mt. Sinai. Our Sages teach (*Midrash Shmuel* 15:3) that Moses transferred the Scroll to Joshua, and that it was then passed down from generation to generation until it reached the hands of King Solomon.

King David is seen here standing, as described in the Midrash, in order to transmit the Scroll to his son Solomon. As the latter looks at the plans for the Sanctuary and the courtyards, King David points to the area of Mt. Moriah, where workers have already begun digging the foundations and transporting large stones for the Holy Temple.

Casting the Menorah for Utmost Precision ››

Various Rabbinic sources teach that the Menorah originally created by Moses was re-cast many times in preparation for the Holy Temple in Solomon's day, in order to reach the precise measure of gold – exactly one *kikar* – required by the Torah. This picture shows the Menorah being conveyed to the furnace for this purpose.

zSMEKHOV

« Solomon's Prayer at the Dedication of the Temple

This painting depicts the historic dedication of the First Temple, which was built by King Solomon. The large congregation that gathered came from all ends of the Land – "from the entrance of Hamath to the Egyptian river" (Kings I 8:65). In the center, King Solomon is seen offering his famous prayer as he kneels atop the bronze laver, as is written: "For Solomon had made a bronze laver. . . and he stood upon it, kneeling upon his knees before the entire congregation of Israel" (Chronicles II 6:13).

It was from this prayer that the Sages derived (*Berakhot* 34a) how individuals must bow in prayer, as well as the obligation of a king of Israel to remain in this position throughout his prayer, as is written: "When Solomon concluded his supplication to God. . . he arose before the altar of God from kneeling on his knees, and his hands were upraised towards the Heavens" (Kings I 8:54).

As can be seen at the top of the illustration, fire descended from the Heavens upon the altar at this momentous occasion, as is written: "And all the Children of Israel saw the descent of the fire, and the glory of God upon the House" (Chronicles II 7:3).

On the right side we see the priests bringing the Ark to the Holy of Holies: "The priests brought in the Ark of the Covenant of God to its place, into the Sanctuary of the house, to the Holy of Holies" (Kings I 8:6). Our Sages explained (*Shabbat* 30a): "When Solomon built the Holy Temple, he sought to bring the Ark into the Holy of Holies. . . He recited 24 passages of joyous prayer, but received no response. . . Only when he said, 'The Lord God. . . Remember the kindnesses of your servant David' (Chronicles II 6:42) was he immediately answered!"

Solomon's Temple ››

The picture shows a general view of the First Temple's Sanctuary (*Heikhal*) and Courtyard (*Azara*). The structure built by King Solomon differed in several aspects from that built later by Herod. In brief, the main differences are these:

The Entrance Hall (*Ulam*), Haulam, seen at the front of the building reached a height of 120 cubits (approx. 60 meters), as stated in Chronicles II 3:4, while the Second Temple was 100 cubits high. The hall in Solomon's Temple was actually the entrance to the Sanctuary, with two openings, one within the other. The outer opening – seen here – was broad, and the inner one was narrower: ten cubits wide.

The Sanctuary seen at the back had three floors of 'cells' or small rooms encompassing it (Kings I 6:5); three floors of windows can be seen in the painting. The top level featured two 'attics' as is written: "...and its storage rooms and upper chambers..." (Chronicles I 28:11), for a total height of 90 cubits, compared to the total height of the Second Temple of 100 cubits.

The Altar (seen at the left) in Solomon's Temple was 20 cubits square (Chronicles II 4:1), whereas in the Second Temple the altar was 32 cubits square.

Solomon's Sea (seen at the right) was used as a reservoir to provide water for the service of the priests. According to the Jerusalem Talmud, it was also used for immersion for the priests. In the Second Temple, however, there was no such 'sea'; it was replaced by the 'Chamber of the Wheel' in the north, from which the water was supplied.

The Basins: In Solomon's Temple, there were ten basins atop small wheeled carts (in the center of picture), in addition to the basin from the times of Moses. We also see a priest filling a basin with water from the "Sea of Solomon." By contrast, the Second Temple had only one basin.

'Jachin' and 'Boaz' – Two pillars of copper stood at the forefront of Solomon's Temple, respectively named Jachin and Boaz. The two were adorned on top with crowns surrounded by pomegranates. These two pillars did not exist in the Second Temple.

Windows: There were windows in Solomon's Temple: 'narrowing windows' (Kings I 6:4), referring to windows that were narrow inside, and widened as they neared the outer walls. Similar windows were likely present in the Second Temple as well.

An Inner View of the Sanctuary in King Solomon's Temple ››

The picture depicts the Sanctuary, as described in Kings I, chapters 6–7. On the inner wall are seen Cherubim, and on the sides are the *timorot* – impressive columns topped by a date palm-like engraving, plated with gold (Kings I 6:35). The floor was also gold-plated.

In addition to the Menorah fashioned by Moses, King Solomon added another ten golden candelabra (on the left). The *Baraita DeMelekhet HaMishkan* (chapter 10) states: "They were all ritually acceptable for the Temple service... R. Yossi ben R. Yehuda says: The priest would light the lamps on all of them" (as seen in the painting).

King Solomon also added ten tables to the one made by Moses, and the *Baraita* similarly explains (chapter 8) that they were all acceptable: "R. Yossi ben R. Yehuda says: The priest would arrange [the showbread] on all of them" (as seen at right).

Regarding the wall dividing between the Holy and the Holy of Holies, the *Baraita* states (chapter 7): "The Holy of Holies made by Solomon had a wall, opening, and doors." Atop the opening was a curtain, and Rashi explains (*Yoma* 72b) that it had eagle- and lion-likenesses, as in the painting. In the Second Temple, there was not a stone wall, but rather two curtains in its place; the area was called *Amah Teraksin*.

The inner width of the Sanctuary in Solomon's Temple was 20 cubits, its length was twice that, and its height was 30 cubits (40, in the Second Temple).

Near the ceiling can be seen windows that were "broad within and narrow without" (Kings I 6:4).

The priests did their various activities of preparing and lighting the lamps, bringing the incense, and arranging the showbread at their various set times, on weekdays and Sabbath; it is simply for the sake of demonstration that the picture shows them being performed simultaneously.

Z. SMEKHOV

The "Solomon's Sea" Water Supply

A huge copper basin known as "Solomon's Sea," ten cubits in diameter, served as the main source of water in King Solomon's Temple. The brass was mined in the Jordan Valley (Kings I 7:46). The pipe via which the water arrived from the Ein Eitam spring, outside Jerusalem, can be seen at right. A priest is seen filling a basin with water from Solomon's Sea.

A Peek into the Holy of Holies as seen at the Temple Institute Exhibit ››

Seen here is the *parokhet* (curtain) of the Holy of Holies. Partially open, it provides a glimpse of the Holy Ark and the cherubim atop it, as they are displayed in the permanent Temple Institute exhibit.

The Holy of Holies in Solomon's Temple ››

In the center of the Holy of Holies built by King Solomon in the First Temple stood the Ark of the Covenant, crowned by the Cherubim made during the times of Moses. Solomon added two large Cherubim – ten cubits high and plated with gold – which he placed at the sides of the Ark, with their wingspans reaching from wall to wall (Kings I 6:23).

The illustration also depicts the High Priest entering the Holy of Holies on the only day he is permitted to do so – *Yom Kippur*, the Day of Atonement. He makes his way towards the Ark between its two carrying-poles, carrying the incense in one hand, and the coals on which to place the incense, in the other.

In Solomon's Temple, the Ark in the Holy of Holies stood atop the Foundation Stone, which appears in the illustration as a large floor tile below the Ark. The Ark's poles extend from the western wall in "back" of the Ark, all the way to the curtain in the east. The poles actually touched the curtain (seen on the right), as stated in the talmud (*Yoma* 54a): "'They extended the poles' (Kings I 8:8) – their impression was seen on the other side of the curtain."

Four items (seen next to the Ark) were placed for safekeeping in the Holy of Holies: The jar of Manna, a vial of the Anointing Oil, Aaron's staff with its flowers and almonds, and the gift of gold sent by the Philistines when they returned the Ark to Israel (*Yoma* 52b).

In the Second Temple, only the Foundation Stone remained in the Holy of Holies. The Ark and Cherubim, and the other items stored there were hidden in the depths of the earth by King Josiah.

Hiding the Ark and Menorah ››

The picture depicts a dramatic scene from the last years of the First Temple: Priests make their way underground to hide away the Holy Ark and the Menorah in a "safe room" prepared many years earlier by King Solomon. King Josiah heard from Huldah the Prophetess that destruction was on its way, and he therefore ordered that the holy items be hidden for protection.

Maimonides (*Beit HaBechira* 4:1) tells us that the hiding spot was directly under the Holy of Holies: "The Ark was placed atop a stone in the western part of the Holy of Holies. . . When Solomon built the Temple, he knew it would end up being destroyed, and so he built a place there to hide the Ark, deep underground. King Josiah gave the order to hide it in the place Solomon built. . . together with Aaron's staff, the jar of manna, and the oil of anointing." The Midrash (*Bemidbar Rabba* 15:10) teaches that the altar fire, *Ruach HaKodesh* (Divine Inspiration), and cherubim were also hidden.

By the Rivers of Babylon

The Midrash (*Pesikta Rabbati* 31) describes a sorrowful scene that occurred when the captives of Jerusalem were exiled to Babylon. The painting portrays the Levites sitting before Nebuchadnezzar, who bids them to play for him while he takes his meal, in the manner that they made music in the Temple of Jerusalem. The Levites show him that their fingers had been amputated and explain that they are not able to play. In the words of the Midrash; "'By the rivers of Babylon, there we sat and wept when we remembered Zion' (Psalms 137:1) – Babylonian King Nebuchadnezzar sacked the Temple and exiled and captured the Jews... They sat and wept, and the king said, 'Why do you cry?!' He then called the Levites and said, 'Ready yourselves: When we eat and drink, I want you to play your harps before me, just as you used to do in your Temple before your God!' They said to themselves, 'Is it not enough that we destroyed His Holy Temple with our sins, that now we must play our harps before this dwarf!?' They then came to a decision: They hung their instruments on willow trees nearby, and, in a tremendous display of self-control, they bit off their fingers... God then said to them: 'For this great deed, by your lives I will restore you to the Land...' And in fact, after 70 years, the Temple was rebuilt and Cyrus declared that the Jews could return... [Ezra said] 'Of the sons of Levi I found none' (Ezra 8:15) when reviewing the returnees – meaning that there were none who could play music, because of their amputated fingers.

In the Wake of the Babylonian Destruction of the First Temple

Two Jews returning from Babylon to rebuild the Holy Temple. The First Temple, built by King Solomon, stood for 410 years, until it was razed by King Nebuchadnezzar of Babylonia. With the Temple's destruction, the Jews were exiled from their homeland – some to Babylon, and some to Egypt, Persia and Media. The Ten Tribes were exiled to far-off places to the north and east, and did not merit to return. The exiles never ceased longing to rebuild the Holy Temple, and we find prayers to this effect in the Bible (Daniel 9).

In fact, after 52 years, the first of the Babylonian returnees arrived in Jerusalem, and renewed the Temple service: They first rebuilt the altar amidst the ruins, and within 18 years – 70 years after the destruction – the entire Temple stood once again.

The Second Temple

Reconstructing the Altar from its Ruins ››

Following the declaration of Cyrus calling upon Israel to return and rebuild the House of God in Jerusalem, Jews immediately began returning from Babylon to the Holy Land – though in relatively low numbers. Just over 42,000 Jews came, headed by Zerubbabel and the High Priest Yehoshua ben Yehotzadak, together with three Prophets: Haggai, Zechariah and Malachi. Even before they finished rebuilding their own homes and towns some of them made their way to Jerusalem and began reconstructing the Holy Temple from its ruins – as depicted here.

The first thing they did was build the stone altar, so that they could begin offering sacrifices as quickly as possible. In the center is seen the work on the ramp of the altar, while on the right we see workers preparing the clay mortar.

The returnees also ordered cedar wood from Lebanon. The wood was in fact delivered by men from Tyre, who received wheat, oil and wine in return (Ezra 3:7), as can be seen on the left. The new altar was built 52 years after the destruction of the First Temple.

Z. SMEKHOV

Starting Work on the Altar ››

This painting depicts the situation of the Temple and the altar as it was on the first *Rosh Hashanah* after the return of the first Jews from Babylon to Jerusalem. It was on this day that they renewed the sacrificial offerings on the newly-rebuilt altar. Even after this Divine Service resumed, the Temple itself still stood in its ruins for another 18 years due to the words of hatred sent to the Persian kings by the surrounding nations. The Talmud teaches, "The offering of sacrifices is permitted even if there is no Temple" (*Zevachim* 62a).

The illustration shows the priests performing their priestly functions, as well as the joyous sounding of the trumpets amidst the ruins. At the same time, however, several of the older returnees who still remembered the glory of the First Temple were unable to fully rejoice: "And many of the priests and Levites and the elders. . . who had seen the founding of the First Temple. . . wept aloud" (Ezra 3:12).

Z. SMEKHOV

The Prophets Guide the Construction

This picture shows the returnees from Babylon, beginning reconstruction of the Holy Temple. The first order of business was to uncover the ruins of the First Temple, and at right are seen three prophets, Haggai, Zechariah, and Malachi, pointing out their detailed memories of the First Temple. The Talmud states (*Zevachim* 62b): "[The] three prophets returned to the Land of Israel with the people: one attested to the size of the altar, the second attested to its location, and the third attested to the law that permits sacrifices to be offered even if the Temple has not yet been built."

These prophets were residents of Jerusalem during the destruction of the First Temple, and their first-hand testimony of the precise details of the Temple and the altar was accepted by the Men of the Great Assembly. The returnees were thus able to start building. They actually began offering sacrifices on *Rosh Hashanah*, even before building the Temple, as is written (Ezra 3:1–6): "The seventh month [Tishrei] arrived. . . They built the altar of the God of Israel, to offer sacrifices upon it. . . From the first day of the seventh month they began to offer sacrifices to God, and the Sanctuary of God was not yet founded."

The Prophet Haggai: "Arise and Build the Temple!"

Haggai is seen here reproving the new returnees from Babylon for not having made the required efforts to rebuild the sacked Holy Temple (on the right). His prophecy was delivered 18 years after the renewal of the sacrificial service on the altar on the right), with the Sanctuary still in ruins.

Haggai asked "Is it the time for you yourselves to sit in your ceiled houses when this House is in ruins?!" (Haggai 1:4). As a result of the prophet's rebuke, Zerubbabel ben Shealtiel and Yehoshua ben Yehotzadak the High Priest (both seen at the right) arose to inspire the people and led them in rebuilding the long-destroyed Holy Temple.

Building the Second Temple

Seen here are the returnees from the Babylonian exile, building the Second Temple. As they transport huge boulders to be used in the construction, the Temple treasurer [in the center] negotiates with a quarry owner. At the same time, one of the workers measures one of the large stones [right] so that it can be properly inlaid.

The Second Temple Sanctuary ››

Depicted here is the magnificent Sanctuary of the Second Holy Temple. The *parochet* (curtain) is seen from afar; standing 40 cubits high, it and another curtain close behind it replaced the wall that separated between the First Temple *Azara* and the Holy of Holies (*Bava Batra* 3a). The High Priest is seen in the foreground bowing down, aided by priests supporting him.

King Ahasuerus Desecrates the Temple Utensils

This painting depicts the lavish feast held by Persia's King Ahasuerus during which he showed off and brazenly used the holy utensils of the Temple. The Sages tell us that the utensils stolen during the destruction of the Temple were stored in the royal Persian storehouses, and the king brought them out for display during his party to gladden the participants (*Megilla* 12a and Midrash *Esther Rabba*).

The Three Days of Fasting: Studying the Laws of the Temple

The painting shows a gathering of Jews in Shushan during the three days of fasting declared by Mordecai and Esther. The Sages tell us that the Jews used these days for the study of Torah, and specifically the laws of the Pesach holiday in the Temple – for the days of fasting began on the 14th of Nissan, Passover eve. The Talmud also teaches (*Megilla* 16a) that Mordecai taught the laws of *kemitza* (taking a handful of the flour-offering), specifically regarding the Omer offering brought on the 16th day of Nisan. Mordecai is seen demonstrating, with his right hand, the proper way of carrying out the *kemitzah*. This was Israel's repentance for the sin of ignoring the Temple.

On the right can be seen Haman standing at the gate. He has arrived with a royal steed to carry out the king's command to lead Mordecai in a grand procession around the streets of Shushan. Once Mordecai saw that Israel had done *teshuva* (repentance), he felt that he was permitted to mount the horse in fulfillment of the king's directive.

The Hasmoneans Purify the Temple

This painting depicts several events that occurred when the Hasmoneans purified the Temple from the Greek defilement, such as the finding and smashing of idols left behind by the defeated Greeks. On the right, priests are seen restoring the golden altar to its place. Another priest (in the center) is seen raising the lone flask of oil, announcing that it still had the High Priest's stamp of purity and could be used to light the Menorah – seen in the background being carried into the Sanctuary. This aspect of the depiction is an error, however, for *Megillat Ta'anit* (written during the Hasmonean period) states that the Menorah had been plundered by the Greeks, and that the lamps had to be kindled in a temporary candelabrum made of iron pipes.

Dedication of the Walls of Jerusalem

Upon completion of the new wall around Jerusalem, Ezra and Nehemiah officially dedicated it, giving official validity to the sanctity of "Jerusalem between the walls." This illustration shows a procession of Jews bringing the thanksgiving offerings, making its way atop the walls.

In accordance with Jewish Law, the wall of Jerusalem becomes sanctified via the offering of two thanksgiving sacrifices. Two priests are seen here carrying two of the thanksgiving loaves, leading the procession.

Maimonides writes: "And how is Jerusalem enlarged [according to Jewish Law]? The Sanhedrin must offer two thanksgiving offerings. Two priests then take the leavened breads from these offerings [and proceed], and the Sanhedrin members would follow them . . . They would stand on every corner and at every single stone in Jerusalem, [playing] harps, lyres, and cymbals, and reciting [from Psalms 30]: 'I exalt you, Lord, for You have uplifted me . . .' [They would proceed] until reaching the end of the place that they wished to consecrate, where they would stand and eat one of the two thanksgiving offerings; the other was burnt" (*Beit HaBechira* 6:12).

Maimonides then adds that this served only as a "remembrance" and to reinforce the status of Jerusalem as the "City of Sanctity and the Temple."

The Menorah Lit by the Hasmoneans After their Victory

As seen here, after the victory over the Syrian Greeks and the re-purification of the Holy Temple, the Menorah lit by the Hasmoneans did not look like any previous Temple Menorah. The golden candelabrum that stood there previously had been stolen by the Greeks, and the replacement was made of seven metal rods. The work *Megillat Ta'anit* (Scroll of Fasts) relates: "Why did they light lamps on the first Chanukah? Because the Greeks had entered the Sanctuary and defiled the utensils. . . and the Hasmoneans came with seven metal spears, which they covered with wood [as well as tin and lead], and lit the wicks there" (chapter 9).

One of the priests is seen here standing atop stone steps to light them, as others complete the assembly of the Menorah.

Chanukah: Lighting in "Your Holy Courtyards"

In our Chanukah prayers, we say that the Jews of the day "lit lamps in Your holy courtyards," in accordance with Jewish Law that states that "non-priests are permitted to light the Menorah" (Maimonides, *Biat HaMikdash* 9:7). In the painting, the priest (seen on the right, leaning forward) brings out the candle from the Menorah, and a non-priest lights it.

The procedure was as follows. First a priest serving in the Sanctuary would "prepare" the lamps (in a process called *hatavat hanerot)* by replacing the oil and the wicks. Next, the priest brings the lamp with the oil and wick to the courtyard of the *Azara* or of the Temple Mount, where it is lit. The priest then returns the burning candle and places it in the Menorah in the Sanctuary. The painting shows Israelites (as opposed to priests), wearing regular clothes in the foreground, holding torches with which to light the lamps held by the priests clad in the priestly garments.

The Sanctity of the Encampments in Jerusalem

Here we see the splendor of the Holy Temple, as it stood proudly in its last years. The Sages stated (*Bava Batra* 4a): "He who has not seen Herod's Temple, has never seen a beautiful building in his life."

The Mishna (*Kelim* 1:6–9) teaches of ten levels of sanctity in the Land of Israel, in ascending order:

"The Land of Israel is the holiest of all lands... Within the Jerusalem walls [more sacred than other walled cities]; "light" sacrifices are eaten there... then The Temple Mount... The *chail* (rampart) [between the low wall around the Mount and the Courtyard wall] is more sacred than the Temple Mount, as idol-worshipers and people who are impure for having come in contact with death are not permitted to enter. The Women's Court is holier than that... The Israelites' Court is yet holier... The Court of the priests is yet holier... The Sanctuary is holier... The Holy of Holies is the most sacred of all, for only the High Priest may enter, once a year – on *Yom Kippur*, during the Atonement Service."

These various levels of sanctity stem from the Camp of Israel in the desert on their way to the Promised Land. Let us consider the four main levels that originated in the desert: Jerusalem, the Temple Mount, the *Azara*, and the Holy of Holies.

The sanctity of Jerusalem outside the Holy Temple is like that of the Camp of Israel in the desert where the Tribes encamped around the Tabernacle. Lepers were not permitted to remain within this area of sanctity; they were sent outside the Jerusalem walls. Similarly, the "light" sacrifices, such as the Pesach offering, must be eaten there and not outside the walls (Maimonides, *Beit HaBechira* 7:11 ff.).

The sanctity of the Temple Mount: The source for this sanctity is the Camp of the Levites in the desert; its parallel in the Temple is the entire plaza seen in the painting, enclosed by a wall of pillars. Maimonides writes: "The Temple Mount is more sacred than the city itself, in that women who have just given birth [and others who are temporarily impure] may not enter it... [On the other hand,] a corpse may be brought there, and certainly one who is impure from having come in contact with death may enter" (*Beit HaBechira* 7:15).

The sanctity of the *Azara* (Court of Israel): The built-up area of the Temple Mount is divided into the Women's Court, on the eastern side, and the *Azara*, in which stands the imposing *Heikhal* (Sanctuary) and the altar. The sanctity of the *Azara* is such that impure individuals who enter are liable for death (Numbers 18:7).

The sanctity of the Holy of Holies: The sanctity of each of the preceding levels derives, essentially, from the Holy of Holies, within the imposing Sanctuary. There the Ark stood, inside of which were the *luchot* (Tablets of the Law given at Mt. Sinai), and there is where the Divine Presence dwells. Maimonides writes (*Beit HaBechira* 6:16): "Why do I say that the holiness of the Temple and Jerusalem, sanctified by Solomon, will never be nullified? ... Because this holiness derives from the Divine Presence, which can never be voided."

The Three Sections of Jerusalem ››

This comprehensive view of the entire city of Jerusalem during the Second Temple period shows its various quarters and walls. The city was divided into three "camps," parallel to those of the Israelites in the desert: The camp of the Divine Presence – the Sanctuary and sanctified courtyard of the Temple, colored in red; the camp of the Levites – the Temple Mount plaza, colored in red; and the camp of the Israelites – the entire holy walled city, colored brown.

A Tour of Herod's Temple ››

This picture gives an overview of the Second Temple as described in the Mishna and Talmud, and in accordance with the archaeological findings of recent decades. Let us "tour" this painting and get to know the Temple in detail.

We begin along the long wall facing us **(a)** – the western wall of the Temple Mount, approximately a half-kilometer long. A bridge is seen about midway, leading from the city to the Kifonos Gate **(b)** in the western section of the Temple (Tr. *Middot* 1:3). The remnants of this bridge are today identified with the Mount's Shalshelet Gate. To the right of the bridge and beneath it is the section of the Western Wall at which we pray today **(c)** – only 80 meters in length.

Continuing to the right, we see another bridge, at the site of what we today call Robinson's Arch, with a staircase underneath it **(d)**. The gate here served pilgrims arriving from the southwest. Turning the corner to the southern wall, we see the two Huldah Gates **(e)** – broad tunnels by which pilgrims entered and exited the Temple Mount.

Above the southern wall stands a large building with a covered roof, named the Royal Stoa [Colonnade] **(f)**. Constructed by Herod, it was one of the ancient world's most magnificent constructions, marked by prominent stone pillars. It served as a waiting area for the many pilgrims on their way into the Temple. We continue eastward, where we see a portico of pillars **(g)** that encompasses the Temple Mount. The Talmud states (*Berakhot* 33b): "The Temple Mount was a double stoa – a colonnade within a colonnade."

In the middle of the colonnade is seen the eastern gate, known as the Shoshan Gate **(h)**. From this gate leads a long bridge (**i**), on which the Mishna says the "High Priest who burns the Red Heifer, and the Red Heifer itself and those who deal with it, go out to the Mt. of Olives" (*Middot* 1:3). Continuing to the north, we encounter the Tadi Gate **(j)** (ibid.). On its left we see a tall structure known as the Antonia Fortress **(k)**, built by Herod for Temple protection.

We now enter the Temple Mount courtyard. The Mishna (*Middot* 2:1) states that the large plaza was 500 cubits square. This was true during King Solomon's time, but King Herod doubled its size by expanding the area in the north, south and west. As we walk into the courtyard and approach the Temple itself, we encounter a fence – the *Soreg* **(l)**, also called the *Cheil* (*Middot* 2:3). Stone signs were placed along this fence forbidding entry to gentiles and those who were impure. Some of these signs have been found in excavations, and upon them was written in Greek and Roman: "The stranger may not pass the *Soreg* and the partition around the Temple. A stranger who enters, does so at his own risk."

Our "tour" ends near the western wall **(m)** of the Sanctuary and of the Holy of Holies, about which the Sages said (*Shemot Rabba* 2:2) that the Divine Presence never moved from it. The famous Western Wall of today has merely "borrowed" the name from this Western Wall of the Sanctuary, and over the centuries, this name has remained.

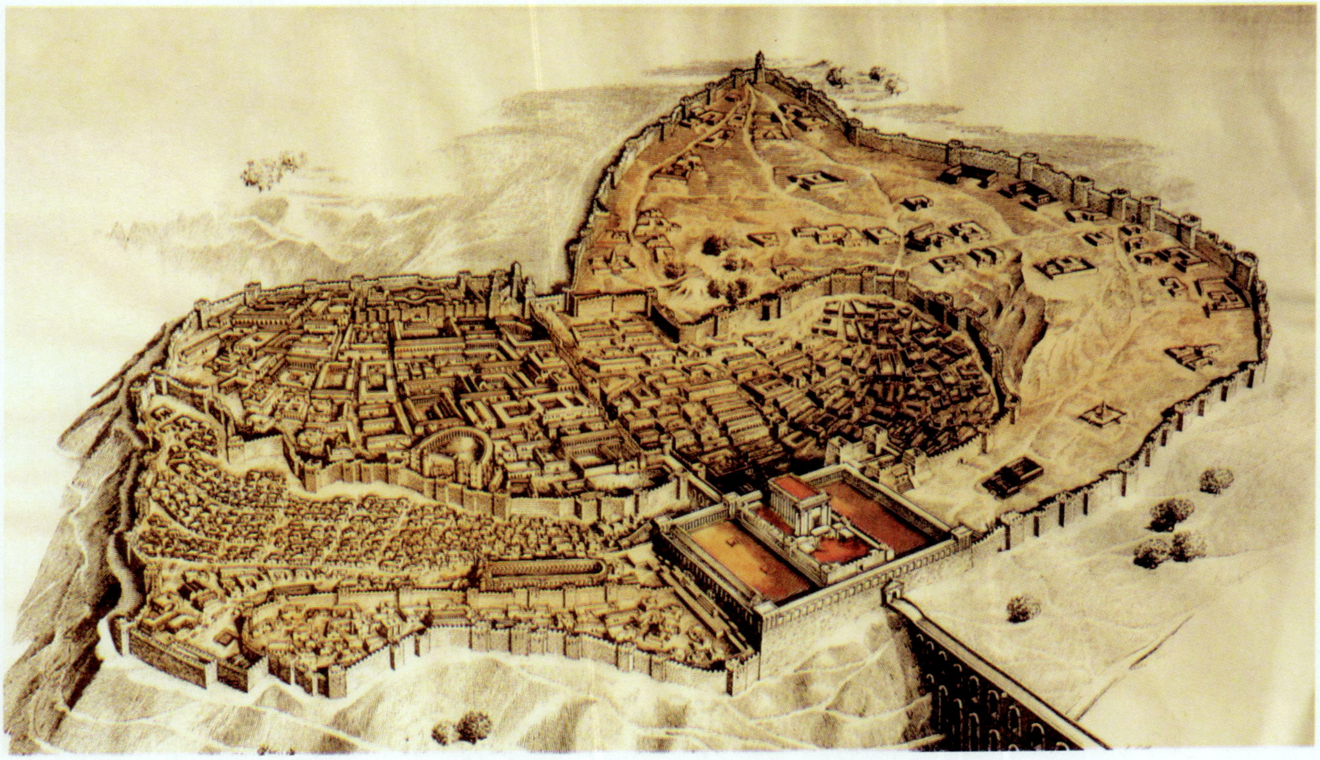

k
j
h
i
l
m
g
f
b
c
a
e
d

The Structure of the Holy Temple

Introduction

When examining the structure of the Holy Temple and its utensils via the pictures in this chapter, we should note an important principle: the uniformity of the Temples. That is, all four of the sacred structures – the Tabernacle, the First Temple, the Second Temple, and the future Third Temple – have a similar structure and form.

Just as every commandment in the Torah has been kept throughout the generations in its original form, so has the Holy Temple. Maimonides ruled in his *Sefer HaMitzvot* (Third Root): "Every mitzvah in the Torah has been permanently set for all time, with all its details." The same is true regarding the Holy Temple and the service therein; these matters are set for all generations, and are not to be changed. Thus, the structure of the Temple is uniform, and pertains to every Temple that will ever be built in the future.

Superficially, one might notice some differences between the various Temples. In truth, however, the principles of the Temple structure are the same throughout; only the outer "shell" is different –with minor changes in non-critical details.

Maimonides wrote briefly and concisely in the introduction to his Commentary on the Mishna that the Beit HaMikdash may be proportionately enlarged, but its essential shape must be retained – "for the proportions are from God, as it is written: 'All this is written by the hand of God Who has instructed me'" (Chronicles I 28:19).

Specifically, in the case of the First Temple built by King Solomon, the *Midrash Shmuel* (15:3) teaches that its structure was determined in the *Megillat Beit HaMikdash*, the Holy Temple Scroll Divinely given to Moses on Mt. Sinai. The Midrash states:

"The Holy Temple Scroll was given by God to Moses, as it is written, 'Now you stand here with Me.' Moses stood and passed it on to Joshua... Joshua stood and gave it to the Elders... to the Prophets... to David... who stood and passed it on to his son Solomon."

This scroll and the plan it details contain the principles for the Temples that would be built throughout the generations The Second Temple built by the returnees from Babylon was constructed according to the exact specifications found in Solomon's Temple. Except for small external details the Temple remains essentially as it was.

Regarding the utensils. We will describe an example of one that underwent a change. The *kiyor* (basin).

During the period of the Tabernacle in the desert, there were only four priests: Aharon, his sons Elazar and Ithamar, and Elazar's son Pinehas. The basin therefore had only to hold enough water for four priests. As Maimonides writes (*Biat HaMikdash* 5:13): "How much water had to be in the basin? Not less than the amount needed to sanctify four priests, as is written: 'Aharon and his sons' – Elazar and Ithamar, and Pinehas with them, for a total of four."

On the other hand, in the First Temple, King Solomon prepared no fewer than ten copper basins. And in the Second Temple, they prepared one copper basin with 12 faucets, so that the entire staff of priests preparing the daily *Tamid* offering could wash at once.

It is self-evident that the one copper basin fashioned by Moses for four priests could not suffice for the Temple period, when thousands of priests, divided into 24 bi-weekly shifts, were engaged in preparing the sacrifices.

Thus, we see that any basin that retains the original principles governing it – namely, that it and its base are made from copper, and that it holds enough water for four priests – is a perfectly acceptable basin for use in the Holy Temple.

Furthermore: King Solomon further improved the basins, building small wagons with wheels on which to move them easily from place to place, thus enabling water to be transported easily and quickly throughout the *Azara*.

The obvious conclusion is that when the Third Temple is built, it will be constructed according to the format of the previous two – and the utensils, as well, will be as they were in the past.

Thus explains Maimonides, in his introduction to the Mishna, why tractate *Middot* – "which is just a narrative of the measurements and shape of the Temple" – was included in a work that is basically one of Jewish Law. The reason is, he writes, "that when the Temple is rebuilt, [we will know] to retain the same shape and proportions."

Similarly, Maimonides includes the *Beit HaBechira* – a description of the Holy Temple as it appears in the Talmud – in his own code of Jewish Law, the Mishneh Torah. These are his words:

"The Temple built by Solomon – is explained in detail in the Book of Kings. And the future Holy Temple, too, [will be built the same way]" (1:4).

This is why the illustrations in this work all depict the Temple as it is described in Tractate *Middot*, and the holy utensils are shown as they looked in the past. In accordance with the Rambam the Third Temple should be built quickly following the plans of the Second Temple.

What about improvements that can be introduced based on the achievements of modern science and technology, such as electricity and computerization? Quite clearly, these will be incorporated into the Holy Temple systems, just as improvements were introduced in both the First and Second Temples. This fascinating topic deserves an essay of its own, in a separate framework.

‹‹ The Sanctuary, the Courts, and the Chambers (view from the east)

Seen here is a marble-and-gold model of the Sanctuary, with the courts around it, as it is displayed in the Temple Institute.

The *Heikhal* (Sanctuary): Standing imposingly in the center of the *Azara*, the Sanctuary is plated with marble and gold. Its front entrance hall is called the *Ulam*, and its height is 100 cubits tall. It is also 100 cubits wide and long (*Middot* 4:6).

The front of the *Ulam* is adorned by a tall entranceway, the largest entrance in the Temple. It is 40 cubits high and 20 cubits wide (3:7). The Mishna describes five beams of precious oak wood placed in parallel above the entrance, like a type of awning.

Atop the roof of the *Heikhal* is a network of sharp golden spikes, known as the *kaleh orev.* Its function was to prevent ravens and other birds from landing and perching there, thus ensuring that they would not drop impure meat in the area and defile the offerings.

The Sacred Court: A vestibule on pillars encompassing the entire *Heikhal.* It measures 187 by 135 cubits. Jewish Law states that one who enters the Court while in a state of impurity – having come in contact with a human corpse or a dead creeping animal – is liable for the grave punishment of *karet* (excision).

The Chambers in the *Azara*: In the north can be seen three chambers, to the right of the *Heikhal*. The easternmost (colored pink is the *Lishkat HaGazit*, where the Sanhedrin convenes. To the left of it is the *Lishkat HaGolah*, which serves as one of the water reservoirs for the Temple. Furthest to the west, the structure with a dome on top is the *Beit HaMoked*, where the priests convene to prepare for the daily service.

On the other side of the *Heikhal* are three other chambers. The easternmost is *Beit Avtinas,* designated for the priests in charge of preparing the incense ingredients.

Ezrat Nashim (the Women's Court): This is the enclosed area adjacent to the *Azara* on the east (in the foreground). It measured 135 cubits square.

The Chambers: One chamber in each corner of the Women's Court: The Chamber of the Nazirites, the Chamber of the Wood, the Chamber of the Lepers, and the Chamber of Beit Shamanya (for storage of the oils and wine).

The Gates: The Mishna (Middot 2:6) notes 13 gates in the Temple: "Thirteen prostrations [were made in the Temple] opposite the 13 gates... The southern gates adjoining the west: The Upper Gate, the Gate of Kindling, the Gate of the Firstborn, and the Gate of Water. Why was it called the Gate of Water? Because a pitcher of water was brought through it for libation on *Sukkot*... And opposite them on the north, adjoining the west: Jeconiah Gate, the Gate of the Offering, the Gate of Women, the Gate of Song... On the east: the Gate of Nicanor, with two wickets, one on its right and one on its left; and two in the west, without names."

On the other hand, another Mishna in the same tractate (*Middot* 1:4) provides another list of gates: "There were seven gates in the *Azara*: Three in the north, three in the south, and one in the east." Some explain the discrepancy between the *mishnayot* in that they are referring to different periods of time: At the beginning of the Second Temple, there were in fact seven gates, but when Herod later expanded the Temple, there were 13. Maimonides (*Beit HaBechira* 5:6) determines that there were seven gates in the Temple, based on the Talmud in tractate *Yoma* 54a and tractate *Ketubot* 106a.

The Temple Court System and Sanhedrin

The Temple was the site of both the judicial system in Israel and the headquarters for teaching Torah to the nation, as is written: "For from Zion shall go forth Torah, and the word of God from Jerusalem." The judicial system included the three Sanhedrin courts: 1) The Great Sanhedrin, located in the *Lishkat HaGazit*, atop the wall opposite the altar, to the right (north) of the *Heikhal*; 2) The Small Sanhedrin, at the entrance to the *Azara* (in the center of the painting, colored pink); 3) The Third Sanhedrin, at the entrance to the Temple Mount, colored pink in the bottom-right corner of the painting.

Maimonides (*Sanhedrin* 1:3) writes as follows: "How many permanent courts should there be in Israel and how many judges should there be in each court? First, a supreme court is established in the Temple, called the Great Sanhedrin, with 71 judges... The judge who is of greatest knowledge is named the head; he acts as the Rosh Yeshiva and is known as the *Nasi* by the Sages... The members of the Sanhedrin sit in a semi-circle so that the *Nasi* and his deputy, the *Av Beit Din*, can see all of them. Two courts of 23 judges each are also appointed, one of which convenes at the entrance to the Temple courtyard, and the other at the Temple Mount entrance."

The Gate of Nicanor

This is the main entrance to the Holy Temple, from the eastern side of the courtyard. The Corinthian bronze gate was named after the man who donated it, as explained in the Mishna (*Yoma* 3:8): "Nicanor experienced miracles with his gates and he was praised."

The Doors: The Jerusalem Talmud (*Yoma* 3:8) states: "All the gates there were changed over to gold, except for the Gate of Nicanor, because a miracle occurred to it; some say it was because its bronze yellows and [becomes] even more beautiful than gold."

The Chambers: The Mishna (*Middot* 1:4) states: "It had two chambers or offices, one on its right and one on its left. One was that of Pinehas the Valet, who was responsible for preparing the priestly garments for the various priestly shifts, and the other was the Chamber of the Griddle-Cake Makers (for the High Priest's daily *Mincha* offering); it was divided in half – one part offered together with the daily *Tamid* sacrifice in the morning, and the other with the evening *Tamid* sacrifice.

The Wickets: The Gate of Nicanor was flanked by two smaller gates, as the Mishna tells us (*Middot* 2:6), one on the right and one on the left.

The Chamber of the Musical Instruments: From the Mishna we learn that this chamber was at the foot of the Gate of Nicanor: "There were chambers underneath the *Azara* that opened into the Women's Court, where the Levites used to keep lyres, lutes, cymbals and all kinds of musical instruments."

The Steps: Leading up to the Gate of Nicanor were 15 steps ascending from the Women's Court to the holy *Azara*. When all of Israel visited the Temple on festivals, such as during the *Simchat Beit HaShoeva* (Joy of the Water Libation) ceremonies, the Levites stood upon these steps as they sang and played their musical instruments. The Mishna states (*Sukkah* 5:4): "Levites with harps, lyres, cymbals and trumpets and countless other musical instruments were there upon the 15 steps leading down from the *Azara* to the Court of the Women, corresponding to the 15 "Songs of ascent" (Psalms 121–135); they stood upon these steps with their instruments of music and sang their songs."

The Slaughtering Area

The slaughtering area, where the sacrifices were prepared, was situated north of the altar. This is because most of the offerings, especially those of higher levels of sanctity, must be slaughtered in the north. Here the offerings were slaughtered, skinned and prepared to be brought upon the altar. The rings, tables and small pillars facilitated this. The animal's neck (or legs, according to Maimonides) was placed in the ring, and on the small pillars – known as *nanasim* – were hung the animals so that they could be skinned. The marble tables were used for washing the meat before it was placed in the fire on the altar.

In the words of the Mishna (*Middot* 3:5): "There were rings north of the altar – six rows of four rings each... Upon them the sacrifices were slaughtered. The slaughtering area was north of the altar, with eight small pillars there, on which were square blocks of cedar-wood. In these were fixed hooks of iron... on which they hung the carcasses, and skinned them over tables of marble between the pillars."

A Golden Grapevine above the Eastern Gate

Atop the entrance to the *Heikhal* a "golden grapevine" was hung, for the purpose of raising donations for the Temple. As the Mishna (*Middot* 3:8) teaches, the golden grapevine was hung atop the *Heikhal* entrance on wooden planks, and when an individual would donate gold for use in the Mikdash, his donation would be fashioned into the shape of a leaf or cluster and these were hung on the vine. The Mishna quotes Rabbi Eliezer son of Rabbi Tzadok as recounting an incident in which 300 priests were once commissioned to clear it – after which the gold would be sold and the funds used for the Temple's needs. The Gemara teaches (*Chullin* 90b) that the number 300 is an exaggeration, coming simply to emphasize the tremendous amount of gold that had been gathered.

The Jerusalem Talmud (*Yoma* 4:4) tells us that when King Solomon built the Temple, he drew all types of tree forms into it, and that when the real trees in the fields would bring forth fruits, the same would occur with the 'trees' in the Temple.

The Beit Avtinas Office

The painting depicts the preparation of the *ketoret* (incense) for the *Yom Kippur* service. The High Priest is seen practicing for the complex procedure (*Yoma* 47b). In the background on both sides are seen members of the Avtinas family grinding the *ketoret*, for which they were responsible (*Shekalim* 5:1), both on *Yom Kippur* and for the daily incense service.

It was also here in the *Beit Avtinas* office that the Sanhedrin elders had the High Priest swear that he would perform the *Yom Kippur* service, including the offering of the incense in the Holy of Holies, precisely as he was taught (*Yoma* 1:5). This office, designated specially for the making of the incense, was located above the Water Gate in the southern part of the Temple, and was one of the three Temple offices guarded by priests (*Middot* 1:1).

Preparing the incense earned the Avtinas family both an honorable mention and a shameful one in the Talmud. They were mentioned in shame for not teaching others how to prepare the incense. On the other hand, "never did a bride of their family walk outside with perfume, lest people assume that the perfume came from the incense – and for this, they were mentioned with honor" (*Yoma* 38a).

The Chamber of the Seals

It is located in the northeastern corner of the Fire Room, known as the *Beit HaMoked* (*Tamid* 3:3). The Mishna also teaches (*Shekalim* 5:4) that when a person wished to bring a sacrifice, he would go to this office to pay for the required additions of wine, flour, and oil, and would receive a receipt – a *chotam*, seal – in the form of a pottery piece marked appropriately. With this seal he would turn to the man responsible for sacrificial offerings, and would take possession of the animal. Rashi explains (*Yoma* 15b): "In the northwest corner of the *Beit HaMoked*, which was a large hall, large fires would be lit by which the priests would warm themselves; they walked barefoot on the [cold] marble floor of the *Azara*... There was the Chamber of the Seals, where would be kept the receipts of those who bought from the Temple treasury. And the Mishna (*Shekalim* 5:3–4) teaches: 'There were four types of seals in the Temple, written on them respectively: Calf, Kid-goat, Male, Sinner' – each one referring to a different quantity of flour/oil/wine, depending on the sacrifice being offered. The person would pay, and receive a seal, and then go to the man responsible for the *nesakhim* (libations), and would receive the *nesakhim* in exchange for his seal."

The illustration shows two people who wish to bring sacrifices. One goes to the treasurer (on the left), pays, and receives a seal; the other on the right has already paid, gives in a seal, and receives the *nesakhim* for the offering.

The illustration also shows the large rocks of the altar destroyed by the Syrian Greeks and placed there for safekeeping by the Hasmoneans (*Middot* 1:6; see the commentaries there).

The Chamber of the Lepers and the Ritual Bath

In the north-west corner of the Women's Court was a special room in which lepers would immerse (*Middot* 2:5). When a leper would arrive at the Temple on the eighth and last day of his purification process, he would immerse in the mikveh (ritual bath) for his purification. From there, he would proceed to the nearby Gate of Nicanor, where he would stand and extend his thumbs into the Court as his special offerings were being sacrificed, so that the priest could place upon them some of the blood and oil from his offerings, and thus complete the purification.

Maimonides writes as follows (*Mechusrei Kappara* 4:2): "Afterwards the priest who receives the blood in his hand comes to the remaining leper, standing inside while the leper stands outside [the Gate of Nicanor]. The leper puts his head inside the *Azara* and the priest places from the blood in his hand on the leper's right earlobe. The leper would then extend his right hand into the *Azara*, and the priest would place [the blood] on his thumb, and the leper would then similarly extend his right foot and the priest would do the same on the big toe..." [A similar process was carried out with the oil.]

Chambers for the Preparation of Sacrifices

The picture shows a model of the Temple, focusing on the southeastern corner of the *Azara*; the Gate of Nicanor (left) leads outward to the 15 Steps. A two-story structure can be seen to the south of the Gate of Nicanor (top of the picture), with three chambers on the ground floor for the preparation of the sacrifices. As we read in the Mishna (*Middot* 5:3): "The Chamber of the Salt, where the sacrifice was salted. The Chamber of the Fur, where the skins would be salted. The Chamber of the Washers, where the innards would be rinsed... From there led a *mesibah* (a winding staircase) up to the roof of the Chamber of the Fur."

On the second floor, above the Chamber of the Fur, was a special room in which the High Priest immersed his hands and his feet on the Day of Atonement.

Purification of the Leper at the Gate of Nicanor

In this illustration we see a man who has come to the Temple to be purified from his leprosy and to bring his purification offerings. He has already shaved off his hair, as required. He now stands in the east of the courtyard at the Gate of Nicanor, where he recites the confession and is about to lean his hands on the head of the animal he has brought for a sacrifice. The Gate of Nicanor is of a lesser sanctity than that of the courtyard to which it leads, and he may therefore perform the "leaning" there, even before he has been purified. The purification process demands that blood of the sacrifice be placed on the thumbs of his hands and feet, and for this purpose he may insert those limbs inside the gate. He is also permitted to place his head inside the Gate, so that blood and oil may be daubed on his earlobes. The reason for this is because of the halakhic rule, "partial entry is not considered entry" (*Zevachim* 33b).

The Chamber of the Nazirites

This chamber, one of the four located in the Women's Court, was where a nazirite would come to complete his period of nezirut. Located in the southeast corner of the Women's Court, it is described as follows in the Mishna (*Middot* 2:5): "The nazirites would cook their *shelamim* (peace-offerings) there, shave their heads, and burn their hair in the fire under the vat." For at the conclusion of his nezirut period, the nazirite would bring three offerings: An *olah* (burnt-offering), a *chatat* (sin-offering), and a *shelamim*. The nazirite would give the priest the shankbone of the *shelamim*, which he would have to first cook – and he did so in the Chamber of the Nazirites (so explains the Meiri).

Maimonides writes (*Nezirut* 8:3): "Where would he shave his hair? In the Women's Court's south-eastern room, the Chamber of the Nazirites. There they would cook their *shelamim* and throw their hair into the fire." This, in fulfillment of the Torah command (Numbers 6:1): "And he shall take the hair that grew on his head during his *nezirut vows*, and place it in the fire that is under the *shelamim* sacrifice... He would not shave his head unless the entrance to the *Azara* was open, as is written: '... at the entrance to the Tent of Meeting.' This does not mean he must shave opposite the opening, for that would be a desecration of the holiness of the Temple [but rather that the entrance must be open]."

For this reason, a special office was placed close to the *Azara* entrance for the nazirites to shave their heads and cook the meat of their offerings."

Repairs in the Holy of Holies ››

This illustration shows a worker, having been lowered into the Holy of Holies inside a large box, to replace floor tiles in the holy area. The Mishna (*Middot* 4:5) relates how such repairs were made, given the special sanctity of the place: "Trap doors in the upper chamber opened into the Holy of Holies by which the workmen were let down in boxes, so that they should not stare at the Holy of Holies."

The Small Rooms Surrounding the Sanctuary ››

This painting shows some of the rooms that surrounded the Sanctuary. There were 38 such rooms, in three floors on the north, south and west. The Mishna (*Middot* 4:3) states: "There were 38 rooms there – 15 in the north, 15 in the south, and eight in the west: Five in each of three floors on the north and south, and in the west, three on the first two floors and two more above them."

Each room had three openings: "One to the room on its right, one to the room on its left, and one to the room above it." In the picture we see a row of rooms open to each other, forming a type of corridor around the *Heikhal*.

‹‹ Behind the Holy of Holies

The back of the Holy of Holies was the western wall of the *Heikhal*, and in back of it – 11 cubits away (*Middot* 5:1) – was the western wall of the *Azara* (just to the right of the Holy of Holies). This area was called "Behind the *Beit HaKaporet*," as it was behind the Holy of Holies in which were the *Kaporet* (Ark Cover) and the Cherubim. The Mishna also notes (2:6) that there were two gates in this wall, "and they didn't have names."

The first Mishna in Tractate Middot teaches that Levites would guard this area at night: "The Levites would guard in 21 places in the Temple, [including] behind the *Beit HaKaporet*."

The *Midrash Sifrei* relates that a special court would convene in this area to check and verify the lineage and genealogy of the priests.

The Gemara (*Yoma* 21a) explains that although this area was in the west, far from the rest of the *Azara*, there were times when Israelites would come here to prostrate themselves: "When the Israelites would make the festival pilgrimages, it would be very crowded when they stood – but when they bowed down, there was much room; they would extend 11 cubits behind the *Beit HaKaporet*."

The Gemara also tells us that there were times when sacrifices had to be slaughtered in this area (*Zevachim* 55b and *Tosefta* 7:1). For this purpose, small windows were built into the western wall of the Holy of Holies (and into the *Beit HaChalifot* in the east side of the *Ulam*), enabling the area behind the *Beit HaKaporet* to be used for the slaughter of sacrifices and the eating of the sacred meat. As the *Tosefta* states: "A small window was behind the *Beit HaKaporet*, eight cubits high, to render the *Azara* kosher for eating sacred meat and slaughtering [other] sacrifices." That is to say, Israelites would enter the area on the Festival for both slaughtering sacrifices and prostrations before God.

A Look Inside the Entrance Hall

The *Ulam* (Entrance Hall) is seen here from the side, to the east (left) of the front of the *Heikhal* (sanctuary). The picture is a composite of several different sources in the Talmud, both Mishna and Gemara. These are the various items in the *Ulam*:

The *Parokhet* (Curtain): The largest opening in the Temple was 40 cubits high, and over it hung the large *parokhet* (in the picture on the right). The source for this is in *Yoma* 54a: "There were 13 curtains in the Temple [including] one for the opening of the *Heikhal* and one for the opening of the *Ulam*."

***Klunsa'ot* (beams):** The Mishna (*Middot* 3:8) teaches: "Cross bars of cedar (at the top of the picture) were affixed from the wall of the *Heikhal* (left) to the wall of the *Ulam* (right), so that the wall would not lean on its side [on account of its great height]."

Chains and ornaments: The above Mishna continues: "Chains of gold were fixed in the roof-beams, by which the young priests [lit., the "flowers of the priesthood") would ascend and check the ornaments." A young priest is seen here atop a golden lift, supported by chains from the ceiling. Opposite him (on the left) are seen the ornaments. This is described by the prophet Zechariah: "The crowns shall be . . . for a memorial in the Temple of God" (6:14).

Chandelier: Hanging down in the center is the golden lamp that was donated by Queen Helene, as recounted in the Mishna (*Yoma* 3:5).

Golden Vine: The Mishna continues: "A golden vine stood at the door of the sanctuary, wound around poles." These are seen on the left.

Windows for knives: On the southern wall are seen windows on which the disqualified slaughtering knives are placed. The Mishna (*Middot* 4:7) states that at the ends of the *Ulam* were rooms called "*Beit HaChalifot*," where these knives were hidden away."

Tables: In the foreground can be seen two tables, on which were placed the showbread (*lechem hapanim*). The Talmud states (*Menachot* 99b): "Two tables were in the *Ulam* at the entrance to the Sanctuary – one of marble and one of gold. The loaves were placed on the marble table when they were brought in, and placed on the golden table when they were taken out – because of the principle that 'we ascend in sanctity and do not descend.'"

Open windows: "Two open windows were in the *Beit HaChalifot*, open to the west (seen in the southeast corner) at a height of eight cubits, in order that the *Azara* should be permitted for the slaughter of sacrifices and the eating of extra-sacred sacrificial meat. Even the area behind the Beit HaKaporet is permitted for eating" (*Zevachim* 55b, *Tosefta* ibid. 7:1).

The Decorative Gold Chandelier

The picture shows the decorative gold chandelier, above the entrance to the *Ulam*, as seen at the Temple Institute. The chandelier is seen shining with the sunrise, and its first reflections appear at the entrance to the *Heikhal*.

The Temple Utensils

Introduction

A famous Rabbinic teaching relates that King Ahasuerus of ancient Persia used the beautiful vessels of the Holy Temple for his feasts. The Scroll of Esther states that "various utensils" were used, and in fact, the Temple was replete with precious vessels of various types needed for the Temple services. Many of the hundreds of utensils made in Solomon's Temple were of silver, and some were made of or plated with gold. Among them were also garments for the priests and musical instruments for the Levites.

The Mishna teaches (*Tamid* 3:4) that each and every day, the priests would bring out **93** different Temple utensils of gold and silver and place them in the Courtyard.

Is the number 93 of any special significance, or was it a chance amount? Many commentaries have attempted to find a source or meaning to this number, but largely without success.

It would seem that precisely 93 utensils were placed in the Courtyard for good reason: Together with the seven permanent utensils in the Sanctuary and Courtyard, a total of 100 utensils were in daily use.

The **seven** permanent utensils are likely these: The large altar, its ramp, and the basin – all in the Courtyard; the incense altar, the table and the Menorah – in the Sanctuary; and the Ark of the Covenant in the Holy of Holies.

However, we can deduce from the words of Maimonides (*Beit HaBechira* 1:6 and 4:1) that he had a different list. He appears to count the large altar and its ramp as one, and the Ark as two: the Ark itself, and the *kaporet* (cover) with the cherubim as another. Indeed, the Torah verses describing the Ark indicate that the *kaporet* is a vessel in and of itself – the last of the seven.

Thus, the Mishna counts 93 vessels that are brought out each day and returned in the evening, and together with the seven permanent vessels, there is a total of 100 Temple vessels in regular use.

These 100 vessels parallel the measurements of the *Heikhal*: 100 cubits wide, 100 cubits long, and 100 cubits tall (*Middot* 4:6). Rabbinic sources indicate that the number 100 represents "awe of God," as is written (*Menachot* 43b): "One must recite **100** (*meah*) blessings each day, as is written, "And now, Israel, what (*mah*) does God, demand of you? Only to **fear** the Lord, your God. . ." (Deuteronomy 10:12).

Thus, just as reciting 100 blessings each day leads to awe of God, so too the holy service in the Temple – which must be held in awe, as is written, "My sanctuary you shall **fear**" – leads to awe of Heaven. The number 100 is even imbedded into the Torah's word for vessels, *kelim*, which is equal to 100 in Hebrew numerology.

The overview in the coming pages encompasses the various Holy Temple utensils that have been fashioned in the Temple Institute. Each one was made after careful research into the various relevant rabbinic texts, as well as the teachings of Maimonides. Use was also made of historical and archaeological sources, which provided various details such as the dimensions of the tools, the manner in which they were used, and the materials from which they were made.

The vessels were made specifically for use in the Torah-mandated Temple service, and are ready to be used on a moment's notice. Nevertheless, they are not considered *hekdesh*, "consecrated for the Temple," which would render them forbidden. When the time comes and all of Israel returns to the Temple Mount for the resumption of the Holy Temple service, the utensils will be consecrated and used for their designated holy purpose.

‹‹ The Ark and the *Kaporet*

This painting shows the Ark of the Covenant that stood in the Holy of Holies, with the Cherubim atop it – their wings raised upward, their faces toward each other. According to the Talmud (*Yoma* 54a), one had a male face and one a female face: "When Israel would come to Jerusalem for the Festivals, the Curtain would be opened and the visitors would be shown the Cherubim . . . and they would be told: 'Like a male loves a female, this is how God loves you.'"

Moses placed within the Ark the *luchot* that he brought down with him at Mt. Sinai. The Sages debate whether the broken Tablets were also placed there, or whether they were placed in a separate Ark. They also discuss whether the Torah Scroll that Moses wrote was placed in the Ark, or was it rather placed on the side of it (*Bava Batra* 14a).

The Ark and the Cherubim are described in the *Baraita DeMelekhet HaMishkan*, chapter 6: "The Ark that Moses made in the desert was two and a half cubits long, one and a half wide, and one and a half tall . . . How did Bezalel fashion the Ark? He made three boxes, two of gold and one of wood. In a golden box he placed the wooden one, and within that he placed the other golden one, and then covered the upper edges with gold, as is written: 'You shall cover it with pure gold.' A *kaporet* of gold was placed atop it . . . and four golden rings were set in the Ark, two on the north and two in the south, and through them they would place the poles there permanently, as is written: 'In the rings of the Ark shall be the poles, they shall not move from it.'"

Maimonides writes (*Beit HaBechira* 4:1): "There was a stone in the Holy of Holies, on its western side, on which the Ark stood, and in front of it the jar of Manna and the staff of Aaron. When Solomon built the Temple, he knew that it would end up being destroyed, and he built within it a place for the Ark to be buried below in deep, maze-like vaults. King Josiah ordered the Ark to be hidden in the place that Solomon built."

The Golden Menorah

The Torah describes the construction of the Menorah: "You shall make a Menorah of pure gold, it shall be fashioned in one piece; its base, stem and decorative cups, spheres and flowers shall be made from it" (Exodus 25:31). The work is described in the *Baraita DeMelekhet HaMishkan*, chapter 10: "How did Bezalel fashion the Menorah? He made it like a beam, and from its stem downward he made cups, spheres and flowers, and then extended two branches from it in both directions... The body of the Menorah – 18 handbreadths high, the legs and the flower were three handbreadths ... Three handbreadths remained, in which were the cups, spheres and flowers... The cups were similar to the cups of Alexandria; the spheres were similar to Beirut apples; the flowers were similar to the flowers of the pillars... Isi ben Akiva says: The Menorah once had an extra dinar of gold, and it was put into the fire 80 times [until the extra amount was consumed]." (See the detailed description of the Menorah in Maimonides, *Beit HaBechira* 3:1.)

The Temple Institute has made a Menorah according to its exact specifications, plated with a *kikkar* (some 43 kilograms) of gold. It is on display for public viewing in the Jewish Quarter of the Old City of Jerusalem.

Preparing the Menorah Lamps ››

This picture shows the several utensils used to clean the Menorah: The *machtah* (shovel, hanging on right), *melkachayim* (tongs, hanging on left), and the bowl for washing the utensils. The Torah mentions "Its tongs and shovels." They were used to shine the golden lamps in the Menorah, and to clean out the oil and wicks of the previous day in preparation for the new day's kindling. The *Baraita DeMelekhet HaMishkan*, chapter 10, explains how the golden lamps were cleaned: "He passes them over the Menorah [into a bowl], then places them in a cleansing agent, and then wipes them off with a sponge. Several priests would thus take care of one lamp. . . The Sages say [differently]: The priest would not move the lamps from their place; he would rather clean them in the Menorah itself."

The Flask of Oil ››

The flask seen here contains oil enough for one day's lighting of the seven lamps of the Menorah, i.e., three and a half *log*. A flask just like this was found by the Hasmoneans when they entered the Temple to purify it, still closed with the seal of the High Priest – proof that it was still pure. In addition, an image of this type of flask was found engraved on an ancient coin from the Second Temple period. Minting a coin with this image was apparently meant to eternalize the discovery of the oil flask in the Temple.

A Small Flask to Measure Oil for the Menorah ››

The golden flask seen here is a unique vessel among the Menorah accessories. It holds a half-*log* of oil, precisely enough to light each of the seven lamps for an entire night, even during the winter, beginning with the first flickers of sundown. As is written: "Aharon and his sons would arrange [the Menorah] from evening until morning before God" (Exodus 27:21). This small "measuring" flask was filled with oil from the larger flask, and it was then poured into one lamp; the process would then be repeated for each lamp. The Gemara teaches (*Yoma* 15a): "Give it its precise measure so that it will remain lit all night until the morning."

‹‹ The Golden Menorah with Straight Branches

This illustration depicts a priest preparing the lights of the Menorah. The branches are straight, not rounded, based on an important find made in our generation: a manuscript of Maimonides' Commentary to the Mishna (*Menachot* 3:7) – with a sketch he drew of a straight-branched Menorah. The discovery has generated a lively debate among the scholars: Did he intend to depict the Menorah precisely as it was, or simply to draw the general structure, without focusing on whether it was round or straight?

The fact is that we have other drawings and depictions of the Second Temple Menorah by people who actually saw it – and in all of them, the branches are rounded. Among these is the likeness of the Menorah on the Arch of Titus in Rome, and another imprinted on a coin from the time of Hasmonean King Mattityahu Antigonus. In addition, the description of the Menorah in the writings of Josephus and other ancient findings indicate that the Menorah branches were rounded.

It is therefore puzzling: Was it Maimonides' considered opinion that the Menorah's branches were straight, and if so, why? Upon closer inspection, we find that the Maimonides's sketch is quite simplistic and general. He himself wrote that it was just to "show its general form." He also wrote that he meant not to depict accurately the Menorah's cups, knobs and flowers, since he had already explained this in his *Mishneh Torah*, but rather to show where they were located on the Menorah. To this end, he set a "key," drawing circles for the button, half-circles to show flowers, and triangles to depict the cups, placing them along lines that stood for the branches. His purpose, he wrote, was to "facilitate the drawing," that is, to enable those who copied the manuscripts to draw the Menorah with maximum speed.

On the other hand, the Lubavitcher Rebbe held that Maimonides' drawing was precise, that the branches were actually straight and not rounded, and that the cups were actually triangle-shaped with the opening facing downward.

This topic was the subject of a Temple Institute research project. One of its conclusions was that it would be acceptable according to Jewish Law to build the Menorah either way, and that the branches may be either straight or rounded. Thus, the Temple Institute's Menorah was fashioned with rounded arms, in accordance with today's findings from the Second Temple period – but at the same time, we also present this painting of a straight-branched Menorah, in accordance with the Maimonides's sketch.

The Table of the Showbread ››

The gold-plated showbread table is seen here as it appears on display in the Temple Institute. The Torah describes it in Exodus 25, where God instructs Moses: "Make a table out of acacia wood: two cubits long, one cubit wide, and one and a half cubits tall. You shall plate it with pure gold, and make a gold rim all around it... and you shall place the showbread on the Table before Me, at all times" (verses 23–30).

The *Baraita DeMelekhet HaMishkan*, chapter 8, explains: "The table made by Moses in the desert was two cubits long, one cubit wide, and one and a half cubits tall... The table was [thus] 12 handbreadths [*tefachim*] long, and its width – six. The showbread was ten handbreadths long, and five in width. The priest places the length of the bread against the width of the table, and folds the bread – two handbreadths on each side, and two handbreadths of space in the middle [between the loaves] so that air could circulate between them."

Regarding the bowls, spoons, branches and half-tubes that formed shelves, Maimonides writes (*Beit HaBechira* 3:13): "The table had four side-frames of gold, known as *k'sot*, split into two at their tops [i.e., they were Y-shaped]. They supported the two sets of showbread – two for each set. There were 28 rods of gold (*m'nakiyot*), each resembling half of a hollow reed – 14 for each set. There were two incense bowls (*kapot*), in which the frankincense was placed inside on the table, alongside the showbread. The molds used to make the showbread are called its *ke'arot*."

The Table and Censers

This painting shows the table standing in the Sanctuary, in which the showbread loaves are placed and remain throughout the week. Each loaf stands on the *m'nakiyot*. According to the *Gra* (the Vilna Gaon), each loaf was placed inside a gold molding. Seen here are the priests bringing the new loaves for the week; they are about to set them on the Table, replacing the ones placed there the previous Sabbath. Two other priests are seen carrying the frankincense jugs, preparing to place them on the Table together with the new loaves.

The Altar of Incense ››

The Altar of Incense, seen here, is made of cedar wood and plated with gold. Its dimensions and shape are described in Exodus 30: "Make an altar for bringing incense up in smoke; out of acacia wood you shall make it. It shall be one cubit long and one cubit wide, a square, and two cubits high, including its corner protrusions. You shall overlay it with pure gold... and you shall make for it a golden crown all around... Aaron shall make incense of spices go up in smoke upon it, every morning."

In the Tabernacle that accompanied Israel in the desert, the altar was made of acacia wood, but in Solomon's Temple, it was fashioned of cedar, as is written in Kings I (6:20): "He covered the altar with cedar." In light of this, the Temple Institute altar was fashioned from cedar. The art of gold-plating wood is quite an intricate task, and only a small number of artisans can actually do it. And in fact, the gold-plating of the incense altar in the Temple Institute was achieved via a method used by the kings of Egypt thousands of years ago.

‹‹ The Frankincense Censers

The two golden censers seen here, containing frankincense, were placed on the showbread table. When the loaves were placed on the table on the Sabbath day, the censers were placed alongside them, as Maimonides writes (*Temidin UMusafin* 5:2): "Alongside each of the two sets [of six loaves each] was a vessel with a handful of frankincense... These dishes had flat bases so that they could be placed on the table." When the 12 showbread loaves were taken to be given to the priests, the censers would be taken as well, and offered atop the fire of the altar.

The Incense Chalice »

The golden incense chalice seen here held the ingredients for the incense offering. The Mishna (*Tamid* 5:4) states: "The priest who earned the privilege of making the incense offering would take the [golden] spoon... It held three *kav*, and the [incense] dish was in it, heaped up with incense. It had a covering [to keep the fragrance from escaping]."

On regular days, two priests would use these utensils: One would hold it by its handles and empty the incense into his hands, while at the same time, the other would hold the spoon/dish under the first one's hands – to keep crumbs from falling to the floor. On *Yom Kippur*, however, the High Priest would do this by himself, alone in the Holy of Holies. This was considered a very difficult Temple service, and the purpose of the handles was to make it easier.

Some feel that the purpose of the "bell" atop this vessel was to fulfill the verse, "Its sound shall be heard when he enters the sanctuary" (Exodus 28:35).

The Incense Bowl

Seen here is a large *kaf*, bowl, used for the burning of the incense. As explained in the Mishna (*Tamid* 5:4), "The priest who earned the right to bring the incense would take the golden bowl... holding three *kav*, with a small *bazakh* [for scooping up the incense] in the middle, heaped up with incense." After bringing the bowl with the *bazakh* in it to the Sanctuary, the priest would offer the incense. He would begin by taking the *bazakh* and emptying its contents into his fist. In order that the incense not scatter, another priest would hold the bowl under his hands to catch the incense crumbs and restore them to the first priest's hands.

The Incense Pan

Seen here is the gold-plated coal pan for incense. Two pans served in the Holy Temple for the incense process: one of silver, and one of gold. The Mishna (*Tamid* 5:5) teaches: "The priest who won the privilege of shoveling the cinders took the silver pan and ascended to the top of the altar [where there was a special fire for the incense] and cleared away the live coals to both sides . . . and then went down and emptied them into the gold pan."

For the High Priest's incense offering on *Yom Kippur* in the Holy of Holies, there was a special golden pan, of a different size and shape than the regular gold pan. As the Mishna teaches (*Yoma* 4:4): "He would generally take out [the cinders] with a silver coal-pan, and empty it into one of gold; but on the Day of Atonement, he took them out with a golden pan, in which he was to bring the incense to the inner sanctuary [the Holy of Holies]. He would generally take them up with a coal-pan containing four *kav*, and empty it into one containing three *kav*, but on this day he would take them out with a three-*kav* pan . . . On other days the pan was heavy, and its handle was short, and it was of yellowish gold, but today it was light, and its handle was short, and it was of red gold."

The Main Altar

The large altar, known as the Altar of Burnt-Offerings, was situated in the center of the *Azara*. On top of it are the wood-piles, which were used as the fuel for burning the offerings. Maimonides details the law of its location as follows (*Beit HaBechira* 2:1): "The site of the altar was most precise; it must never be moved . . . Isaac was bound for sacrifice on [what was to be] the site of the Temple, as is written: "Go to the land of Moriah" (Genesis 22:2). It is also written, "Solomon then began to build the House of the Lord in Jerusalem, on Mt. Moriah . . ." (Chronicles II 3:1). Three prophets returned to the Land with the people: one attested to the site of the altar, and another attested to its dimensions."

The Mishna (*Middot* 3:1) tells us the dimensions of the altar: "The altar was 32 by 32 cubits. It ascended one cubit [from the floor] and then went in one cubit (on each side), thus forming the foundation, leaving 30 by 30. It then ascended five cubits and went in one more – this is the *sovev* – leaving 28 by 28. The corners were one cubit square, leaving 26 by 26. A cubit on every side was allowed for the priests to walk, thus leaving an altar of 24 by 24 cubits for the wood pile [for the fire]."

The Golden Jug ››

This is a likeness of the golden cup used for drawing water from the Siloam pool on the *Sukkot* festival. The cup contains three *log* of water (*Sukkah* 4:9), which would be brought up to the Temple for the water libation ceremony as the *Tamid* sacrifice was offered.

The Three-Pronged Fork

A fork of this type is mentioned in Samuel I (20:13) in connection with the Shiloh Tabernacle service performed by the sons of Eli the Priest. According to Rashi, the fork had *unkliyot* (prongs), with which the Priest would turn over the sacrificial meat on the fire so that it would be totally consumed.

The Sages termed this pitchfork-type vessel a *tzinor.* So writes Maimonides (*Temidin UMusafin* 2:13): "After the one who removed ashes from the altar descended, his priestly brethren would run and quickly sanctify their hands and feet. They would take the rakes and forks and ascend to the altar top, and would place all of the sacrificial parts that had not been consumed by the fire during the night, on the side of the altar."

The *Mizrak*, a Receptacle for Blood

Shown here are two *mizrakim*, one of silver and one of gold. The blood of each sacrifice is thrown by a priest onto the corner of the altar, and therefore the utensil in which the blood is received and from which it is then thrown is called a *mizrak* (from the Hebrew root meaning "throw").

The Torah thus teaches (Numbers 7:13): "One silver *mizrak* [weighing] seventy shekels according to the holy shekel." It was fashioned with a rounded bottom, so that it could not be placed on the floor and cause the blood to congeal; the priest always keeps it in his hand, thus keeping it in constant motion.

So states the Mishna (*Pesachim* 5:5): "The Priests would stand in rows holding basins of silver and of gold (in which to hold the blood). A row that was entirely of silver was of silver, and a row entirely of gold was of gold; they were not mixed. The basins did not have flat bottoms, lest the priests put them down and the blood become congealed."

The Measuring Utensils ››

Seen here are eight different measuring utensils used in the various offices of the Temple. For instance, wine had to be measured in different amounts for different sacrifices, and the same for oil. The kindling of the Menorah also required measuring oil, and milled flour was measured for individual and public offerings. Some of the utensils were used for dry items, such as flour – an *isaron,* half-*isaron,* etc. – and others measured liquids, in units of *hin*: a half-*hin*, a third of a *hin*, etc.

‹‹ A Meal-Offering Vessel

This is a special copper utensil – a bowl with a cover – used to bring a mincha offering of a mixture of finely-milled flour and oil, topped with a handful of aromatic frankincense. The offering would be brought in this vessel to the corner of the altar.

Silver Shovel for Removing Ashes ››

A silver shovel was fashioned in the Temple especially for removing ashes from the altar. This is the first act of the Temple service of the day, performed at dawn. The Mishna (*Tamid* 1:4) teaches: "He would sanctify his hands and feet from the basin, take the silver shovel, go to the top of the altar, and clear away the cinders on either side. He would scoop up the ashes in the center, and go down... he would make a heap of the cinders on the floor, three handbreadths away from the ascent."

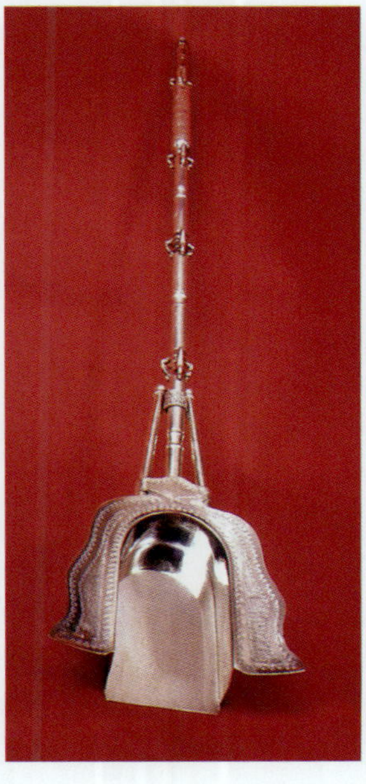

The Copper Cart

This special utensil, called a *pesakhter,* was used to cart away the ashes that piled up on the altar. Its wheels helped it maneuver easily and efficiently around the altar and on the ramp. With the help of chains, two priests would wheel the cart which was full of ashes outside the Temple, so that it would not tip over.

The Mishna (*Tamid* 5:5) teaches: On the Sabbath he would put a pesakhter over the aches. The *pesakhter was* a large vessel holding a *letekh* (approx. 28 gallons). It had two chains: with one he would draw it down, and with the other he would hold it above so that it would not roll over. It was used for three purposes: for placing over live coals, and over a [dead] creeping animal on the Sabbath, and for drawing down the ashes from the top of the altar.

The ashes that amassed atop the altar were taken to the *Beit HaDeshen* (the place of the ashes), a "pure place outside the Temple" (Leviticus 6:4), on the Mt. of Olives outside the city walls, or to the large *Beit HaDeshen* in the north of Jerusalem (*Tosefta Zevachim* 11:4).

The Copper Laver ››

This is the laver fashioned by the Temple Institute. Every priest must begin his Temple duties by sanctifying – washing – his hands and feet, as written: "Fashion a washstand of copper and its base of copper for washing; place it between the Tent of Meeting and the altar, and put water therein. Aaron and his sons shall wash their hands and feet from it, when they enter the Tent of Meeting. . ." (Exodus 30:18–20).

The laver was comprised of the water receptacle and the stand. In the model before us, we also see a third part on top: the *mukheni* ("machine"). Water that remained in the basin overnight was disqualified for use and would have to be discarded. This *mukheni* contained water that would occasionally go into the basin, so that it did not contain only water that was there all night (see Maimonides, *Beit HaBechira* 3:18 and *Biat HaMikdash* 5:14).

During the Second Temple period, a High Priest named Ben-Katin enlarged the laver and added 12 faucets. This enabled the 12 priests involved in the daily *Tamid* offering to sanctify their hands and feet simultaneously.

The *Yom Kippur* Lottery Box

Two lots were drawn on *Yom Kippur* to see which of the two goats would be sacrificed to God upon the altar, and which would be hurled to Azazel in the desert. On the lot on the right was written God's Ineffable Name (cannot be spoken), and on the second one was written "for Azazel." The lottery box would be presented to the High Priest, and he would put both his hands inside, picking up a lot with each hand – without looking. If the lot in his right hand was for God, then the goat on the right would be for God; and vice-versa.

The lots were originally made of box-tree wood, but during the Second Temple period, the lots were made of gold, at the initiative of Ben-Gamla the High Priest; the Sages praised him for this, as they were taught by the Mishna (*Yoma* 3:9).

Silver and Marble Tables

Seen here are two tables on the western side of the altar. On the right is the silver table, on which a priest is arranging Temple vessels, and to his left is the marble table on which a priest is seen preparing the limbs to be sacrificed. The Mishna (*Shekalim* 6:4) lists 13 tables in the Temple, their functions and locations. Among them are the above two, which Maimonides also mentions (*Beit HaBechira* 2:15).

In addition, these two tables mark the spot where the priests would stand during the sounding of the trumpets. When the Levites heard these blasts, this was their signal to begin singing the Song of the Day. As the Mishna (*Tamid* 7:3) teaches: "Two priests stand on the Table of the Fats [the marble table] with two silver trumpets in their hands, and blow *tekia*, *terua*, *tekia*. . ."

Stone Vessels for the Red Heifer Ash

This picture shows several stone vessels – very functional in the Temple and in priests' homes, because halakhically, stone cannot become impure. These vessels were used in the Temple for various steps in the process of preparing the red heifer ash in purity, including: crushing the ash of the heifer after it was burned on the Mt. of Olives (tool seen in top-center), and a cup used for drawing water from the Siloam spring (right). A pitcher for Siloam water is seen as well (in the foreground), and a jug made of marble (top) in which the ashes were stored until they were used to purify those who had come in contact with death.

Vessels for the *Omer*

Seen here are the utensils needed for the harvest of the *omer*. On top we see the *kupa*, a wicker basket, holding barley grains harvested in accordance with the *omer* commandment. To its right is a scythe, and in the foreground is a sifter.

The Harp

The harp pictured here is the Temple Institute's reconstruction of an ancient harp, based on research of ancient harps. A harp similar to this one – one of the musical instruments in the Holy Temple – was found in archaeological digs and in various finds from the Biblical period. This harp has 22 strings, corresponding to the 22 letters of the Hebrew alphabet. The Levites stood on the platform as the daily *Tamid* offering was brought, holding musical instruments, singing and making music as the wine libations were offered on the altar when the sacrifice was concluded.

Maimonides (*Kelei HaMikdash* 3:4) writes about the Levites' song: "There would be no fewer than two harps and no more than six." The Levites also played their instruments at the Festival of the Water-Drawing ceremony, as well as on other festive occasions in the Holy Temple.

The Lyre

The Temple Institute reconstructed the lyre pictured here based on an ancient coin featuring the imprint of a Temple lyre. Mentioned many times in the Book of Psalms, the lyre was one of the instruments often played by King David, who also instituted the Holy Temple music with harps and other instruments, accompanying the daily sacrifice. No restriction was placed on the number of lyres played, but the minimum was nine (Maimonides, *Kelei HaMikdash* 3:4).

The lyre has ten strings, based on Tractate *Arakhin* (13b): "The lyre in the Temple had seven strings... but in the World to Come, it will have ten, as is written, "Upon a ten-stringed harp... with speech upon a harp" (Psalms 92:4). On the bottom can be seen both sides of an ancient coin issued by King David, as explained in *Bereshit Rabba*: "David's coin had a cane and a satchel on one side, and a tower on the other."

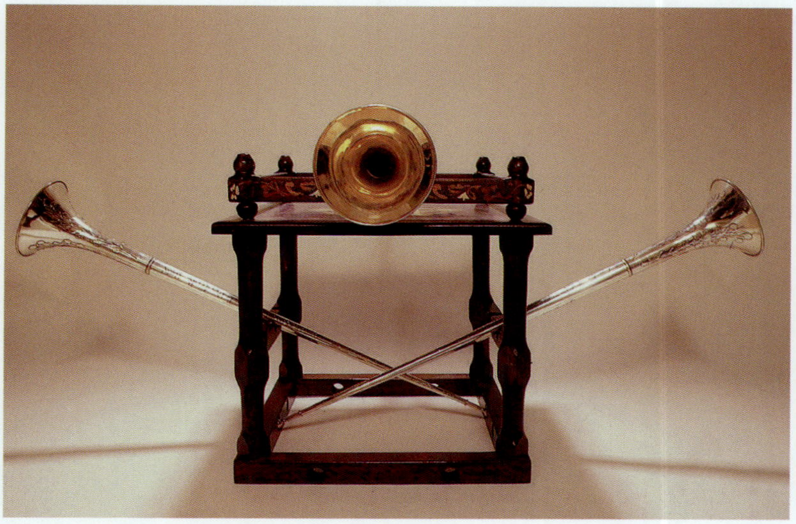

‹‹ The Silver Trumpets

The trumpets seen here were prepared in the Temple Institute, reconstructed based on the likeness seen on the Arch of Titus in Rome. There were many such trumpets in the Temple, used widely by the Levites on the platform. The Talmud tells us (*Arakhin* 13b) that at times, there were as many as 120 trumpets, sounded on many different occasions. They were also used to alert the people and arouse them to repent, as Maimonides teaches (*Ta'anit* 1:1): "It's a positive Biblical commandment to cry out and sound the trumpets whenever the community is engulfed by tribulation . . . such as drought, locusts, and the like."

The Ram's Horn ››

The *shofarot* in the Temple were sounded on *Rosh Hashanah* (the New Year) and on days of fasting. The Mishna (*Rosh Hashanah* 3:3) teaches that the *shofarot* were plated with silver or gold, up to the spot where the mouth was placed: "The shofar used on New Year was an antelope's horn and straight, and its mouth was overlaid with gold . . . On communal days of fasting they would blow [two] curved ram's horns, the mouths of which were overlaid with silver."

The Priestly Vestments

The White Garments of an Ordinary Priest ››

The illustration shows the "four white garments" of an ordinary priest. Of the four, only the belt (or sash) is colored, because of its embroidery, as it is written: "You shall make a sash, a work of embroidery" (Exodus 28:39). Maimonides writes (*Kelei HaMikdash* 8:1) that there are 4 basic priestly garments: Pants, tunic (cloak), hat, and sash, all made of bleached flax. Every thread in the garments is woven of six threads. Because the Torah says that these clothes should be symbolic of honor and glory" (28:40), Jewish Law requires that they must be new and beautiful, certainly without stains, and precisely fit to the measurements of the priest.

How were they made?

The tunic was woven of plaid squares (28:4), and its sleeves were woven separately and then sewn on to the tunic. The gown reaches down to the feet, slightly above the heel (as seen here), while the sleeves reach the palm of the priest.

The pants are worn around the waist, close to the heart, reaching down to the knees; the priest ties them on under the tunic with ribbons.

The hat is actually a turban, some 8 meters of material in length.

The sash is three fingers wide, and 16 meters long. It is wound around the waist many times. It is unique in that it is adorned with embroidery in blue, purple and red-colored woolen thread upon a length of flax.

The Splendor of the Priest's Hat ››

Shown here is the hat worn by regular priests, in accordance with the view of several commentaries that it was a type of large cap covering the entire head. Atop it is a round piece of material that some commentaries say must be added to the hat – for the Torah uses the word *pa'arei* (Exodus 39:28), from the same root as "splendor," indicating that a splendorous aspect must be added.

The Garments of the High Priest According to Rashi ››

The illustration shows the High Priest adorned in his eight priestly garments, in accordance with Rashi's approach (Exodus 28:4). The **vest** covered the Priest from waist to feet, like an apron the width of his back. The **belt** was connected to the top of the apron across its width, and was embroidered. The **shoulder-straps** were attached from the belt, one on each shoulder, to the edge of the apron in back. The **sardonyx stones** are placed in the shoulder-straps, with twelve gold-settings for the precious stones, one for each tribe. And two **braided gold cables** were emplaced in two rings on the top width of the breastplate, one on each side; two gold chains on each side are attached to each setting on the shoulder-straps.

The *Ephod* (Vest) According to Maimonides ››

Seen here is the *ephod* as Maimonides depicts it. It covers the High Priest's chest and back (not from his waist down, as according to Rashi), and its function was to hold the breastplate and keep the chains tight. Its width is as a man's back, and its length is from his elbows to his feet. It is fastened by two bands extending from it on both sides, called the *cheshev* [belt] of the *ephod*. The entire garment is woven with gold, sky-blue wool, red wool, scarlet wool, and linen with 28 threads, as with the breastplate.

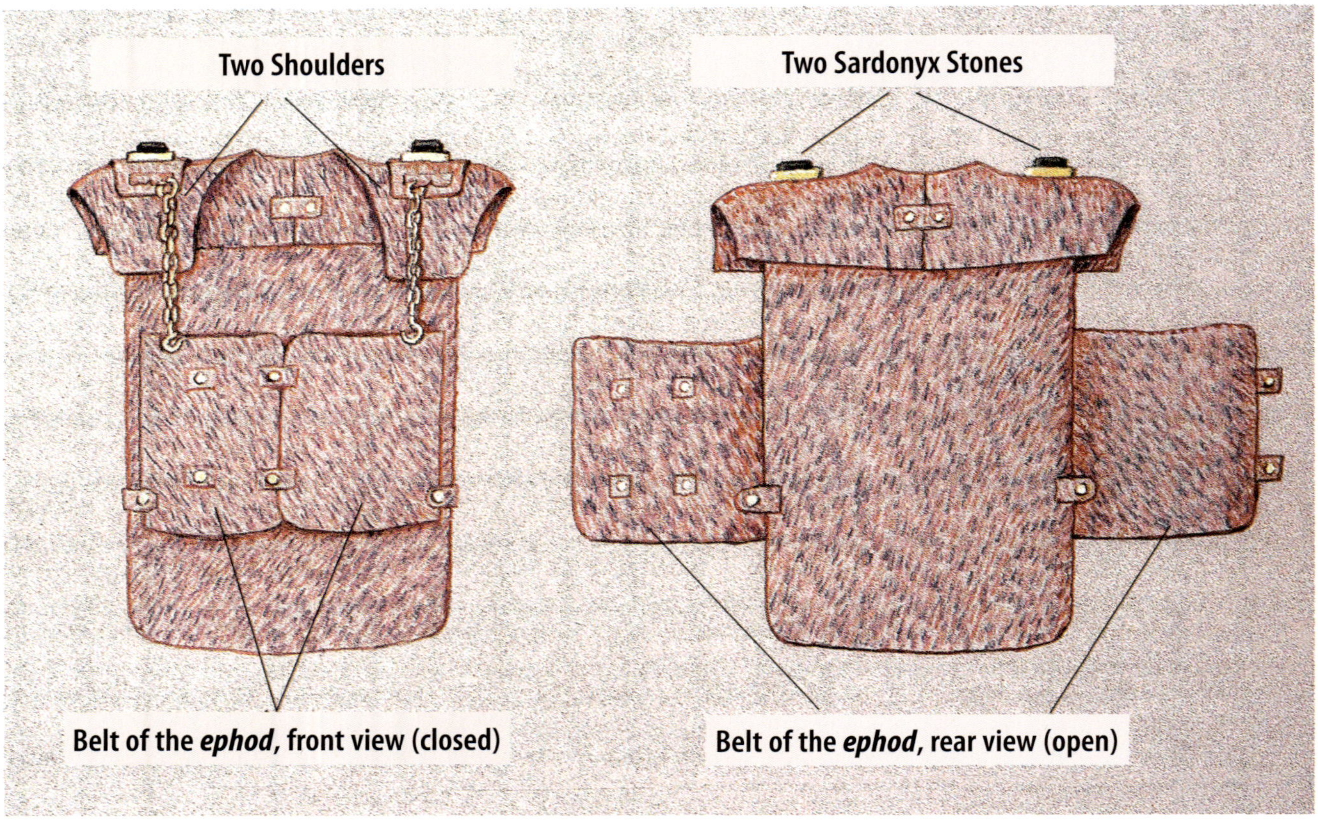

The Components of the *Ephod* ››

The illustration shows the front of the *ephod*, according to Maimonides, in three positions:

At the right: Both the belt and the *ephod* are open.
In the Center: The belt closes the *ephod*.
Facing Page: The breastplate has been placed on the front of the *ephod*, using the gold chains connecting it to the rings above. Sky-blue strands connect the bottom ends of the breastplate to the *ephod* on his back.

Two shoulder straps are sewn upon the *ephod* so that it will extend to the High Priest's shoulders. To each shoulder is affixed a square sardonyx stone in a setting of gold. The tribal names are engraved on the two stones, six on each stone, in age order. On each shoulder are two rings, atop and below the shoulder. The two golden cords, called chains, are placed in the two upper rings. The breastplate is thus flat over his heart and the *ephod* is behind him, and the *ephod* belt is tied over his heart below the breastplate. The two *ephod* shoulders lie on his two shoulders. The two cords of gold extend down from his shoulders to the breastplate rings, and the two sky-blue wool strands are tied below his elbows (Maimonides, *Kelei HaMikdash* 9:9–11).

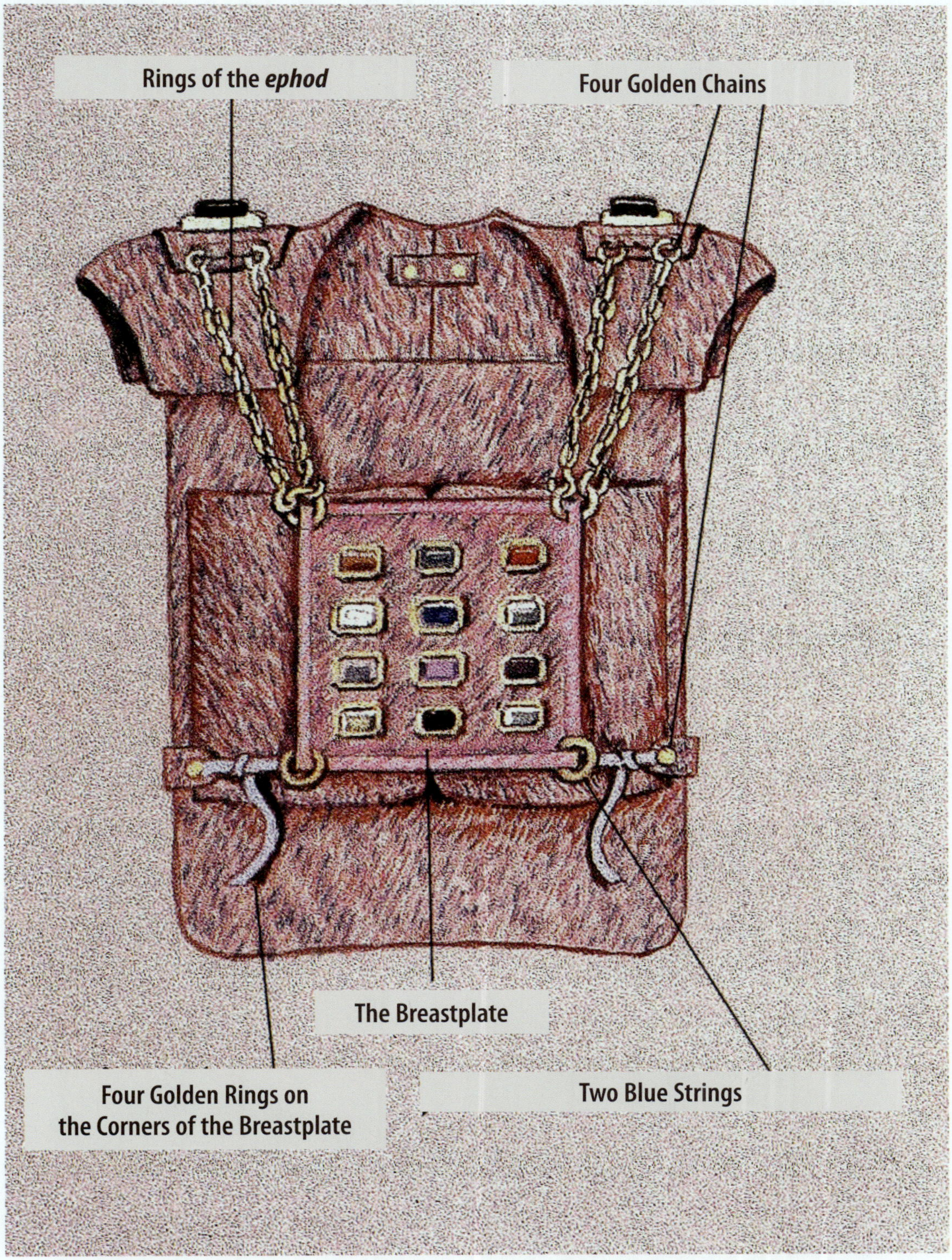

Rings of the *ephod*
Four Golden Chains
The Breastplate
Four Golden Rings on the Corners of the Breastplate
Two Blue Strings

The Sardonyx Stones on the *Ephod* Straps ››

Seen here are the two precious stones as they were prepared in the Temple Institute. As the Midrash describes (*Bemidbar Rabba* 2), the stone's color was "very black." Upon them the artisans engraved the names of the 12 Tribes, in chronological order; the Gemara (*Sota* 36) discusses precisely how the names were arranged. Twenty-five letters were engraved on each stone. The stones were set in the golden rings, and then attached to the *ephod*'s shoulder straps.

The Precious Stones

These are the 12 Precious Stones of the High Priest's Breastplate, as gathered by the researchers of the Temple Institute. They were polished, engraved with the tribes' names, and emplaced in the gold settings.

The precise identification of the stones is a difficult endeavor, and was the subject of intense Temple Institute research for nearly a decade. Some experts claim the stones came from Egypt and environs, others say they were imported from across the ocean. Some attempt to identify them by their medicinal properties, others by their hardness; the Midrash says that when a prospective buyer attempted to check the strength of a sapphire stone [2nd row, 2nd stone], he broke both the hammer and the anvil, while the stone remained whole. In reality, all that we know with absolute certainty is the color of each stone – for the Midrash (*Bemidbar Rabba* 2:7) states that each tribe's breastplate stone matched the background color of its flag. Accordingly, the following list appears to be the most accurate:

Row 1 (r-l): Ruby (red, Reuben); Emerald (green, Simon); Topaz (white, black, red – Levi).

Row 2: Carbuncle (sky-blue, Judah); Sapphire (bluish-black, Issachar); Quartz crystal (white, Zebulun).

Row 3: Jacinth (bluish-black, Dan); Agate (gray, Gad); Amethyst (purplish-wine, Naftali).

Row 4: Chrysolite (aqua, Asher); Onyx (dark black, Joseph); Opal (all colors, Benjamin).

The High Priest's Breastplate

Seen here is the breastplate, with the precious stones attached to its embroidery. The stones are set in golden squares arranged in four rows. The embroidery, described in detail in the Torah (Exodus 28), was fashioned by various artisans and craftsmen: A weaver, goldsmith, stone polisher, and engraver. Maimonides (*Kelei HaMikdash* 9:6) explains that for the breastplate, a garment was woven from 28 strands of gold, sky-blue and crimson wool, and twisted linen; it was a cubit long and a finger wide, folded into two, forming a small square. On it were affixed four rows of precious square stones, set in a setting of gold. On the stones are engraved the names of the tribes in order of birth; the names of Abraham, Isaac, and Jacob are engraved on the stone with the name of Reuben, and below Benjamin are the words *Shivtei Y-ah* [The Tribes of God], so that all the letters of the alphabet appear there. Four golden rings are made on the four corners of the breastplate: In the two upper rings, from which the breastplate is suspended, are two golden cords, called chains, and in the two lower rings are two cords of sky-blue wool.

The Robe

The High Priest's robe, with no sleeves, was made of one piece of long, wide fabric, colored completely blue. The upper part encompasses the neck, and is reinforced with stitching so that it will not tear.

The robe is woven of blue woolen strings, each of which is woven of twelve threads.

Around the bottom edge of the cloak were 72 gold bells with clappers inside, and 72 pomegranates – 36 of each on each side.

In between the bells were small bulbs of wool in the shape of pomegranates. Each string of the bulb was woven of 24 threads: Eight each of blue, scarlet and purple, all interwoven into one strand, and then wrapped into a pomegranate-like bulb. They were hung between the bells, as is written: "A golden bell and a pomegranate, a golden bell and a pomegranate, around the hem of the coat" (Exodus 28:34; Maimonides, *Kelei HaMikdash* 9:3).

How the Crown was Attached

The picture shows how the *tzitz* was attached to the sky-blue turban (based on Rabbinic sources and the writings of Josephus, himself a priest). The Torah states: "Attach a strand of sky-blue wool to it so that it can be worn next to. . . the front of the turban" (Exodus 28:37). According to Rashi, there were six sky-blue strands on the *tzitz,* covering the head like a hat, while Maimonides states that one strand connected the two holes on either side of the *tzitz*, as seen here.

The Talmud (*Chullin* 138a) states: "A woolen skullcap was on the High Priest's head, with the *tzitz* on it. . ." Though Maimonides does not cite this passage, Josephus describes it centuries earlier in his *Antiquities of the Jews* (III 7:6): "Regarding the High Priest's hat, it was similar to the hats of the common priests – but above it was sewn another hat of sky-blue material, encompassed by a golden crown."

The Golden Headband

Here is seen the golden headband, the *tzitz*, set on a stand, as fashioned in the Temple Institute. The words *Kodesh LaHashem*, Sacred unto God, are clearly visible. The headband is adorned as a crown, in accordance with the Biblical verse describing it as a "sacred coronet" (Leviticus 8:9).

How was it fashioned? Maimonides (*Kelei HaMikdash* 9:1–2) writes: A plate of gold is made, two fingerbreadths wide; it extends from one ear to the other. Upon it is written the words *Kodesh LaHashem* in two lines, *Kodesh* on the lower line and *LaHashem* on the upper line. If both are written on one line, it is valid... The letters project outward. A craftsman would engrave the letters on the back of the plate while it was pressed into beeswax and hammered until they protruded."

The Golden Bells

Seen here are two of the golden bells – including a view from the inside of one – that were attached to the bottom of the sky-blue robe. The bells alternated with colored woolen "pomegranates" on the robe.

The High Priest's Garments According to Maimonides ››

Shown here are the eight garments of the High Priest according to the Maimonides, as they appear in the Temple Institute's permanent exhibit. The *ephod* covers the High Priest's chest and back, and the *choshen* breastplate is seen resting on the *cheshev* (the closed straps) of the *ephod* on his chest; the straps are attached with gold chains to the *ephod*'s shoulder-straps, and with strands of sky-blue from below. Under it is the *me'il* (coat), with bells and pomegranates on the hem. The coat has a flap in front and one in back, with no sleeves (Maimonides, *Kelei HaMikdash* 9:3–9; 10:11).

‹‹ Weaving the Priestly Garments

Seen here is a professional weaver entwining six threads of flax into one thread. The garments of the common priests were made of such threads, and were thus known as Garments of Six *(shesh*, in Hebrew).

The Loom ››

This is a photo of an elaborate, hand-operated weaving machine that was used for various purposes, such as preparing a crisscross pattern. The picture shows preparation of one of the white garments worn by the priests.

‹‹ The Spindle

This picture is of a spindle for spinning and weaving linen (flax); the threads of wool about to be woven can be seen. In the background one can see a bundle of processed and bleached linen; spools of woven thread; and a priest wearing his four vestments.

Daily Service in the Holy Temple

Introduction

The daily Temple service was run according to a strict regimen. Each priest and Levite knew his job and his schedule, and all worked together with great coordination.

There were, of course, many priests and Levites in Israel, with not enough jobs and functions to go around. They were therefore divided into 24 annual shifts, or *mishmarot* – as Maimonides writes: "Moses, our teacher, divided the Priests into eight shifts... and thus it remained until the time of the prophet Samuel. He and King David then divided them into 24 shifts, each of which was headed by one supervisor. Every shift would ascend to Jerusalem for one week [every half-year], and switch with the previous one every Sabbath" (*Kelei HaMikdash* 4:3).

The same occurred with the Levites. Each shift was divided into families, each of which served on an assigned day of the week. Each family had a *rosh beit av*, a leader, to oversee the priests' service for the day.

Some of the priestly and Levitic functions were assigned permanently to specific individuals in order to ensure that they were performed, with all their details, precisely and correctly. As the Talmud states (*Arakhin* 11b): "It once happened that R. Yehoshua ben Chananya went to assist R. Yochanan ben Gudgeda in the fastening of the Temple doors, whereupon R. Yochanan said to him: 'My son, turn back, for you are of the singers, not of the door-keepers.'" The commentaries explain that each man was to perform only his specific function in order to ensure that it was done properly.

During the course of the day, the priests and Levites performed their duties in the *Azara*, the main courtyard, upon the altar, and in the Sanctuary. These main activities occupied some 50 priests and 50 Levites, in addition, to many others who worked in other areas of the Temple.

The daily schedule of the priests is largely delineated in the *mishnayot* of Tractate *Tamid*. It began with three priests guarding the main chambers throughout the night.*Beit Avtinas*, *Beit HaMoked* (Place of the Hearth), and *Beit HaNitzotz* (Place of the Spark).

The service in the *Azara* began before dawn, when the first priest set out to do *Terumat HaDeshen*, cleaning out the ashes that had accumulated on the altar over the night. Other priests would go out to check the *Azara* when dawn broke, to make sure that all the vessels were ready and in their places. Two priests would then enter the Chamber of the Griddle-cakes to prepare the daily offering for the High Priest.

Two priests would then ascend to the top of the altar to arrange that which was not burnt over night, and others would arrange the *tapuach*, the pile of coals in the center of the altar.

To remove the ashes that accumulated over night, three priests would ascend to the altar carrying a *pesakhter*, a wheeled copper cart in which they would cart away the ashes and coals to the Beit HaDeshen, a place of purity outside the city.

Once the altar was readied for the daily service, a line of priests would ascend to the altar carrying wood for the new day's altar fire. Other priests would bring up two larger pieces of wood for the same purpose.

Lots were chosen for other priestly activities, obviating any possibility of discord among the priests as they performed the Divine service. To this end, they gathered in the *Lishkat HaGazit*, the Chamber of Hewn Stones, where the Sanhedrin convened, and cast the lots.

Thirteen priests were chosen by lottery to carry out the morning part of the daily *Tamid* sacrifice: Some of them prepared the animal for the actual offering: Slaughter, skinning, washing the limbs and body parts that are to be sacrificed, and more. Others brought the organs to the altar, and others entered the Sanctuary to prepare the oil and wicks for the Menorah and to prepare the Golden Altar for the incense.

Once the sun rose a priest was sent to the Temple roof in order to announce to all that the east had lit up. At the same time, other priests brought out the 93 gold and silver vessels from the Chamber of the Vessels for the *Tamid* service, while still other priests were dispatched to the Chamber of the Lambs to bring the day's offering. It was there that the priests carefully checked the animal for any blemishes or defects, and gave it water to drink.

When the time came, the priests of the shift opened the large Sanctuary gate; the sound of it was heard at a great distance. This was the signal to begin the slaughtering and the other activities.

Another lottery was then held, in which one priest was chosen to bring the incense, and eight others were tapped to bring the limbs and the libations to the top of the altar.

The Levites also divided up their various Holy Temple jobs. Some of them were guards throughout the night, in 21 different locations in the Temple. Other Levites served as gatekeepers, responsible for opening the entry gates supervising entry to the Temple, and closing the gates at night. Other Levites were singers and musicians; they would head for the Chamber of the Musical Instruments, and then to the *dukhan* (platform) where they would accompany the sacrificial offerings with song and music. Finally, still other Levites were in charge of various offices and chambers in which vessels, garments, oil, wine and wood among others were prepared.

Thus, each Levite fulfilled the duty assigned to him by the head of the shift during the week he and his family spent in the Temple.

The Place of the Hearth

The illustration depicts a general view of the *Beit HaMoked*, the Place of the Hearth, where a fire burned all night and warmed the area for the priests who slept there.

When dawn broke, the supervisor would come and knock on the gate (seen at left) to awaken the priests for ritual immersion and the daily lottery (*Tamid* 1:1–2). Across the center of this room were stones jutting out of the floor, delineating between the two different levels of sanctity within the chamber: To the right was the holy area of the Sanctuary, while on the left was the outer, less sanctified area. From this area, the priests would descend the steps (bottom-left) to the Ritual Immersion area in the lower floor. Lamps in the wall would light the priests' way.

A detailed description of the *Beit HaMoked* is provided in *Middot* (1:6–9). It was a large, domed building, with a hearth in the center. It also had "layers of stone" where the elders of the shift's family slept; below them slept the "priestly flowers," i.e., the younger priests. At the right in the picture a priest is seen lifting a large floor tile in order to remove the key to the gates.

The Chamber of Pinehas the Valet

In this area were stored and organized all the priestly garments to be used by the weekly shift. Priests are seen here dressing for the morning *Tamid* service.

Garments for 24 shifts were stored in special cabinets in the chamber. At sunrise, the priests would enter this room to receive their clothing, each one according to his size. Waiting for them there were *chazanim* who would remove the clothing from the cabinets and distribute them to the priests. The clothing was divided into four groups: turbans, cloaks, pants, and sashes. At right can be seen a priest helping a colleague put on his sash, which was 32 cubits long.

Night-Guarding in the Temple

The priests and Levites who guarded in 24 different Temple locations every night were carefully supervised. In the picture we see the Officer of the Temple Mount and his escorts coming upon a Levite who has fallen asleep on his watch.

The purpose of the guard duty in the Temple was to show honor to the holy site, as taught in the Midrash: "A palace that has no guards is not the same as one that has guards" (*Sifrei*, *Bemidbar*).

The Mishna (*Middot* 1:2) describes the guard duty procedures: "The Officer of the Temple Mount would go round to every watch, with lighted torches before him. If any watcher did not rise [at his approach], he would say to him, 'Peace upon you,' – and if he did not answer, it was clear that he was asleep, he would hit him with his stick. He was also at liberty to singe his clothes. People in the Temple would say, 'What is that noise in the *Azara*? It is the cry of a Levite being beaten [or] having his clothes singed, because he was asleep at his post.' R. Eliezer ben Yaakov said: They once found my mother's brother asleep, and they burnt his clothes."

Preparations for the Morning *Tamid* Offering

The illustration shows two rows of priests carrying torches before dawn, ensuring that the *Azara* is ready for the daily service. As explained in Tractate *Tamid*, the supervisor would awaken the priests in the Place of the Hearth, and they would proceed to ritually immerse in the ritual bath reserved for priests. From there they held the lottery for the removal of the altar ashes, and afterwards they proceeded in two rows to check the *Azara* as stated above.

The Mishna (*Tamid* 1:2–3) teaches: "Those who desired to remove the ashes from the altar would rise early and immerse before the supervisor came... He did not always come at the same time; sometimes he came at cock-crow, sometimes a little before or a little after... He took the key and opened the small door in the Main Gate and went into the *Azara*, and the priests followed him, carrying two lighted torches. They divided into two groups: one went along the portico to the east, while the other went along it to the west. They went along inspecting [that every vessel was in its place], until they came to the place where the griddle-cakes were made [for the High Priest's daily offering], where they met and said, 'Is all well? All is well.'"

Bringing the Offering of Thanksgiving

A frequent occurrence in the Temple was the bringing of the *Toda* (thanksgiving offering). The early commentaries discuss the various cases in which a *Toda* is offered. Rashi (to Leviticus 7:12) says it is brought when one benefits from a miracle, such as successfully crossing the ocean or desert, being freed from prison, or recovering from a dangerous illness. These four cases require an expression of thanks to God, as written, ". . . will thank God for His mercies and wonders to people, and bring thanksgiving offerings and relate His deeds with joy" (Psalms 107:21,22).

Rabbeinu Bachyei adds (Leviticus 6): "The offering of thanksgiving is brought as thanks for a miracle, such as recovering from a sickness. . . or other joys, such as a wedding, as is written, 'The sound of joy and the sound of happiness. . . of groom and bride. . . the sound of bringing thanks to the House of God'" (Jeremiah 33:11).

Maimonides rules (*Ma'aseh HaKorbanot* 3:15) that when one brings a *Toda*, he leans on it with both hands, as with other sacrifices, "and recites words of praise." R. Meir Simcha writes in *Or Same'ach* that the recitation must include Psalm 100, *Mizmor L'Toda*, "A Song of Thanksgiving," as noted in the *Targum* of that chapter.

The Lottery

The illustration shows the lottery in progress for participation in some of the daily service activities. Maimonides (*Temidin UMusafin* 4:3) explains how it worked, based on the Mishna in *Yoma* (2:1): "The priests stand in a semi-circle, and agree on a number [such as 80, or 100, or any other number]. The supervisor would then tell them, 'Extend your fingers,' and they would stick out one or two [or three] fingers... The thumb may not be used, because of the deceivers; for the thumb is small and easy to stick out or hide [when the priest sees the count nearing him]. The supervisor begins counting from the priest whose turban was removed [first on the left, in the painting]. The extended fingers are counted, repeatedly if necessary, until the agreed-upon number is reached – and the priest upon whose finger the counting was completed is the one chosen."

The Removal of the Ashes

This picture depicts the *Terumat HaDeshen* activity, taking place at dawn, involving the removal of the ashes that accumulated overnight on the altar and bringing them to a set-aside place. The Mishna (*Tamid* 1:4) tells us:

"The one chosen by lot to clear the ashes made ready to do so. The other priests would say to him: 'Be careful not to touch any vessel until you have washed your hands and feet from the laver. . .' No one entered with him, nor did he carry any light; he rather walked by the light of the altar fire. No one saw him or heard him until they heard the noise of the wooden machine (*mukheni*) that Ben Katin had made for hauling up the laver (see the wooden wheel, top of the picture). He would wash his hands and feet from the laver, take the silver firepan, ascend to the top of the altar, and clear away the cinders on either side and scoop up the ashes in the center. He would then descend, and upon reaching the floor he would turn to the north, walk along the east side of the ascent for about ten cubits, and then make a heap of the cinders on the floor (see the small pit, bottom of the picture) three handbreadths from the ascent."

The Priestly Washing of Hands and Feet

Seen here are priests beginning their day at dawn with the sanctification of their hands and feet from the laver in the *Azara*. After the removal of the ashes, the Mishna tells us (*Tamid* 2:1), "the priests would rush to wash their hands and feet, then would take the shovels and forks and go up to the top of the altar. Whatever had not been consumed through the night, they removed to the sides of the altar."

Chamber of the Wood

This is the room in which the wood for the altar was stored and prepared before being placed on the altar. The Chamber of the Wood was the north-eastern chamber in the Women's Courtyard. Priests who were not fit to serve in other capacities in the Temple would check the logs to make sure they were not worm-infested and thus not suitable for the honor of the sacrifices. Other priests were assigned the task of removing the logs and bringing them to the altar.

Placing the Two Additional Pieces of Wood

In the foreground of this picture one can see a priest ascending to the altar, carrying two pieces of wood for the altar. It is a Biblical commandment to add these two blocks of wood for both the morning and evening *Tamid* sacrifices. Each of the two wood pieces measured a cubit square. Maimonides writes (*Temidin UMusafin* 2:2) that two priests would carry up the two blocks in the evening, but in the morning, only one priest would carry up both blocks.

The Chamber of the Vessels

Many priests gathered in the Chamber of the Vessels to bring out the 93 gold and silver vessels that would be used in the course of the day (*Tamid* 3:4).

The Mishna (*Shekalim* 5:6) mentions another wing of this room that was used for contributions from the public: "Whoever wished to contribute a vessel to the Temple would cast it into the Chamber of the Vessels, and once in 30 days, the treasurers would open it" and review the contributions for suitability. The location of this Chamber is not specified precisely in Rabbinic sources, but it appears to have stood in the Women's Courtyard, where it would be most accessible to the public. In addition, it appears to have stood adjacent to the Chamber of the Musical Instruments (based on the use of the plural "chambers" in *Middot* 2:6).

The Chamber of the Lambs

This illustration shows priests, early in the morning, feeding and tending the animals that are to be offered as sacrifices on the altar. Some of the priests check for blemishes and defects that would render the animals unfit for sacrifice. The Mishna (*Middot* 1:6) tells us that this Chamber was in the south-west corner of the Place of the Hearth. The sheep and bulls/cows were brought here four days before they would be offered as sacrifices. According to the Mishna (*Arakhin* 2:5), there must always be at least six lambs in the Chamber of the Lambs ready to be offered on the altar.

The Chamber of Musical Instruments

A large number of musical instruments were used in the Temple, as recorded by the verse (Chronicles II 5:12): "And the Levites who were singers… with cymbals, harps and lyres stood to the east of the Altar… with them were a hundred and twenty kohanim blowing trumpets… and when the sound of the trumpets and cymbals and other musical instruments sounded out, with praise of God…"

These instruments were kept in chambers that were near the Nikanor Gate, close to the platform in the Court upon which the Levites stood during their singing and playing (*Middot* 2:6).

In this illustration the Levites receive the various musical instruments from the overseers of the chamber, in preparation for their recital of the Daily Song upon the platform.

Opening the Side Door

As seen here, four priests were sent to open the main gate (left) of the Sanctuary at dawn. First, a priest would open the side door (center), in two stages: He would first open the small window at the bottom of the door using one key, and then, holding the second key, he would insert his entire arm through the window and unlock the door via a bolt on the floor. Once this door was opened, the priests would walk through it and unlock the main gate.

The Dawn Call: *Barkai!*

In the center of this picture a priest is standing watch high above on the east side of the Temple. His task was to identify the first rays of sunshine of the day and thus make known the exact moment at which the day began. The Mishna teaches (*Yoma* 3:1): "The supervisor [foreground] would tell them, 'Go out and see if the time for slaughtering has arrived.' The moment it arrived, the sentry would cry out, '*Barkai*,' meaning, 'The sun has risen!' This was the signal for the beginning of the Temple service for the day."

Priests Ascending to the Temple and Levites to the *Dukhan* ››

Seen here are the priests and Levites in the *Azara*, rushing to their respective positions and tasks. The priests (at right) are on their way to bow down in the Sanctuary – part of their service during the *Tamid* offering. At the same time, the Levites (left) are making their way to the *dukhan*, the platform, to their accompaniment of the *Tamid* sacrifice with their singing and music.

The Levites and priests were called to their positions via an instrument known as a *magrefa*. The Mishna (*Tamid* 5:6) teaches that it was "thrown between the hall and the altar" (center-right in the picture), making a noise so loud that "one could not hear his friend speak in Jerusalem... When a priest heard the sound of it, he knew that his brother priests were going in to prostrate themselves, and he would run to join them; when a Levite heard it, he knew that his brother Levites were going in to sing and he would run to join them."

Opening the Main Gate ››

The picture shows the priest opening the Main Gate of the Sanctuary at dawn. As the Mishna explains (*Tamid* 3:7), after the small door to the side was opened, the priests would enter a small, built-in cell and from there they would go to the Sanctuary, which they traversed until they reached the Main Gate. There, a priest would draw back the bolt and the latches and open it. The slaughterer did not slaughter until he heard the sound of the Great Gate being opened – a sound that was heard all the way to Jericho.

Inside the Sanctuary, the slaughtering priest is seen slaughtering the morning *Tamid* offering. His back is towards the sun, to negate the custom of the idol-worshipers who specifically bow to the sun. This is stated in the Mishna (*Tamid* 4:1), which adds that the morning *Tamid* was slaughtered near the north-western corner of the altar, on the second ring – as can be seen here in the picture.

Bringing and Sprinkling the Blood

The four main activities in every sacrificial offering are: Slaughtering, receiving the blood in a receptacle, bringing it to the altar, and sprinkling it on the altar. Seen here are the latter two: The priest on the right is bringing the blood to the corner of the altar, and the priest on the left is sprinkling it. As Maimonides writes, "The priest casts it from the receptacle twice, [once] on each of two of the altar's corners, northeast and southwest, on a diagonal, on the bottom half of the altar. When doing so, his intention should be that the blood will surround the corners" (*Ma'aseh HaKorbanot* 5:6; *Tamid* 4:1).

Another form of sprinkling is by pouring it [in the picture: the priest in the center], as is done for certain sacrifices. Maimonides writes (*Ma'aseh HaKorbanot* 5:17): "The first-born, and the tithed animal, and the Passover offering – their blood is given by pouring it on the bottom of the altar next to the foundation."

‹‹ Ascending the Altar

This picture depicts the priests making their way, in an orderly manner, with the various parts of the sacrificial animal to be placed on the fire atop the altar. The Mishna (*Tamid* 4:3) stipulates the precise order in which the parts were distributed to the priests and how they were to ascend to the altar. Here one can see a priest leading the way carrying a golden pitcher for wine libation, followed by one carrying flour for the Mincha offering, then a priest with the High Priest's griddle-cake offering. Next in line [though they actually preceded the previous three] are the priests carrying the parts of the *Tamid* offering: First the head and back leg, then the two front limbs, etc. In all, nine priests carried the various parts.

Tossing the Limbs of the Sacrifice ››

After the priests brought the limbs of the animal to the altar, they threw them, as required, on to the large fire. The priests actually stood on the ramp when they threw the limbs, with some distance between them and the fire, as the Talmud states (*Pesachim* 77a): "There was a small empty space between the ramp and the altar" (*Kesef Mishne* commentary to Maimonides, *Beit HaBechira* 2:13).

Keriat Shema on the Mt. of Olives

The picture shows Pilgrims on their way to the Temple stopping at the Mt. of Olives. They wait at dawn to see the rays of the rising sun strike the chandelier at the Sanctuary entrance. When the chandelier shines, it signifies to the pilgrims that the moment has arrived to recite the morning *Keriat Shema*, together with the people of Jerusalem (*Yoma* 37b). In the picture, the sun has risen just enough to illuminate the chandelier.

The Temple Chandelier Signals the Time for *Keriat Shema* ››

Shown here are the sun's early-morning rays striking the chandelier atop the Sanctuary's main gate. The chandelier was precisely placed so that the residents of Jerusalem, and in particular those visiting in the *Azara*, would see the sparks of light and know that the time for the recitation of *Keriat Shema* has arrived, as the Mishna (*Yoma* 3:10) states: "Queen Helene [the righteous convert], mother of King Munbaz, had a golden chandelier placed above the entrance to the Sanctuary." The Talmud adds that when the sun shone upon it, everyone in Jerusalem would know that the time for *Keriat Shema* had arrived.

‹‹ Daniel Facing Jerusalem in Prayer

The Book of Daniel relates how Daniel would pray in the direction of Jerusalem from his kingly home in Persia. The Sages learned three lessons from Daniel's prayer, as can be seen in the picture: 1) It is laudable to pray in a house with windows. 2) One must face Jerusalem during prayer. 3) While praying to God, it is appropriate to bow down on one's knees, for this is a form of "Divine service."

Three Types of Prostration

Seen here are three stages of bowing, as was customary when praying both inside and outside of the Temple: falling to the knees, sitting while kneeling, and bowing while kneeling. The fourth and main stage of bowing, that of full-body prostration, is depicted in other Temple Institute paintings, such as those depicting the *Yom Kippur* service. All four stages are listed in the Jerusalem Talmud (*Berakhot* 1:5).

Kneeling Stones

Father and son kneel just outside the Temple courtyard on an *Even Maskit*, one of several kneeling stones, sculpted and decorated especially for bowing. The Torah expressly forbids doing so (Leviticus 26:1) everywhere except in the Holy Temple. The Sages instituted 13 locations in which visitors to the Temple were to bow down in this manner, opposite the 13 breaches of the wall made by the Syrian Greeks and later closed up by the Hasmoneans (*Middot* 2:3; Mishna 2:6). In the picture is seen a sign, in Greek, banning Gentiles and ritually impure Jews from continuing past a certain point.

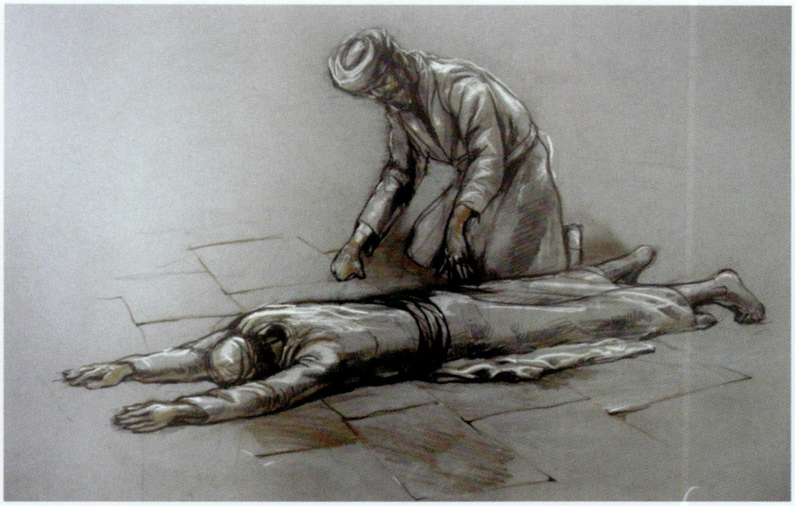

Stages of Prostration

This painting shows the procedure of bowing down, stage by stage. The person first bows on his knees, and then prostrates himself totally, spreading his arms and legs on the floor. Maimonides states (*Tefilla* 5:10): "Bowing down [means] spreading out one's arms and legs, until one is lying face-down on the ground."

Kidda

One of the forms of prostration in the Temple was *kidda*, and very few people were able to execute it properly. The Talmud explains (*Sukkah* 53a): "It was said about Rabban Shimon ben Gamliel that when he celebrated the Celebration of the Drawing of Water (*Simchat Beit HaShoevah*) on *Sukkot*, he would... bow down, place his two thumbs on the ground, kiss the floor, and then stand upright; no one else could do this feat, known as *kidda*."

The *Tamid* Sacrifice in the Temple Courtyard ››

Many Israelites gather in the *Azara*, in the early morning, to participate in or witness the offering of the daily morning *Tamid* sacrifice. A priest can be seen here on top of the altar supervising the offering. Other priests, wearing white, are carrying out other functions of the Temple service. At left, on the platform, the Levites stand at the same time with their musical instruments and sing the Daily Song.

Many Israelites can be seen as well, bringing their own sacrifices and offerings for various purposes; they were permitted to enter the Priestly Courtyard for the purpose of slaughtering their sacrifices and performing *semikha*, laying hands on them.

When the chandelier on the Main Gate was lit up by the rays of the rising sun, this was the signal to recite *Keriat Shema*.

The sashes of the priests are seen in various shades of blue, purple and red, which were the colors of the embroidery thereof. Josephus writes that different colors stood out more at different times.

The Priestly Prayers

In the middle of the *Tamid* service, the priests would stop and gather in the Chamber of the Hewn Stones to recite the *Keriat Shema*. The appointed leader is seen here beginning the prayers by saying to his colleagues, "Recite one blessing!" (*Tamid* 5:1). This took place even before the community at large recited the *Keriat Shema*. The priests in this forum would also recite the Ten Commandments – the foundations of faith – as well as some blessings of the *Amida* (*Retzei* and *Sim Shalom*).

Teaching the Priests to Light the Menorah ››

The priest responsible for priest-training in the Temple is seen here giving a lesson in lighting the golden Menorah. He shows priests, both old and young, the art of kindling the lamps on a model candelabrum, while another priest (right) shows how the oil is poured into each lamp. If the Western Lamp – the one closest to the Holy of Holies – is already lit, the wick next to it is brought close so that it will catch fire, and so on with the other lamp-wicks, each one in turn. If, however, the Western Lamp had become extinguished, fire is brought from the altar to light that lamp, and the others are lit as above.

The term "Western Lamp" is explained in various ways; this painting portrays one of them.

Lighting from Wick to Wick ››

This picture shows how the Western Lamp (on the left) was lit from the fire of the altar (on the right). The priest has brought fire from the altar, and he nears it to the wick of the candelabrum lamp that is first on the right. The priest then continues to the next lamp, bringing its wick close to the existing fire and kindling it. He continues in this manner until all seven lamps are lit.

The Incense Offering

Seen here are three priests preparing the daily incense offering. The Mishna (*Tamid* 6:2) relates the procedure:

"The one who had been chosen for the firepan (at left) made a heap of cinders [from the large altar] atop the [inner golden] altar, then spread them about with the end of the firepan, prostrated himself, and went out. The priest chosen to offer the incense (center) took the dish (after taking a handful of incense) from the bowl (held by the priest at right) and gave it to his friend or relative (at right). If some of the incense spilled into the bowl, the friend would put it into the (center) priest's hands... He would then begin to scatter the incense [over the coals] and would then go out. The one who burnt the incense did not do so until the superior said to him, 'Offer the incense.' ... The priests departed [from the Sanctuary], and he would offer the incense, prostrate himself, and go out."

Cleaning and Lighting the Menorah

It is a daily Biblical commandment to clean and remove the previous day's wicks and ashes from the Menorah, and to kindle the lamps once again. Maimonides details the process (*Temidin UMusafin* 3:10–13): "How much oil should be put in each lamp? Half a *log* (6–10 oz.) ... Every lamp that has burnt out, its wick and its [remaining] oil are removed, and it is cleaned. The priest places another wick and other oil in it, and lights it; this is *hatavat hanerot*... He would not light all seven lamps at once, but rather stops after five... and then returns and lights the remaining two [for this enhances the beauty of the commandment]."

The Chamber of the Oils

The chamber seen here is where the oil and wine needed for the Temple services were stored It was located in the south-western corner of the Women's Court, unroofed just like the other three chambers here. On the right are priests engaged in pouring wine and oil into larger flasks for storage.

The Levites on Their Way to Sing ››

The Levites, carrying their musical instruments, are seen on their way to sing the Song of the Day. They pass through the *soreg* fence encompassing the Courtyard as they near the Sanctuary, and then walk through the Gate of Song as they make their way to the platform.

The Priestly Blessing in the Temple

This illustration depicts the Priestly Blessing in the Holy Temple. The blessing recited here differs in several respects from the Priestly Blessing recited outside the Temple. As the Mishna (*Tamid* 7:2) describes, the priests "went and stood on the [12] steps of the *Ulam* (in the drawing they are seen standing on the top step). The first set [the five who had entered with the utensils for lighting the lamps and cleaning the incense altar] now stood to the south of their brother priests (in the center of the drawing and south of the steps), holding the five utensils... They recited the Priestly Blessing as a single benediction, and not three (as it is recited outside the Temple) ... In the Temple the priests raised their hands above their heads, except for the High Priest (seen on the left), who did not raise his hands above the *tzitz*." In this picture, the priests are seen raising their hands as high as their heads, in accordance with Targum Yonatan to Leviticus 9:22.

The Song of the Levites

This picture depicts the Levites' daily song in great detail. On the right, the Levites play and sing on the platform during the wine libation over the altar. On the left, many Israelites prostrate themselves, fully extending their arms and legs.

Every day of the week had its own *Shir Shel Yom* (Song of the Day), and each song was divided into three parts; after each part, the priests would sound the trumpets, and the people in the *Azara* would bow down towards the Holy of Holies.

The Mishna (*Sukkah* 5:5) teaches: "There were no fewer than 21 trumpet blasts a day in the Temple: . . . Three for opening the gates, nine for the morning *Tamid* [three for each song-part], and nine for the evening *Tamid*."

The Mishna (*Tamid* 7:3) states: "The Deputy High Priest stands on the corner (of the altar, seen here at top left), with the flags in his hand. Two priests stood on the table of fats [west of the ramp], holding two silver trumpets [which they sounded three times]. The two priests came and stood on either side of Ben Arza, who held the cymbals. The priest atop the altar bent down to pour the wine, and the deputy waved the flags, and Ben Arza sounded the cymbals, and the Levites sang the song. When they reached the end of the first part of the song, the priests blew the trumpets, and the people prostrated themselves. For every part of the song – a trumpet blast, and for every trumpet blast – a prostration."

The Trumpet Signals the Onset of Sabbath

Six trumpet blasts were sounded in the Temple on the Sabbath eve: "Three to announce the end of weekday work, forbidden on the Sabbath, and three to differentiate between the weekday and the holy Sabbath" (*Sukkah* 53b, and Maimonides, *Kelei HaMikdash* 7:6).

Josephus notes that the trumpet was similarly sounded to mark the end of the Sabbath. He writes (*The Wars of the Jews* 9:12) that the fourth tower built by Herod in the Temple "was built atop the Temple's Chambers, where one of the priests would stand every Sabbath eve and sound a trumpet to announce the onset of the Sabbath; he would do the same the next night [to signal the Sabbath's end]. The first blast would tell the people to stop their work, while the second would tell them to return to their work."

Recent archaeological excavations at the Temple's south-eastern corner uncovered a fragment with the Hebrew inscription "to the *Beit HaTekiya* [Place of the Trumpet Blast]," indicating the place where the priest stood and proclaimed to pilgrims, visitors, and residents the onset – and departure – of the Sabbath.

A Fistful of Frankincense

The painting depicts the procedure of *kemitza*, which took place when the Showbread was brought to the Sanctuary on the Sabbath, just before the offering of the incense upon the altar. Maimonides writes (*Temidin UMusafin* 5:2): "A vessel containing a handful of frankincense is placed next to each set of loaves, as is written (Leviticus 24:7), **'You shall place pure frankincense next to the arrangement.'** This vessel is called a *bazakh*. There were thus two fistfuls of frankincense in the two dishes."

The priest picks up a fistful of incense or milled flour in his three middle fingers, and uses his thumb and little finger to brush away the extra amount; that which remains between his three fingers is called by the same name, *kemitza*.

The procedure of *kemitza* was required for various parts of the Temple service, and mainly for the bringing of the Mincha offerings to the altar.

Sabbath in the Temple

On the Sabbath two activities were added to the priests' daily tasks: First, The *Musaf* offering – "On the Sabbath day, two yearling lambs, unblemished" (Numbers 28:9) – and second, the placing of the Showbread on the *shulchan* (table) in the *Heikhal*.

The illustration shows priests bringing the two lambs from the Chamber of the Lambs to be sacrificed on the northern part of the altar. Behind them, other priests bring the Showbread and the frankincense from the Chamber of the Showbread Makers. Both chambers were in the *Beit HaMoked*.

Bringing the Showbread

Every Sabbath the priests would bring 12 newly-baked loaves and place them on the *shulchan*, opposite the Menorah. Maimonides writes (*Temidin UMusafin* 5:1) that it is a positive Biblical commandment to arrange the new Showbread loaves every Sabbath. He explains the procedure:

Four priests enter, two holding one set each of six loaves, and two holding two small vessels [of frankincense]. Four priests enter before them, two to take the two [old] sets of loaves, and two to take the two small censers that were on the *shulchan*. Those who enter stand in the north and face south, and those who leave stand in the south and face north. [Precisely as] these remove [the previous week's Showbread, the others place down [the new breads], and they stand within a handbreadth of the other, as written: "[You shall place Showbread] before Me continually" (Exodus 25:30).

To arrange the bread, they would dismantle the *shulchan* on Friday (as seen in the foreground), and put it back together after the Sabbath.

« The Incense Censers

This painting shows two golden censers and their covers; the incense was kept inside them. Placed on the Showbread Table, they would remain there all week, together with the loaves of Showbread. When the priests removed the bread, on the Sabbath, to distribute among the priests, the censers were brought to the altar. Only after the frankincense was placed atop the altar for burning would the priests be permitted to eat the loaves in the *Azara*.

Consulting the *Urim VeTummim*: Rashi »

This painting shows a Davidic king of Israel (right), asking the High Priest (left) whether to go to war or not. According to Rashi, as opposed to Maimonides, the question need not be asked in a particular place; it is critical only that the king face the High Priest and the Breastplate on which the Divine answer is to be revealed.

Both Maimonides and Rashi agree that the questioner must face the Divine while asking the question. However, Maimonides says this means he must face the Holy of Holies, while according to Rashi, he must face the Divinely holy Breastplate and its twelve precious stones.

Consulting the *Urim VeTummim*: Maimonides ››

As seen here, the King of Israel and the High Priest stand by the entrance to the Holy of Holies as they consult the Urim VeTummim – on the High Priest's breastplate – for a Divine answer to their question of national importance. This happened frequently during the First Temple, often involving questions of whether to go out to war. During the Second Temple, with the removal of prophetic spirit, the *Urim VeTummim* were not consulted.

It was forbidden to enter the Holy of Holies, of course, and they therefore made sure to stand only at the entrance. A stone wall (on the right) separated the Holy of Holies and the Sanctuary, with an opening covered by a curtain, which they opened. Thus, the question was presented "before the Divine Presence" – opposite the Holy Ark and the Cherubim.

The High Priest opens the curtains and stands between the rods of the Ark at the entrance to the Holy of Holies, facing the place of Divine inspiration. The king stands slightly behind him, and asks briefly and in a low voice, "Shall I go up [to war]?" The Divine Presence immediately comes over the High Priest, he reads the answer from the sparkling letters on the breastplate, and responds to the king: "Go up!"

In general, only priests performing their Temple duties are permitted to enter the Sanctuary. This case is special, however, because the commandment of consulting the *Urim VeTummim* must specifically be done opposite the Holy Ark, and the king or a representative of the nation, i.e., a member of the Sanhedrin, are to bring the question "before the Divine Presence." That is, for the purpose of a national question that requires a Heavenly answer, it is permitted for the king to enter this area – for that is how this commandment is to be fulfilled (based on Maimonides, *Kelei HaMikdash* 10:11, and his commentary to Mishna *Yoma* 7:5, and a discussion with an expert on Maimonides, Rabbi Yosef Kapach of saintly blessed memory).

The Sanhedrin in the Chamber of Hewn Stone

Introduction

The Beit HaMikdash embraces and unites two central concepts of the Divine mandate given the Jewish People at Mt. Sinai: Torah and worship.

The first is found in the Holy of Holies, in the form of the *Luchot* (Tablets of the Law) given to Moses and placed for safekeeping in the Ark of the Covenant. The Ark also holds the Torah Scroll that Moses wrote at the conclusion of the 40 years in the desert.

The second concept is worship. Expressed today mainly in prayer, it is manifest in the Holy Temple in the priestly service at the altar and in the Sanctuary. This includes the offering of regular and special sacrifices, by both individuals and the community, and other activities as well, all performed with joy and awe.

In addition, the seat of the Great Court (Sanhedrin) is also in the Holy Temple. The Talmud (*Sanhedrin* 88b) derives from the verse, "These are the laws that you shall place before them" (Exodus 21:1) that the Sanhedrin must convene near the altar, in the shadow of the Divine Presence. This is because the Sages of the Court required Divine supervision and special inspiration in their efforts to reach the best decisions. As Nachmanides wrote (Deuteronomy 17:11), we are bidden to "adhere to the Great Court, standing before God in the place He chose, in everything they instruct regarding the Torah . . . for the spirit of God is upon the servants of His Sanctuary, and He will not abandon His followers and will ever save them from mistakes and errors."

Furthermore, there are two important Halakhic issues that can be judged only in the Sanhedrin in the Temple's Chamber of Hewn Stone (*Lishkat HaGazit*). The first is capital punishment. Maimonides writes (*Sanhedrin* 14:11–13): "Cases of capital punishment are adjudicated only when the Temple is extant, and when the Great Court hold sessions there in the Chamber of Hewn Stone . . . Oral Tradition taught that only when priests offer sacrifices on the altar, and the Court holds sessions in its place, are capital punishment cases judged . . . Capital punishment was nullified 40 years before the Temple's destruction, because though the Temple was still standing, the Sanhedrin had gone into exile and was not in its place in the Temple."

The second important matter that can be judged only by the Sanhedrin is *zaken mamre*, the "rebellious elder" – a Sage who issued a ruling in opposition to the Sanhedrin. Under certain circumstances he is put to death, because of the critical importance of assuring "one law" in Israel. However, if the Sanhedrin was not in its place when he rebelled against it, he is not liable, for the "place" is a critical element (Maimonides, *Mamrim* 3:7).

Similarly, when the High Priest was asked questions of national import that would be answered via the *Urim VeTummim*, Maimonides wrote that these would be asked in the Holy Temple, before the Holy of Holies.

The Tent of the Sanhedrin in the Desert

This painting depicts the Tabernacle in the times of Moses, at the foot of Mt. Sinai. The tent of the Seventy Elders stood adjacent to the Tabernacle gate. Here Moses taught the laws that he received on Sinai and in the Holy of Holies to the elders and to all of Israel.

Moses first taught the priestly family, Aaron and his sons, and then the tribal leaders and the judges, followed by the entire nation. The Talmud explains the procedure (*Eiruvin* 54b): "Moses learned from God; Aaron then entered, and Moses taught him. Aaron then sat at Moses' left, and Aaron's sons entered. Moses taught them, and they sat near Moses and Aaron, Elazar to Moses' right and Itamar to Aaron's left. . . The elders then entered, and Moses taught them. The people then entered, and Moses taught them. Thus, Aaron heard the laws four times, his sons – three, the elders – twice, and the people – once." From there, the elders went to their respective tribal Sanhedrins, and taught God's word to the "ministers of the thousands and the hundreds" (Exodus 18:25), who then taught them to the 600,000 Israelites.

Moses Transfers Mantle to Joshua

This picture shows a special occasion in the Plains of Moab, where Moses placed his hands (the act of *semikha*) upon the head of Joshua bin Nun. He thus transfers the national leadership to his student, as God commanded, as the nation is about to cross the Jordan River into the Holy Land after 40 years of wandering.

According to Maimonides, it was here that rabbinic *semikha* – the transfer of rabbinic leadership and scholarship – was first introduced. The Mishna (*Avot* 1:1) states: "Moses received the Torah at Sinai, and gave it to Joshua, and Joshua gave it to the Elders. . ."

Moses thus taught all future generations: "Just like I appointed Joshua as leader with both my hands, you shall do the same. Continue the *semikha*, and thus guarantee the existence of the Oral Law for all generations." Maimonides thus rules that the authority of all authorized rabbis, even today, stems from Moses and Joshua. Others, however, state that Moses transferred only the royal leadership to Joshua at this time, but that the appointment of Sanhedrin judges can be carried out in all generations even without *semikha*.

King David and the Sanhedrin

This illustration shows King David asking for the Sanhedrin's authorization to go to war against Moab and Aram (Mesopotamia). The Midrash (*Bereshit Rabba*) teaches that the king removed his crown and mantle, showing that he came not as a king but as one of the sages. Following a debate, the Sanhedrin granted him the authority, and King David set out for war.

With the ascendance of David as King of Israel, the judicial system in general and the Sanhedrin in particular were strengthened, and the commandment of "Appoint judges and officers in all your gates" was carried out. David appointed Yoav and the military as a police force ensuring the execution of the judges' rulings, as explained in *Midrash Tanna'im* (Deuteronomy 16).

Solomon Judges the Two Mothers

The painting shows King Solomon shortly after he became king, at the age of 20, sitting in the Sanhedrin in the royal palace. One of the first cases that came before him was that of the two mothers; the baby of one of them had died, but both claimed to be the mother of the one who still lived. Solomon, in his wisdom, asked for a sword with which to "divide" the baby in two; one mother refused to allow the baby to be killed, thus making clear that she was his mother. The wisdom of King Solomon was thus revealed to all (Kings I 3): "All Israel heard the verdict delivered by the king, and they feared him, because they saw that the wisdom of God was in him to do justice."

As did his father King David, King Solomon established the High Court in Jerusalem, and prayed as follows (Kings I 3:5–28): "A small boy am I, I do not know to come and go... Please grant Your servant an understanding heart to judge Your people, to understand right from wrong."

Shimon HaTzaddik and the Great Assembly ››

Seen here is Shimon HaTzaddik (Simon the Just), dressed in priestly garments, leading a delegation of priests to greet Alexander of Macedonia. As a result of the honor shown him, Alexander bolstered the status of the Temple and the Sanhedrin.

Shimon HaTzaddik (*Avot* 1:2) marks the end of an era in the history of the Great Court: the end of the Great Assembly, which was established as a continuation of the Sanhedrin, and the beginning of the period of the "Pairs" (*Avot* 1:2–8). The Assembly was founded immediately upon the return of the Babylonian exiles to the Holy Land, at the beginning of the Second Temple period.

Maimonides writes (introduction to the Mishna): "The Men of the Great Assembly are Haggai, Zechariah, and Malachi... and Ezra the Scribe and Nehemiah ben Hachaliah... Altogether, 120 elders." These great Sages of Israel during the first years of the Second Temple had no choice but to establish the Great Assembly, because the Babylonian Exile had led to widespread abandonment of the Torah, and many commandments were simply not being observed (Nehemiah 8:1–16). Ezra the Scribe convened the returnees from Babylon in the Temple courtyards, and re-taught them the commandments and laws that were forgotten – thus restoring the crown to its former glory.

The Sanhedrin in the Days of Shimon ben Shatach ››

This painting depicts a dramatic scene that occurred in the Sanhedrin: The sage Shimon ben Shatach stands next to King Alexander Yannai during a trial of a royal slave accused of murder. Shimon ben Shatach demands that the king stands up, but the other judges, for fear of the king's wrath, hide their faces and do not second the demand.

It was around this time that the Sanhedrin underwent a traumatic jolt: It was taken over by the Sadducees, Jews who did not accept the authority of the Oral Law and the Sages. Shimon ben Shatach acted tirelessly to replace the Sadducee judges with others who were loyal to the Torah of Moses, and worked in general to strengthen the Court's status vis-à-vis the royal house (which also inclined towards the Sadducees).

The Talmud (*Sanhedrin* 19a) relates the dramatic events of the trial of King Yannai's slave, which was initiated by Shimon ben Shatach: "The Court summoned the slave, as well as the king – just as when an ox gores a man, the Torah requires the owner of an ox to testify. The king came, and sat before the judges. Shimon ben Shatach said to him, 'King Yannai! Stand on your legs!' The king responded, 'What do your colleagues say about this demand?' The king looked to his right, and the judges buried their faces in the ground; he looked left, and the judges there did the same. Shimon ben Shatach said, 'Are you men of thought!? The Master of Thoughts will come and exact payment from you!' Whereupon Gabriel came and smote them to the ground and they died."

The Sanhedrin in Kerem B'Yavneh ››

Seen here is a stormy session of the Sanhedrin in Kerem B'Yavneh in which a famous question was debated: Is the Evening Prayer obligatory or merely optional? Rabban Gamliel, the President of the Court, is seen sitting on the left, instructing Rabbi Yehoshua to stand and state his dissenting opinion. Rabbi Chutzpit HaMeturgeman (the elucidator is seen in the center.

"Give Me Yavneh and its Sages!" The establishment of Kerem B'Yavneh as the center of Torah study and its dissemination after the destruction of the Temple is credited to the great Sage Rabban Yochanan ben Zakkai. As head of the Sanhedrin, it was he who had made the request of the Roman general Vespasian: "Give me Yavneh and its Sages." Rabban Yochanan then served as president of the academy during the ensuing critical period, until he transferred the mantle of leadership to Rabban Gamliel. The latter's leadership style was soon considered to be too strict, and the Sages chose R. Elazar ben Azariah to succeed him.

Rabbi Yehuda ben Bava Ordains His Students Despite the Ban ››

This picture depicts Rabbi Yehuda ben Bava and his five students at the moment when he ordained them despite a ban on doing so. The location chosen for this momentous occasion was between Usha and Shefaram (seen in the rear of the picture), two places the Sanhedrin met for several years (*Rosh Hashanah* 31a) In his willingness to risk his life conducting the ordination, Rabbi Yehuda was trying to send a message that the end of the Sanhedrin was a fundamental issue that put the continuity of the Torah at risk. On the right one can see Roman soldiers charging in the direction of Rabbi Yehuda and his pupils.

At the time the Sanhedrin was in Usha and Shefaram, most religious life revolved around local courts, rather than in the Sanhedrin, which met only infrequently. This can be seen from the Talmud (*Sanhedrin* 32b): "One should follow the best, most prestigious court of the generation. For example, follow after Rabbi Eliezer to Lod, after Rabban Yoḥanan ben Zakkai to Beror Chayil… after Rabban Gamliel to Yavne, after Rabbi Akiva to Bnei Brak… after Rabbi Yehuda HaNasi to Beit She'arim."

In other words, a person with a question of Jewish law should find the best court, with the best reputation for decisions it renders. The Sanhedrin was a thorn in the eyes of the Romans, as they understood it to be the source of power for the Jewish nation. Therefore, they banned rabbinical ordination. Rabbi Yehuda ben Bava risked his life in order to fulfill the commandments of "Judges and officers" (Deuteronomy 16:18) as cited in the Talmud (*Sanhedrin* 13b): "Indeed, that man will be remembered favorably, and Rabbi Yehuda ben Bava is his name, as had it not been for him the laws of fines would have been forgotten from among the Jewish people… One time the wicked kingdom of Rome issued decrees of religious persecution against the Jewish people [with the aim of abolishing the chain of ordination and the authority of the Sages]. They said that anyone who ordains judges will be killed, and anyone who is ordained will be killed, and the city in which they ordain the judges will be destroyed… What did Rabbi Yehuda ben Bava do? He went and sat between two large mountains… between Usha and Shefaram, [a desolate place not associated with any city, in order not to endanger anyone else], and there he ordained five elders. And they were Rabbi Meir, and Rabbi Yehuda, and Rabbi Shimon… People say about this incident that the Roman soldiers did not move from there until they had inserted three hundred iron spears into him, making him appear like a sieve pierced with many holes."

‹‹ The Half-Circle, According to Maimonides

Manuscripts written by Maimonides and found in Yemen show another approach to the seating arrangement of the Sanhedrin: The President and Av Beit Din sit at the head, and opposite them sit the other members of the Sanhedrin as students in front of their teacher (Rav). This arrangement enables the entire tribunal to follow the testimonies and arguments most efficiently (*Sanhedrin* 1:3). On the left can be seen an opening to the *Azara* through which one can see the altar.

The Chamber of the Hewn Stone

The illustration shows the 71 members of the Sanhedrin in session. They sit in a half-circle and their students sit opposite them. The *Nasi* (President) of the Sanhedrin and his deputy, the *Av Beit Din* (left), listen attentively as the two litigants present their respective cases before the judges (center). Two court stenographers (foreground) record the testimony and the final ruling.

The Chamber of Hewn Stone, *Lishkat HaGazit*, was located in the north-eastern side of the Sanctuary Courtyard. Half of it was considered more holy than the other, and the judges and spectators in fact sat in the less holy side. To reach the altar and the Courtyard (seen behind the curtains), one had to walk through the more-holy part of this Chamber (*Sanhedrin* 88b, and Maimonides, *Beit HaBechira* 5:17).

"Arise and Go to the Place"

This painting shows a session of the Sanhedrin in the *Lishkat HaGazit*, presided over by the *Nasi* and the *Av Beit Din* (sitting in the center). The other members are each seen with a golden table standing in front of them, as the Talmud states (*Sukkah* 51b). At issue here is a question that was unable to be solved in the local court where the question first arose. In such a case, the law is that the question must be decided by the High Court in Jerusalem (Deuteronomy 17:8). There were actually three courts in the Temple: One at the Temple Mount entrance, one at the entrance to the *Azara*, and one in the *Lishkat HaGazit*, from where Torah goes out to all of Israel. The *Sifrei* quotes this verse: "You shall do according to that which they will tell you from the place chosen by God."

A Mistaken Sanhedrin Ruling

If the Sanhedrin issues a mistaken ruling, leading a majority of Israel to act errantly, the judges of the Sanhedrin must offer a special set of sacrifices, known as the Forgotten-Law Bull. Twelve bulls are brought, corresponding to the Tribes of Israel. Seen here are members of the Sanhedrin placing their hands on the heads of the sacrifices and confessing to the error they made. The confession on the part of five of the elders, as Maimonides states (*Ma'aseh HaKorbanot* 3:10), is the first step of repentance, and leads to atonement.

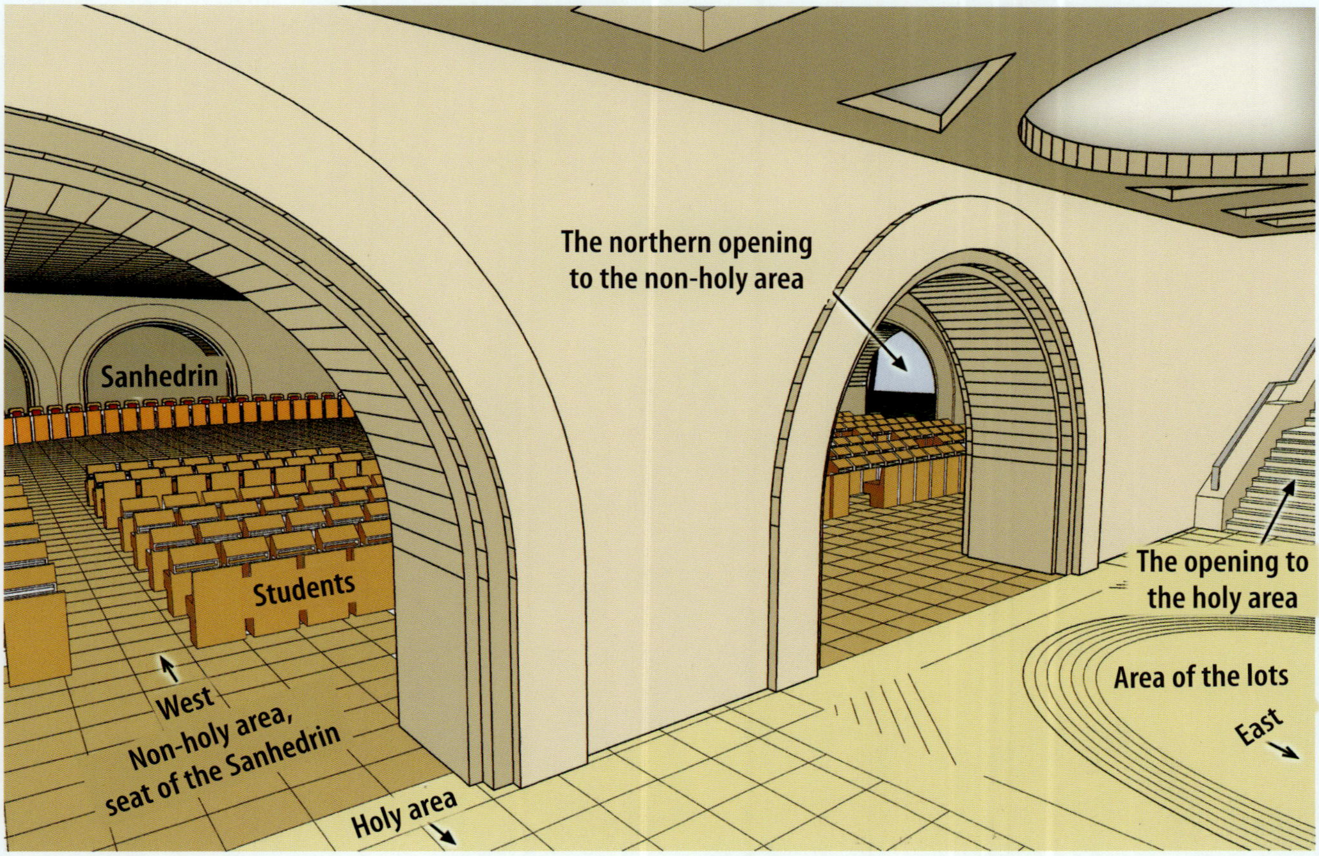

The Chamber of Hewn Stone and its Entrances

Seen here is a plan of the Chamber of Hewn Stone especially drawn up for the Temple Institute by architect Rabbi Shmuel Balsam. The plan shows the Chamber of Hewn Stone (*Lishkat HaGazit*) beneath the Courtyard floor, under the slaughtering area, thus that it is very close to the altar – in accordance with the law that the Sanhedrin must be close to the altar (*Sanhedrin* 88b).

The *Lishkat HaGazit* is divided in two parts, with passages to different parts of the Temple (*Yoma* 25a). The eastern part is "holy," because it has an entrance to the holy courtyard. This is where the priests draw lots each morning to determine their tasks; they must stand for this procedure, because of the sanctity of the site. The western part of the *Lishkat HaGazit* is "non-holy," because of its passage to the non-holy *Cheil* (rampart) area in the northern Temple Mount, and the 70 judges, and others, are permitted to sit there.

Women in the Holy Temple

Introduction

What role did women play in the Holy Temple? What were their obligations vis-à-vis the sacrifices, the prayers, and the various ceremonies and special occasions held in the Temple?

We must begin by remembering that when the first Temple – the Tabernacle (Mishkan) – was built, it was the women who so eagerly donated their gold and silver. As it is written, **"The men accompanied the women"** (Exodus 35:22) – that is, the women preceded the men in their desire to help build the Sanctuary. Nachmanides explains that the women rushed to immediately donate their jewelry, while the men merely followed after them. The Midrash teaches that the women of the desert generation were rewarded for their generosity in that they entered the Holy Land, while the men did not.

Thus, when the Mishkan was built, paving the way for the dwelling of the Divine Presence amidst Israel, the women had a decisive role: It was their characteristically deep faith that played a major role, and made its imprint on the nation for generations to come.

A careful perusal of the wide-ranging network of Temple mitzvot shows us that women were assigned a significant role in the Temple, in a manner befitting both their femininity and their responsibilities as mothers and wives.

From the very first days of the Mishkan, women are recorded to have entered the Tent of Meeting for prayer. It occurred famously in the times of Eli the High Priest in Shiloh, as we know from the story of Hannah. During the Second Temple period, women often entered the *Azara* for either prayer, repentance, or sacrifice, and a special "Women's Gate" was built. This was in addition to the separate Women's Courtyard where women congregated in the Temple for prayer – a central part of a Jewish woman's life – or for other needs. *Tosafot* (*Kiddushin* 52b) says that when necessary, a woman can enter the *Azara* freely to slaughter or "wave" a sacrifice, just as men do.

Many of the Temple sacrifices could be offered by either men or women. Among these were the Passover offering, a peace-offering (*shelamim*), a thanks-offering, a nazirite woman's sacrifice, and of course, the required post-birth offerings.

Women were full partners, like men, in construction of the Tabernacle and the Temple. They were also employed in the Temple's workshop, sewing curtains, priestly garments, and the like. Maimonides, in fact, rules that women are obligated in the commandment of building the Holy Temple: "Temple construction work takes place from dawn until dusk. And all are required to take part in the building, **both men and women**, financially and otherwise, just like in the Temple in the desert" (*Beit HaBechira* 1:12).

Thus, many commandments in the Temple – and even its very construction and maintenance – are incumbent upon women and men alike.

‹‹ The Israelite Women in the Desert

The picture shows women bringing their bronze mirrors to the priest in the Tent of Meeting, as donations for the Mishkan. Other women are seen praying towards the Holy of Holies, including one who prostrates herself on the ground in the Tabernacle courtyard. The Bible tells us that the women also brought donations of their silver and golden jewelry.

The laver (center), from which the priests washed their hands and feet, was fashioned entirely out of the bronze mirrors brought by the women. The Torah saw fit to note this at length: "He made the copper washstand and its copper base out of the mirrors of the women who had set up the legions (*hatzovot*), who congregated at the entrance of the tent of meeting" (Exodus 38:8). Rashi comments: "The daughters of Israel had mirrors they used when adorning themselves, but even these they did not hold back from donating towards the Tabernacle. Moshe did not want these mirrors, because they were used to serve the Evil Inclination [of lust]. God then told him: 'Accept them! They are most beloved to Me of all, for with them the women produced many hosts (*tzevaot*) [of children] in Egypt. . . and of these mirrors will be made the washstand, to be used to restore peace between man and wife, for its waters will be used to test a suspected adulteress.'"

Nachmanides comments: "The brass of the mirrors was burnished brass, resplendent and very beautiful, and he therefore set it aside from the start for the making of this utensil. When the women saw this, they gathered and came in all together (*tzevaot tzevaot*) to give their mirrors for this purpose."

Jonah's Wife in Jerusalem

The wife of the prophet Jonah brings her sacrifice, arriving via the Women's Gate, as recounted in the Talmud. Several Sages are surprised, but do not protest.

A woman is permitted to bring a *re'iya* burnt-offering on the three Festivals, though only men are commanded to do so. The Talmud (*Eiruvin* 96a) relates that Jonah's wife made the Festival pilgrimage to Jerusalem, and the Meiri adds that she also brought the *re'iya* burnt-offering – for a woman may take upon herself a positive commandment that only men are actually commanded to fulfill.

The trip was difficult and dangerous, for the wicked kings of Israel of the time had erected barriers to prevent the Ten Tribes from bringing sacrifices in Jerusalem; whoever crossed them would be severely punished (*Ta'anit* 28b). Jonah's wife braved these dangers and made it safely to the Temple.

Hannah Prays at the Tabernacle in Shiloh

One of the most famous Biblical examples of a woman praying in the Sanctuary is that of Hannah in Shiloh. Eli the High Priest is seen here sitting "next to the doorpost of the Sanctuary of God" (Samuel I 1:9), that is, in the courtyard of the Tent of Meeting. The verses continue: "She made an oath, saying, 'God of Hosts, if You look on the affliction of Your handmaiden . . . and give Your handmaiden offspring of man, I will give him to God all of his days. . .'" After Eli was assured that she was sincerely praying to God, and not simply drunk, he blessed her: "Go in peace, and may the God of Israel grant your request that you asked of Him."

Facing the Temple, Praying for Rain

Abba Chilkiya and his wife are seen here facing the Holy Temple and praying for rain. As related in the Talmud (*Ta'anit* 23a-b): "Once, during a drought, the Sages sent two Torah scholars to Abba Chilkiya's house to ask him to pray for rain. He saw them and said to his wife, 'I know they have come because of the drought. Let us go up to the roof and ask for mercy; perhaps God will bring rain, and they won't know that it was in our merit.' They went up and prayed on the roof, each one in a different corner – and rainclouds began to appear... The scholars realized that the rain had come because of Abba Chilkiya, but asked him why the clouds came first from his wife's direction. He explained, 'My wife is at home and gives food to the poor, which they can use immediately, while I give only money – therefore, her prayers were answered immediately.'"

The New Courtyard

When the First Temple stood, during the reign of King Jehoshaphat, a "new courtyard" was built outside the Sanctuary – and during the Second Temple days, it became the *Ezrat Nashim*, the Women's Court. The king is seen here standing at the Sanctuary gate, as priests sound the trumpets next to him and the congregation stands in prayer. Men stand on one side, and women on the other.

The new courtyard is mentioned (Chronicles II, 20:2) "Jehoshaphat proclaimed a fast throughout Judah... and he stood in the assembly of Judah and Jerusalem in the House of the Lord, before the **new court**... And all the Judeans stood [there] before the Lord, also their infants, **their wives**, and their children..."

That very day, the Sages renewed a law in connection with this courtyard, namely, that one who has immersed for purification may not enter the Levite camp, i.e., the Women's Court, until the sun has set.

The Women's Gate ››

In this picture the Women's Gate is seen from the north. The Women's Gate (the middle one) is where women who wished to bring a Festival sacrifice would enter. The gate on the left is known as the Gate of Song, through which the Levites pass on singing and making music on their way to the *dukhan* (platform).

The Women's Gate from the Inside – 2nd Temple

This picture provides a view of the gate through which women would enter the Temple to pray, give thanks, or bring a sacrifice. Located on the north side of the *Azara*, the women would enter through this gate to watch as the priests offer their sacrifices upon the altar – as is required. Women are even obligated to slaughter the Passover offering, unless a family member does it instead. The women would accompany their sacrifices with prayer, confession, repentance, prostration and thanks to God for His kindnesses.

The Four Chambers of the Women's Court ››

The picture shows a bird's-eye view of the *Ezrat Nashim* (Women's Court) and the Four Chambers at its corners. Maimonides explains that the chambers were built inside the Women's Court, one in each corner. This illustration, however, is in accordance with the Rosh (Rabbeinu Asher), who wrote (*Middot* 2:2) that the chambers were actually outside the Women's Court – leaving a large area inside for the holding of special events. The *Simchat Beit HaShoevah* (Water Drawing Festivities) and the *Hak'hel* ceremonies, for instance, took place in the Women's Court, where a large multitude of people could take part.

The Rosh's approach also explains why this was specifically a "women's" court: The male priests and Levites were busy with Temple service matters in the various chambers, as were male Israelites at various times, thus leaving the inner Court empty and available for women to spend time in prayer, prostration, and Divine worship.

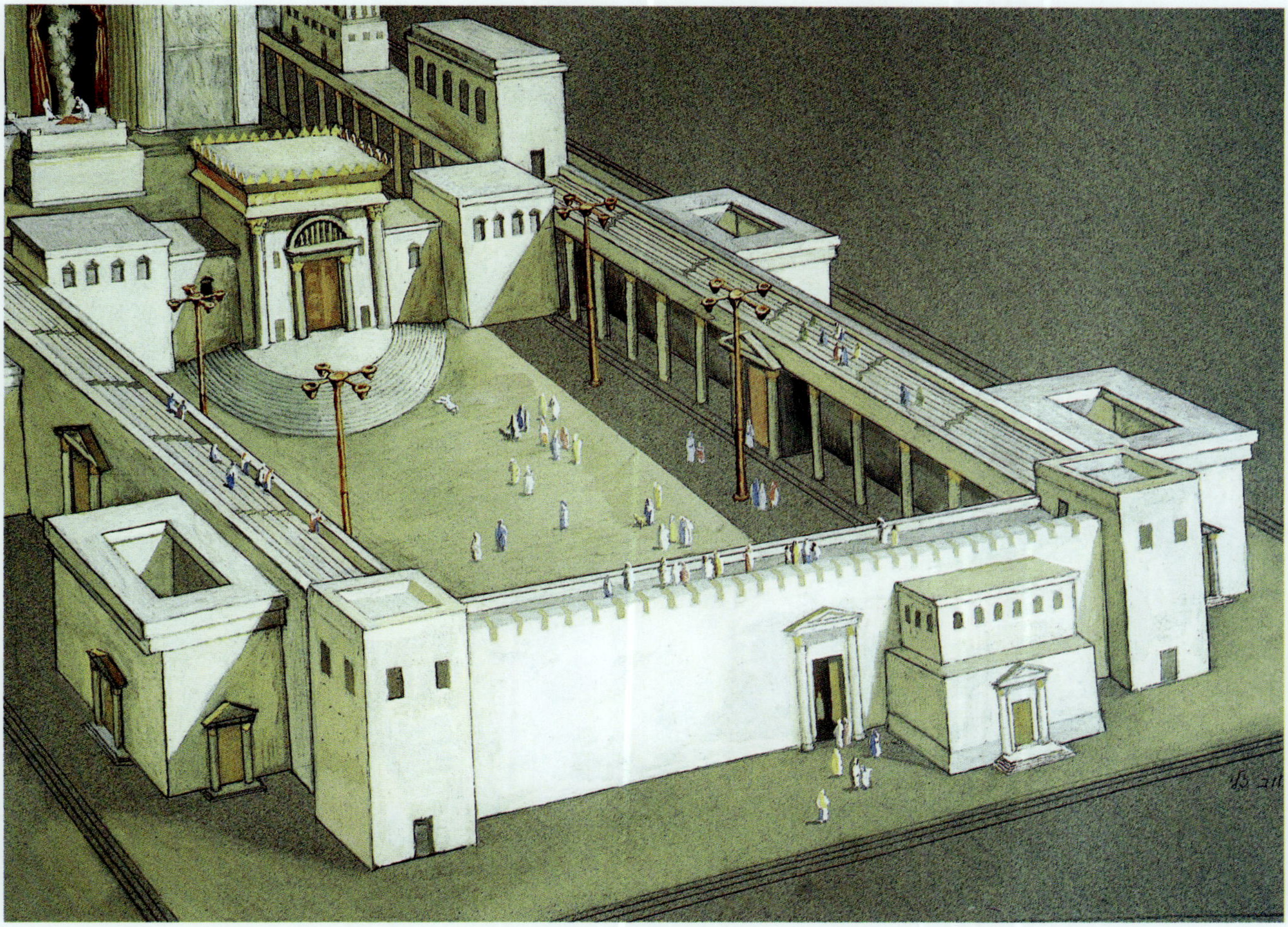

‹‹ Women's Prayer on the Temple Mount

The Sages teach that special consideration was given to downtrodden visitors to the Temple. The Mishna (*Middot* 2:2) states: "All who enter the Temple Mount come in from the right and go out on the left, except for one to whom something [sad] has happened, who would enter from the left." The latter would meet the others along the way, and they would ask him, "Why do you come from the left?" If he said he was a mourner, they would say, "May He Who dwells in this house comfort you." If he said he had been excommunicated, they would say, "May He Who dwells in this house inspire you to listen to your colleagues [the Sages] and they will bring you close again."

The picture shows women in need of salvation or consolation arriving at the Temple and receiving a blessing from other women. In Tractate *Semachot* (6:11), it states: "It happened that a woman came because her daughter had taken sick. She came from the left and went around the Sanctuary, and did not move from there until she was told that her daughter had been cured." It was similarly told about one who lost a Torah scroll worth 100 *maneh*, and came to the Temple from the left and did not leave until he was told that it had been found.

At right is seen a woman circling the Mount from the right, offering to pray for a friend she meets coming from the other side. On the left, one woman holds her ailing baby, while a second woman comes towards her and blesses her.

The Sacrifices Offered by Women after Giving Birth

The picture shows women arriving at the Gate of Nicanor after having giving birth, bringing their required sacrifices. In the center we see a mother giving her sacrifices to the priest. A wealthy woman stands at right, with a lamb and pigeon for her offering, while at left stands a lesser well-off woman, required to bring only two turtle-doves.

The Torah stipulates that a woman who gave birth must bring offerings to the Temple, dependent on her financial status. Maimonides (*Shegagot* 10:2) states: "If the new mother was wealthy, she brings a yearling lamb and a pigeon or a turtledove. If she does not have the means, she brings two turtledoves or two young pigeons." If her family cannot afford even that, or cannot afford the travel expenses, she need bring only the flour offering of a "poor man's sacrifice."

The woman stands outside the Gate of Nicanor and watches the priests as they offer her sacrifice – for until they do so, she is not permitted to enter the Sanctuary.

To facilitate matters for a new mother, she may simply give money to the priests, who will purchase sacrifices for her and offer them on the altar (Maimonides, *Mechusrei Kappara* 1:12). The Midrash teaches that the sons of Eli the Priest sinned, inter alia, by taking money from the new mothers but delaying their sacrifices, thus forcing the women to wait an extra day in the Mishkan. As a result, strict procedures were enacted to ensure that all such sacrifices were offered on the day they were brought.

Women and "*Semikha*"

A priest stands on the steps of the Women's Court, at the Gate of Nicanor, after having given over a sacrifice to women so that they could "lay their hands" – the act of *semikha* – on the consecrated animals.

It is a matter of Talmudic dispute whether or not a woman may perform *semikha* on the animal's head before it is placed upon the altar. The Talmud (*Chagiga* 16b) relates that Abba Elazar told R. Yosei: "We once had a calf for a peace-offering that we brought to the Women's Court, and women placed their hands on it – not because they are required to, but rather to provide them with contentment." The Meiri comments: "The Sages said that women do not place their hands, while R. Yosei said they may do so if they wish. The Ra'avad ruled that they should not place their hands, even on their own sacrifices . . . Others rule that they may if they wish."

The Sacrifices of a Woman Nazirite

Becoming a nazirite is one method by which a man or woman can achieve a spiritual uplift. At the end of the naziriteship, generally 30 days, he or she must bring sacrifices, as seen here.

Maimonides counts ten Biblical commandments associated with a nazirite, including bans on cutting one's hair, partaking of the produce of a vine, and coming near a corpse. A woman is specifically included in these commandments – and in fact one of the most famous nazirites was Queen Helena of the late Second Temple period. The Talmud (*Nazir* 19b) relates that she once vowed that if her son would return safely from the wars, she would be a nazirite for seven years – and she in fact did so.

When the period of being a nazirite is completed, the nazirite makes his or her way to Jerusalem and has a haircut in the Holy Temple. He or she then brings the appropriate sacrifices, ceremoniously "waving" them before God. Maimonides (*Nazir*, 8:1): "When the nazirite completes his naziriteship, he brings three animal sacrifices: A sheep as a burnt-offering, a lamb for a sin-offering, and a ram for a peace-offering… and 20 loaves – ten matza loaves and ten matza wafers… He has his hair cut in the Chamber of the Nazirites in the southeast corner of the Women's Court; there, his *shelamim* are cooked and their hair is thrown into the fire… The priest then takes the cooked foreleg of the ram and one of each matza, and gives them into the hands of the nazirite, and waves their hands – and then they are permitted to drink wine and come in contact with a corpse."

The Oath of the *Sota*

The picture shows a woman coming to the Temple to prove that she has not been unfaithful to her husband – in the face of his claim, buttressed by witnesses, that she secluded herself with a particular man despite his warnings not to do so. If she proclaims her innocence, she must undergo a special oath at the Gate of Nicanor, opposite the Holy of Holies. In the background we see the priests holding the special curse-bearing waters that she must drink to prove or disprove her innocence. The suspected adulteress is known as a *Sota*.

The Scroll of the *Sota* and the Waters

Three priests are seen here preparing for the *Sota* oath. One writes down the oath that she must take, copying it word-for-word from a golden plaque donated by Queen Helena (right). Another priest (left) removes the woman's hair-covering, and a third priest (inside the courtyard) prepares the curse-bearing waters that she must drink. The Sages discontinued the *Sota* procedure towards the end of the Second Temple period.

In the Chamber of the Curtain

This Chamber, adjacent to the Temple, is where women prepared the various curtains used in the Temple. Three activities are seen here: The weaving of material to be used in one of the curtains, the manufacturing of thread by spinning, and mixing and cooking dyes such as purple and turquoise. Here, too, the many priestly vestments used in the Temple were sewn and manufactured. Particular expertise was required to form the High Priest's golden vestments.

This Chamber was constantly guarded, possibly because of the inflammable materials used there.

Weaving and sewing were an important part of the Temple activities. The Talmud teaches (*Ketubot* 106a): "The women who wove and embroidered would receive their pay [a monthly salary] from the Temple funds [raised by public contributions] . . . There were 13 curtains in the Second Temple: Seven for the seven Court gates, one for the entrance to the Sanctuary, one for the entrance to the *Ulam*, two at the entrance to the Holy of Holies, and two above them in the upper floor."

Elsewhere, the Talmud (*Tamid* 29b) tells us that knitting and weaving the main curtain, the *parokhet*, between the Sanctuary and the Holy of Holies, was quite complex: "The *parokhet* was one handbreadth thick, formed of 72 strands each made of 24 threads. Its length was 40 cubits, its breadth was 20 cubits, and it was made by 82 young girls. Two were made each year, and it took 300 priests to immerse it." The Jerusalem Talmud adds that the new curtain would be spread on top of a roof on the Temple Mount so that the people would see the beautiful finished product.

‹‹ Woman Bringing First-Fruits

Women also participated in the festive bringing of the first fruits (*bikkurim*) of the harvest – and when they did, they also brought a lamb for a sacrificial offering, as seen here. Women were exempt, however, from reciting the *bikkurim* passage (Deuteronomy 26:5–10). Maimonides, however, indicates that they were required, like men, to recite aloud the introductory words professing that they have come "to the Land that God swore to our fathers to give us" (verse 3).

The person bringing the fruits, "even if he is a great King in Israel" (Maimonides, *Bikkurim* 3:3), carries them in a basket on his shoulder, walks into the *Azara*, and places them near the southwest corner of the altar, bows, and leaves. At that point, the fruits receive the status of "*bikkurim*," and are permitted to be eaten by the priests.

Women Bearing the First-Fruits

The picture portrays women bringing their first fruits (*bikkurim*) to the Temple; one woman (center) is fulfilling the commandment of "waving" them.

The first fruits are brought to a defined area in the Courtyard: the place known as "between the *Ulam* and the altar." The process has three steps: 1) Waving – the woman holds the handles of the *bikkurim* basket, while the priest places his hands underneath the basket, and they wave it together back and forth, up and down. 2) Placing the basket near the corner of the altar. 3) The woman then bows down on the ground, facing the Sanctuary.

The Maidens of Shiloh

Seen here are the daughters of the town of Shiloh, wearing white and dancing in the vineyards as they welcome the others bringing their first-fruits from around the country to the Tabernacle in Shiloh.

A verse (Judges 21:19) describes the "Feast unto God" that was held in Shiloh: "A sacrifice from time to time before the Lord in Shiloh, which is to the north of Beit El, on the east side of the highway going up from Beit El to Shechem, and to the south of Levona." Some commentaries imply that this was a holiday on which sacrifices were brought, such as one of the Three Festivals or *Yom Kippur*. Others say it was the 15th of Av, about which the Sages say, "There were never greater days of joy in Israel than the 15th of Av and the Day of Atonement. . . [On the former,] the Tribe of Benjamin was permitted to again marry into the Congregation of Israel." The joy in Shiloh at this time of year was also connected with the grape harvest, accompanied by the bringing of the first-fruits to the Tabernacle there.

Women at the Seder

The picture shows a Passover Seder in Jerusalem, with women fulfilling their obligation alongside the men. A child asks the 4 *Ma Nishtana* questions, while in the background, the roasted Passover offering is being brought in.

The obligations of women on Passover include ascending to Jerusalem and partaking of the Passover offering. Maimonides states (*Korban Pesach* 1:1): "It is a positive commandment to slaughter the Passover offering on the 14th of Nisan after midday. . . Both men and women are obligated in this commandment" – and both are liable for the extreme punishment of *karet* (excision) if they do not fulfill it. If a man is exempt from the commandment because of sickness and the like, his wife is still obligated.

Regarding the Seder, women may, if they wish, form their own group, taking care to fulfill the various commandments such as eating in purity and not breaking a bone of the lamb.

Women's Preparing for Tu B'Av Celebration

"There were never greater days of joy in Israel," states the Talmud (*Ta'anit* 26b), "than the 15th of Av and the Day of Atonement, when the daughters of Jerusalem would walk out in borrowed white garments – in order not to shame those who had none." This picture shows women borrowing from each other. They would purify the garments, even those that had been folded and put away, in order to ensure that they would mark the day in purity.

The Talmud continues: "The daughters of Jerusalem came out and danced in the vineyards, exclaiming: 'Young man, lift up your eyes and see what you choose. Do not set your eyes on beauty, but rather on good family. . .'"

Women at the Festivities of Water-Drawing

The picture shows women watching the *Simchat Beit HaShoeva* (Water Drawing festivities) from above. They are standing above the Women's Court, in a balcony made specifically so that men and women would not mingle together in an atmosphere of light-headedness. The introduction of this balcony was thus considered a "great enactment," the Sages say.

Maimonides (*Sukkah* 8:12): "There was an additional celebration of joy in the Temple on *Sukkot*... On the eve of the first day, they made a place for the women above so that there would be no inter-mingling. They would begin the festivities when the first day concluded, and then every night of the holiday, beginning after the offering of the afternoon daily *Tamid* sacrifice and all through the night... The flute would be sounded and songs played on the harp, lute, and cymbals. Everyone would play the instrument that he knew, and those who could sing, would sing, and they would dance and clap their hands, whistle, and the like... The more joy, the better. It was not performed by the common people or anyone who simply desired to take part; only the greatest of Israel's wise men did so: the Yeshiva heads, the members of the High Court, the pious, the elders, and the men of stature..."

The Matriarch Rachel Weeps over Her Exiled Sons ››

This striking picture depicts Rachel praying, as in the verse (Jeremiah 31:14), "A voice is heard on high, lamentation and bitter weeping – Rachel weeping for her children, she refuses to be comforted for her children for they are gone."

A sacked and burning Judean city can be seen at right (top), and the exiles are seen making their sad way out of the Land, carrying the Temple menorah. Men (bottom right) are seen grabbing onto the boulder of Rachel's Tomb, praying to be allowed to return, in fulfillment of verse 16: "The sons shall return to their border."

In his commentary (Genesis 48:7), Rashi explains what Jacob told Joseph regarding his mother Rachel's burial site: "I buried her there, on the road to Bethlehem, by Divine counsel, so that she could be of aid to her children exiled by King Nebuzaradan of Babylon as they pass by there. Rachel will stand outside her grave, crying and asking for Divine compassion for them [as in the above-quoted verse]. God will then answer: 'There is reward for your actions; the sons will return to their border.'" This idea is found, as well, in the *Midrash Pesikta Rabbati*, which states that the exiled children will embrace the Tomb of Rachel and ask for the prayers of the Forefathers.

Rosh Hashanah in the Mikdash

Introduction

Rosh Hashanah, the holiday that marks the new Jewish year, has two names in the Torah: Day of Remembrance, and Day of *Terua* [Shofar blast]. Both remembrance and shofar-blasts are integral parts of the significance of this holy day.

It is a Day of Remembrance, because according to the Sages it is a day on which every creature is brought before God for judgment. There is no more appropriate day than *Rosh Hashanah* for introspection, repentance, and atonement, for on that day Adam was created and took his first steps on earth. The Midrash teaches (*Pesikta DeRav Kahana* 23:1):

"On the 25th of Elul the world was created. 'This is the day of the beginning of Your works… the day on which it will be determined which country will face sword and which will be at peace; which will face hunger and which will be satiated; which is headed towards death, and which to life. All of creation will be noted for life or death…' On this first day, Adam sinned, and was judged, and was exempted from punishment. God said to him: 'Adam! This is a sign for your descendants, that just as you were tried and exempted from punishment, so too they will be tried on this day and will be exempted from punishment – on the first day of the seventh month [*Rosh Hashanah*].'"

This, then, is the significance of the Day of Remembrance: All of Creation is reviewed and judged. Thus, the New Year and the new month of Tishrei [both begin on the same day] are intrinsically bonded, in that both the moon and all of Creation are renewed – as is man himself, who renews himself with repentance and good deeds.

On *Rosh Hashanah*, Isaac was bound on the altar on Mt. Moriah – and then replaced with a ram after God exempted Abraham from carrying out the test any further. On this Day of *Terua*, the ram's horn is sounded, a reminder of the binding of Isaac and its ram.

The Midrash states as follows: "Abraham called that site **'God will see'** (Genesis 22:14). When Isaac's sons come to pray before You on this day [*Rosh Hashanah*], let it be **seen** before You as if Isaac's ashes are gathered there, and please forgive their sins."

The fact that the shofar is specifically a ram's horn reminds us of two things: The day of Creation, and the Binding of Isaac and the laying of the foundation of the Holy Temple in Israel – for it was on this occasion that the first sacrifice was offered, the ram, by the Patriarch Abraham, on the spot of the future Temple.

These concepts and others find their expression in the following series of paintings and pictures, and the accompanying explanations. These ancient insights are intrinsically intertwined with the Day of Judgment, and they help us truly delve into the deep significance of this day and arouse our thoughts towards a proper understanding of it.

‹‹ The Exiles Return to the Temple to Repent on *Rosh Hashanah*

Following the Babylonian Exile, when some 42,000 Jews returned to the Land of Israel, many of them gathered in the Holy Temple on *Rosh Hashanah*. Ezra the Scribe (wearing orange, at left) read the Torah aloud, reminding them of the many Divine commandments they had neglected over the years such as the commandments of Sukkah and Lulav. There were those seen in the crowd in the crowd who "transmitted" Ezra's words to the others, and were even able to answer questions. It was on this occasion that a covenant was contracted to observe the commandments of the Torah, and especially those mitzvoth having to do with the Temple.

In the Bible (Nehemiah 7:72) we read: "...and the seventh month arrived, and the Children of Israel were in their cities. All the people gathered as one man to the square before the Water Gate [in the southern part of the Courtyard]," as can be seen in the picture. The gates and buildings in the picture are designed and colored in the style to which the returnees had grown accustomed in Exile in Babylon.

***Rosh Hashanah*: From Mourning to Rejoicing**

The passage continues: "Ezra the priest brought the Torah before the congregation, both men and women... on the first day of the seventh month, and he read it aloud... And Ezra the scholar stood on a wooden platform that they had made for the purpose." Six priests stood on his right and six on his left, "and Ezra blessed the Lord, the great God, and all answered, 'Amen, Amen,' with the uplifting of their hands, and they bent their heads and prostrated themselves to the Lord on their faces to the ground."

Thus *Rosh Hashanah* became, during the times of Ezra and Nehemiah, the beginning of the process of repentance in the Temple, and it continued throughout the month of Tishrei.

When those assembled in the Temple courtyards heard what was written in the Torah, they began to cry and mourn regarding their sins. Ezra and the Levites with him calmed them down and said, "Today is a holy day unto the Lord your God, do not mourn and do not weep... Go and eat and drink delicacies and sweets... For God's joy is your strength" (Nehemiah 8:9).

Sounding the Shofar and Horns at the East Gate of the Temple

The priests sound the shofar and the trumpets in a special order on *Rosh Hashanah*. They stand on the steps of the Eastern Gate of the Sanctuary before a gathering of Temple visitors, who are in the *Azara*, as is written (Psalms 98:6): "With trumpets and the sound of a shofar, raise your voices before the King, the Lord" – indicating that it must be before the Sanctuary. The Mishna (*Rosh Hashanah* 3:3) teaches that the "shofar of *Rosh Hashanah* [in the Temple] – its mouth was overlaid with gold. There were two trumpets, one on each side of it. The shofar[-blower] gave a long blast and the trumpet[-blowers] a shorter one," to show that the mitzvah of the day is specifically with the shofar.

The *Musaf* Offering for the New Month on *Rosh Hashanah* ››

This painting shows a shepherd making his way to the Chamber of the Sheep in the Holy Temple, bringing his animals to be used for the *Musaf* (additional) offering for Rosh Chodesh (the New Month) and handing them over to the priests.

From the moment the Beit Din declared the onset of the new month of Tishrei, based on witnesses who testified that they had seen the new moon, preparations began for the Rosh Chodesh *Musaf* offering – which was to be offered on the same day, but prior to, the *Rosh Hashanah Musaf* offering. Maimonides writes (*Temidin UMusafin* 7:1): "On Rosh Chodesh, including *Rosh Hashanah*, the *Musaf* is brought after the morning *Tamid* sacrifice. It comprised eleven animals: two bulls, one ram, and seven sheep as burnt-offerings, and one goat for a sin-offering."

‹‹ The *Musaf* Offering on *Rosh Hashanah*

Here we see a shepherd on his way to Jerusalem to bring the sheep for the *Rosh Hashanah* sacrifices to the priests. The *Musaf* offering on the New Year includes ten animals, offered together following the Rosh Chodesh offerings. Maimonides writes (*Temidin UMusafin* 9:1): "On the first of Tishrei, the *Musaf* is brought: a bull, a ram, and seven sheep as burnt-offerings, and a goat for a sin-offering, to be eaten – in addition to the regular *Musaf* offering for Rosh Chodesh."

The Uniqueness of Jerusalem on *Rosh Hashanah* ››

Although in general, the Sages decreed that the shofar was not to be sounded on *Rosh Hashanah* when the holiday fell on the Sabbath, Jerusalem was different: Both in the Temple and in the city as well – and even in nearby villages within seeing distance of the Temple – the shofar was blown on the Sabbath of *Rosh Hashanah*. This law only applies when the Temple exists.

« *Rosh Hashanah* Shofar Blowing

Here we see priests blowing the shofar on *Rosh Hashanah*. This time, it is outside the *Azara*, for the benefit of those who were ritually impure and could not enter. The large stone engraved with the warning that the impure may not pass that spot can be seen at the lower left. Here, too, the shofar was accompanied by trumpets on either side, but the shofar blast was longer.

Waiting for the Witnesses

As the Beit Din can declare a new month based only on eyewitness testimony of a new moon sighting, the witnesses' arrival is anxiously awaited every month. Here, as the afternoon sun nears the horizon on *Rosh Hashanah* eve, the priests and Levites are unsure of what to do next for no witnesses have yet arrived. If they arrive before sundown, the day can be Rosh Chodesh and *Rosh Hashanah*: the waiting Levites (on the left) can begin to sing the appropriate Song of the Day (*Shir Shel Yom*), and the priests (center and right) will bring a *Musaf* sacrifice before the afternoon *Tamid*. If they do not arrive, however, today is a regular day and *Rosh Hashanah* will take place only tomorrow.

In light of this problem – which actually occurred at least once, as described in Tractate *Rosh Hashanah* – the Sages instituted the following regulation: If the witnesses have not arrived by the time of the afternoon Mincha offering, the day is officially not *Rosh Hashanah*. In such a case, the regular *Tamid* sacrifice is to be offered, the Levites will sing the weekday Song of the Day, and the next day will officially be declared *Rosh Hashanah*.

New Moon Testimony on the Sabbath

This painting shows witnesses on their way to Jerusalem to testify that they have seen a new moon and that the new month can thus be declared. One witness, riding a donkey, is ailing, while others are helping him, carrying food and weapons. All this can take place on the Sabbath as well: Witnesses may travel and helpers may do all that is needed to protect and help him on his way, as stated specifically in the Mishna (*Rosh Hashanah* 1:9).

The reason the Sabbath may be desecrated for this purpose is because Israel is commanded to declare the festivals at their appointed times, as written (Leviticus 23:4): "These are God's festivals that you must declare at their appointed times." For Rosh Chodesh, as well, the priests must know what sacrifice to bring that day, and so witnesses who saw the moon may set out for the Temple even on the Sabbath.

Eye Witnesses Detained Along the Way

This painting depicts an incident recounted in the Mishna (*Rosh Hashanah* 1:6): Forty pairs of new-moon witnesses, on their way to Jerusalem, arrived in Lod on the Sabbath. They were about to proceed along their way, in accordance with the law that such witnesses may travel on the Sabbath – but Rabbi Akiva stopped them, saying that certainly other witnesses had already testified and that their testimony was not necessary. Rabban Gamliel later told Rabbi Akiva that he had erred, because it would discourage future witnesses. The Gemara quotes an opinion that it was not Rabbi Akiva who stopped them, but rather Zefer, the Mayor of Geder – seen here arguing with the witnesses. The Gemara states that Zefer was later removed from office as a result.

Attempted Sabotage

This painting depicts an incident recounted in the Gemara (*Rosh Hashanah* 22a): Members of the Boethusian sect, whose goal it was to disrupt the Rabbinic way of life and cause Rosh Chodesh to be determined on the wrong day, bribed two men to testify that they had seen the new moon when in fact they had not. They did not realize, however, that one of the "witnesses" was in fact loyal to the Sages and the Torah way of life – and he showed the money to the judges and told them what the Boethusians tried to do. The judges praised the "witness," and sentenced the one who gave the bribe (on the left) to be flogged.

The Beit Ya'zek Courtyard

In Tractate *Rosh Hashanah* (23b) we read that in light of the many new-moon witnesses who came each month, the Sages instituted the construction of Beit Ya'zek – a courtyard in Jerusalem where the witnesses could rest and be generously fed. This would encourage them to continue coming in the future. The painting shows witnesses who have already testified resting and eating, while two new witnesses (in the center) have just arrived and are being shown the way to the Holy Temple (background) where they will give their testimony.

The Court of Rabban Gamliel During the Sanctification of the New Moon ››

Rabban Gamliel headed the Sanhedrin court in Yavne, where he would receive witnesses who claimed to have seen the new moon. He would question them thoroughly, asking them, "Did the moon look like this?" while pointing to one or another of the pictures hanging on the wall for that purpose (*Rosh Hashanah* 2:6–8).

The judges would first question one of the witnesses, then the other. If the witness said that he saw the light side of the moon facing the sun, as in the right-hand picture, he was believed. If he said, however, that he saw something similar to the left-hand picture – an impossibility, since the by definition the sun cannot illuminate the dark side of the moon – his testimony was rejected. The center picture was simply for the purpose of study and clarification, enabling the witnesses to answer questions such as, "In what direction was the crescent facing and at what angle? How wide was it when you saw it?"

Torches On The Mountain Tops Signifying the New Moon

This painting shows one man with a small fire and flammable materials, from which another would light a larger torch that could be seen from afar. The same process would then be repeated on the "next" mountain along the route, signaling from hilltop to hilltop that a new month had been declared. The torch on the last mountain would be seen by the residents of Pumbedita in Babylon, each of whom would light their own in response; the Mishna says the last torch would be waved up and down until all of Pumbedita would be lit up as if it were a great bonfire (*Rosh Hashanah* 2:3).

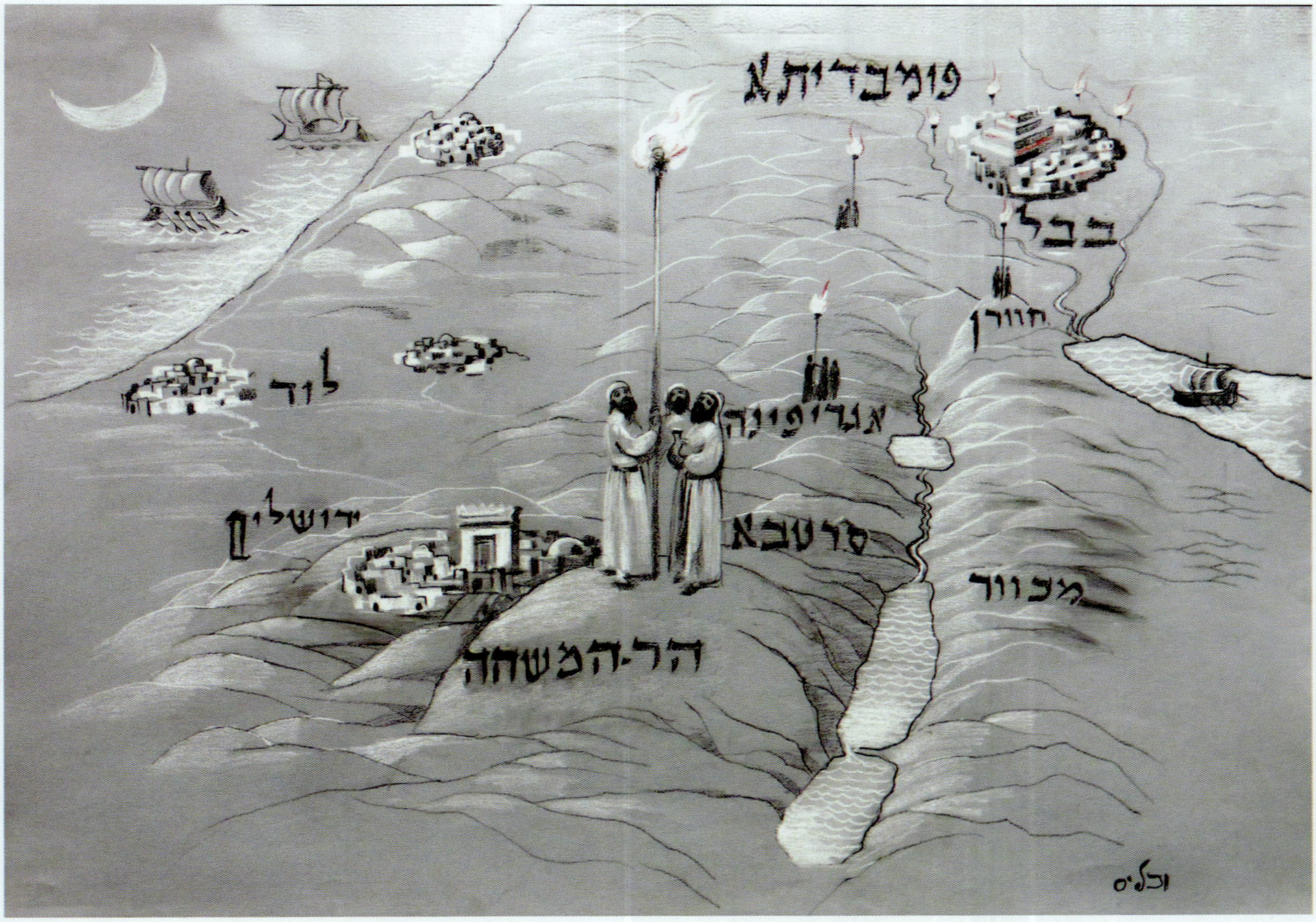

Mapping the Torches

The Mishna (*Rosh Hashanah* 2:4) lists the mountain-tops on which large torches would be lit in order to signal that a new month had been declared. The first torch would be lit near Jerusalem (in the center), and would be seen by appointed watchers on the next mountain to the north, where a torch would then be lit, and so on, all the way to Babylon (upper right).

Among the mountains listed in the Mishna are Sartava, Gerofina, and Chavran; the Jerusalem Talmud adds others such as Geder in Transjordan. Also noted there is the fact that the Cutheans purposely disrupted the New Month declaration process by lighting their own torches at the wrong times; this happened during the times of Rabbi Yehuda HaNasi, who changed the system as a result.

Rabban Gamliel Welcomes Rabbi Yehoshua

The head of the Sanhedrin, Rabban Gamliel, embraces a leading scholar of his generation, Rabbi Yehoshua – in celebration of the settling of the dispute between them regarding the determination of the day of Rosh Chodesh.

The Mishna (*Rosh Hashanah* 2:8–9) recounts that a disagreement had arisen whether or not to believe and accept certain witnesses. Rabban Gamliel's court in Yavne accepted them, while Rabbi Yehoshua thought this was a mistake. At stake was the very calendar, as the new month would begin on different days according to the two of them. Fearful of a long-standing dispute that would mar national unity, Rabban Gamliel ordered Rabbi Yehoshua to "come before me on the day that is *Yom Kippur* according to your calculation, with your cane and coins" and thus show that it was not a holy day. Rabbi Yehoshua did so, and when he arrived at the Sanhedrin, Rabban Gamliel "stood and kissed him, and said: 'Come in peace, my rabbi and student – my rabbi in wisdom, and my student because you accepted my ruling.'"

The Messengers are Dispatched

Once the torch system was no longer used, horseback messengers were used instead to inform the Jews in far-off countries of the date of the new month. This had to be done with all speed, especially in the months of Tishrei and Nisan, when the Jews there had to prepare for their festival pilgrimage to Jerusalem and to make sure to arrive in time (*Sukkot* and Passover both begin on the 15th of the month).

Yom Kippur: The Day of Atonement

Introduction

All the holy activities that took place in the Holy Temple all year round were but a lead-in to the ultimate climax: the *Yom Kippur* service.

The service of this holy day was the only one in the Beit Hamikdash that was fully and sequentially carried out by one specific priest: the High Priest. The Talmud (*Yoma* 60a) stipulates that if any part of the service was performed out of order, it must be redone.

This really special Day of Atonement service, for which the High Priest alternately wore his golden garments and white garments, is completely enveloped in glory and secrecy.

The Gemara (*Berakhot* 7a) vividly describes the climactic and solemn *Yom Kippur* entry of the High Priest into the Holy of Holies – the one time each year that anyone may do so. Reading the account, one gets the sense that the High Priest is actually entering the Sanctuary on High, and is standing before the very Divine Throne of Glory. The Gemara states, in the name of the High Priest and great Torah giant, Rabbi Yishmael ben Elisha: "I once entered the Holy of Holies to bring the incense, and I saw there Akatriel Ya, the Lord of Hosts, seated upon a high and exalted throne, and He said to me, 'Yishmael, My son, bless Me!' I replied, 'May it be Your will that Your mercy overcomes Your anger and Your mercy may prevail over Your attributes, so that You may deal with Your children according to the attribute of mercy and stop short of the limit of strict justice!' And He nodded to me."

Another dramatic description of the entry into the Holy of Holies is provided in Tractate *Yoma* (39b): "During the year in which Shimon the Righteous died, he predicted his death. They asked how he knew, and he said: 'On every Day of Atonement, an old man, dressed in white and wrapped in white, would join me as I entered and left [the Holy of Holies]. But today, I was joined by an old man who was dressed in black and wrapped in black; he entered with me, but did not leave with me.' After *Sukkot*, he was sick for seven days, and then he died." It appears that the man who accompanied the High Priest was none other than the Patriarch Abraham (*Bava Kamma* 50a). Escorting and helping the High Priest in his mission to arouse Divine compassion and atonement for Israel was a special mission assigned to none other than the Father of the Nation, Abraham.

As he performs the uniquely sacred *Yom Kippur* service, the High Priest is simply an emissary for the entire nation. The Talmud (*Yoma* 18b) states: "The elders of the Beit Din [who accompanied the High Priest on *Yom Kippur*] gave him over to the Elders of the Priests, who brought him to the Chamber of Beit Avtinas, and told him: 'Sir, High Priest, we are agents of the Beit Din and you are our agent and the agent of the Court. We adjure you by He that had His name dwell in this house not to change anything of what we have told you.'" Perhaps this is why the image/soul of the Patriarch Abraham escorts the High Priest into the Holy of Holies – to support him that he not fail in this tremendous mission that has been placed upon him on this very holy day.

Although the precise actions of the High Priest in the Holy of Holies are performed far from any human eye, they are not at all secret. Not only the other priests, but all of Israel who gather in the *Azara* at dawn of *Yom Kippur* follow every move the High Priest makes. In addition, the passages describing his actions are studied in detail in all Yeshivot, and have been recited aloud by generations of Jews throughout our centuries of Exile. Even little children learn the *Seder HaAvoda*, the order of the *Yom Kippur* service, and know its details, just as did the High Priest.

Throughout the service, the High Priest would purify himself and immerse in a ritual bath no fewer than five times, and would wash his hands and feet ten times from a golden basin. He would walk back and forth in the *Azara* and Sanctuary forty-two times in order to fulfill all the mitzvot of the day, which were performed in various locations: The mikveh, the *Azara*, atop the altar, in the Sanctuary, and in the Holy of Holies – up until the point that he would "safely leave the Holy."

The following illustrations and explanations will help us to understand something of the vast expanse of the holy *Yom Kippur* service – and perhaps even help us to understand its true depths.

The High Priest Prepares for the *Sed HaAvoda* on *Yom Kippur*

The High Priest is seen here teaching his fellow priests the laws of *Yom Kippur* and the order of the Temple Atonement service. He holds in his hands the incense utensils that he will bring in with him to the Holy of Holies on the holy day itself, to fulfill the commandment of offering the incense. On the table before him are other utensils he will need for lighting the lamps on *Yom Kippur*, and the silver goblet from which to pour wine on the altar – activities that he will have to rehearse before *Yom Kippur*.

The Mishna (*Yoma* 1) describes the High Priest's seven days of preparation: "Seven days before the Day of Atonement, the High Priest would leave his house in Jerusalem and go to the Parhedrin Chamber [in the northeast corner of the Sanctuary]," where he would be protected from most impurities. He would spend these seven days reviewing the details of the laws of the *Yom Kippur* service with the Elders of the Sanhedrin.

Appointing a Deputy High Priest

One of the preparations just before *Yom Kippur* involved appointing a Deputy High Priest – someone who could fill in for the High Priest in case he became impure or otherwise unfit for the service. In this picture we see the head of the Sanhedrin introducing the Deputy to the other members.

The High Priest Studies Torah on *Yom Kippur* Night

The High Priest would remain awake throughout the night of *Yom Kippur*, to ensure that he not become impure. He would spend the night studying and teaching Torah. The picture shows leading Jerusalem residents, as well as Torah scholars of the Sanhedrin and others, gathered together in Beit Avtinas to study with him. If the High Priest happened not to be a Torah scholar, the Sages would teach him the laws of the Avoda Service and read chapters from the Bible to him.

Appointing the *Ish Iti*

The High Priest has recited his confession over one of the goats, and is seen here appointing the *Ish Iti* – the priest who will accompany the goat to Azazel in the desert. The Talmud explains that though a non-priest may serve as the *Ish Iti*, the priests took this job upon themselves and would not allow a non-priest to do it. On the other hand, "R. Yossi testified that an Israelite from Tzippori, a non-priest, once served as the *Ish Iti*."

The High Priest Takes an Oath

Before the *Yom Kippur* service began, the judges of the Sanhedrin would adjure the High Priest and have him swear that he would fulfill his duties properly. This ceremony took place in Beit Avtinas, above the Water Gate in the southern part of the *Azara*. The elders said to him: "Sir, High Priest, we adjure you by He Who had His name dwell in this house [the Sanctuary is seen through the window] not to change anything of what we have told you," and specifically not to bring the incense as the Sadducees did. The Mishna (*Yoma* 1:5) describes how he would turn aside and cry, because they suspected him, and they too would cry (below right and left), for having had to raise the suspicion.

It was in Beit Avtinas that the Avtinas family prepared the ingredients for the coming year's supply of incense and for *Yom Kippur* (the tools can be seen at right). During the seven days of preparations here, the High Priest would learn from the other priests (dressed in white, at left) the intricacies of taking a handful of incense and its various laws.

Ritual Immersion on *Yom Kippur*

The High Priest is seen here ascending the winding staircase to the High Priest's Ritual Bath, on the second floor of the *Azara*, above the Parva Chamber (with the open door, where the animal hides were processed). At the top of the stairs, two priests spread a linen sheet between the High Priest and the people, to remind them that the *Yom Kippur* service is performed, in part, with white linen garments, and that all are obligated to "whiten" themselves of their sins.

Of the High Priest's five *Yom Kippur* immersions, the last four took place here, in the "holy" ritual bath. The first time, however, he would immerse in the "profane" ritual bath, near Beit Avtinas (seen at right, outside the gate, above the tall window).

At left are seen three doors, to the Chamber of Salt, the Parva Chamber, and the Washing Chamber, from where the winding staircase ascended. The High Priest, climbing to the ritual bath, wears his golden garments, and is followed closely behind by a priest carrying his white garments, which he will wear after the immersion.

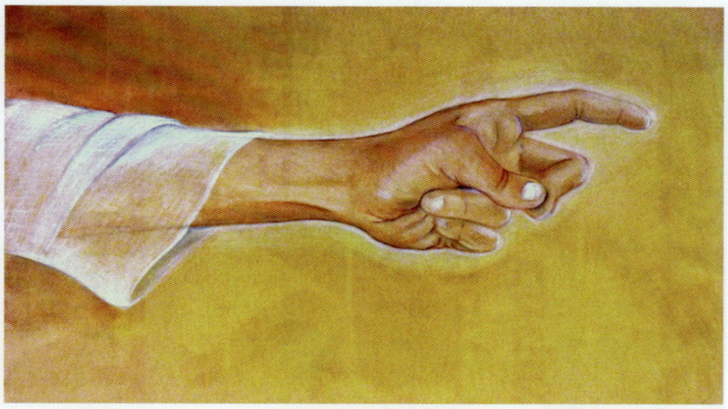

Snapping Fingers

The Mishna discusses the measures taken to make sure the High Priest does not fall asleep on *Yom Kippur* night: "If the High Priest seemed to be falling asleep, the young priests would snap their fingers [as seen in the picture] and say, 'Your honor, the High Priest! Stand up on the cold floor,' and they would keep him occupied until the time for slaughtering the daily sacrifice arrives."

The High Priest Reviews the Animal Sacrifices

Another aspect of the High Priest's preparations for *Yom Kippur* involved a review of the animals from which he was to offer the next day as sacrifices. One commentary states that he was to decide which specific animal would be most suitable for each sacrifice. Bulls, rams and sheep would be brought before him, outside the Gate of Nicanor on the morning before *Yom Kippur*, "so that he would learn and become familiar with the service."

This illustration shows 16 animals that he will encounter the next day in the *Azara*: Two sheep for the *Tamid* sacrifice; two oxen, two rams and seven sheep for the *Musaf* offering; two goats for a sin-offering; and one goat for Azazel (which is not offered on the altar).

The Talmud (*Yoma* 18a) states that in actuality, the two goats offered to atone for the sins of Israel were not brought before him, so that he would not be discouraged by the thought that Israel might not repent and his service will not be accepted.

The Incense Offering in the Sanctuary

The High Priest is seen here offering the incense on the golden altar in the Sanctuary during the daily *Tamid* sacrifice ceremony.

The incense offering began when the supervising priest would say, "Sir, High Priest – bring the incense!" (*Tamid* 6:3) Whoever heard this call would make sure to leave the area, as the Torah states: "No person shall be in the Tent of Meeting when [the High Priest] comes to atone in the holy place." The priest would make sure, when spreading the incense upon the fire, not to come too close, since the incense ingredients are flammable. The Mishna states, "They tell him to be cautious. . . so that he should not suffer a burn."

The Gemara explains that the smoke of the incense "rose straight up like a stick" (*Yoma* 38a). This was due to an ingredient named *ma'ale ashan*, "smoke raiser." The smoke would rise to the ceiling, from where it would spread over the walls and cover them.

‹‹ Immersion in the Mikveh. Changing from White Garments to Golden Garments

The High Priest is seen here preparing to immerse by washing his feet and hands with water from a golden vessel. He will remove his white garments, immerse in the ritual bath, and then change into his golden garments, held for him by two priests standing behind him. He will then again wash his feet and hands (Maimonides, *Yom Kippur* 2:2).

The Mishna (*Yoma* 31:2) states: "If the High Priest was either old or of delicate health, warm water would be prepared for him [before *Yom Kippur*] and poured into the cold, to warm it." Another method for warming the water is described by Maimonides (*Yom Kippur* 4:5): "They would heat up thick metal pieces in a fire before *Yom Kippur*, and the next day they would place them in the mikveh" (see priest at left).

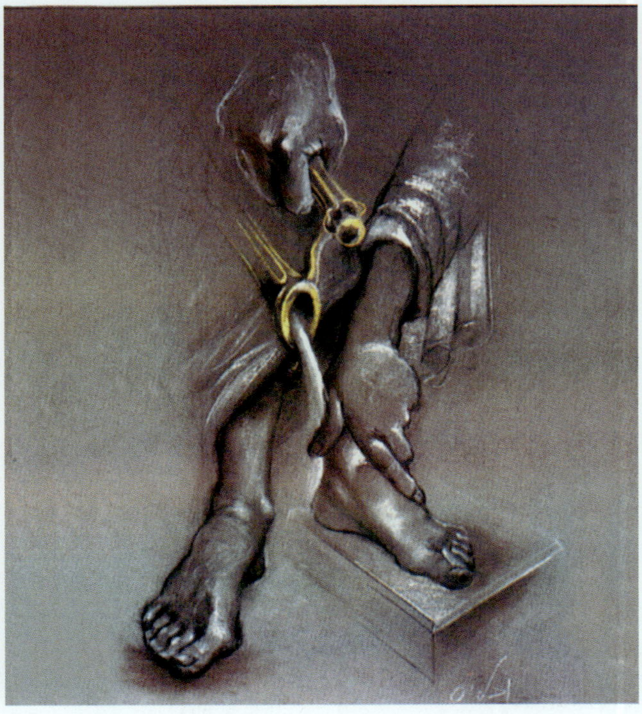

‹‹ Sanctifying Hands and Feet Using a Golden Utensil

The High Priest sanctified his hands and feet a total of ten times on *Yom Kippur*. He would normally do this, like the other priests, from the water of the copper laver in the *Azara* – but on *Yom Kippur*, to honor him, he would use this special golden utensil with a handle.

When washing from the laver, he would hold both feet with both hands and wash; but when washing from this golden utensil, he would first wash his right foot and then his left foot.

« Observing the *Yom Kippur* Service

During the year, non-priests were allowed into the *Ezrat Yisrael*, but generally only 11 steps past the Gate of Nicanor. On *Yom Kippur*, however, so many people wanted to watch the High Priest perform the *Yom Kippur* service that they were allowed to take up every available space in the area, even around the altar and the *Heikhal* (Sanctuary). This, after all, was a day of repentance for all, and the people wished to take part in the ten prostrations – one for every time the High Priest would mention God's Ineffable Name – and confess their sins.

As the Gemara (*Yoma* 20a) states: "By the time the cockcrow approached, the Temple court was full of Israelites."

The *Tamid* and *Musaf* Sacrifices

This illustration depicts the priests bringing the animals into the *Azara* for the *Tamid* (daily sacrifice) and the *Musaf* (additional offering). The two sheep on the left are for the *Tamid* – one in the morning and one in the evening – and the bull and the seven lambs are for the *Musaf* (Numbers 29:11).

The High Priest's Confession

This painting depicts the scene in the *Azara* during the High Priest's confession on *Yom Kippur*. Twice on this day, he would rest his hands on the head of the bull, face the Sanctuary and the Holy of Holies, and confess – first his own sins, and the second time, those of his fellow priests. He stands between the altar on the (left) and the Sanctuary, while the other priests ascend the 12 steps to the sanctuary.

The manner and order in which the High Priest confessed – twice on the bull and once on one of the goats – is outlined in the Mishna (*Yoma* 3:8) and Maimonides (*Avodat Yom HaKippurim* 4:1). When he confesses for himself and his family, he specifically mentions the sins that he knows he committed. He then turns to the east where he would draw the lots over the two goats, and then returns to the bull and confesses a second time, this time for his fellow priests. The bull would stand looking south, with his face turned to the west, while the High Priest would stand in the east and face west.

The High Priest would begin both confessions with a prayer: "Please, God." He would pronounce the Ineffable Name of God, and when he did so, the priests and all those who heard would prostrate themselves on the floor, extending their arms and legs. During the two confessions, he would pronounce the Ineffable Name a total of six times, and those present would prostrate themselves each time.

Drawing Lots

The High Priest places both hands in the box with the two lots, which was only "as big as both his hands" (*Yoma* 39a). He was supposed to quickly pick up one lot with each hand and then quickly remove his hands. This, so that he would not purposely try to "arrange for" a good omen for Israel by taking take the lot with God's Name in his right hand.

Raise Your Right Hand!

Whichever lot came up in the High Priest's right hand would be applied to the goat on his right, and the same for the left. The Deputy High Priest would check both hands; if he saw the lot with God's Name in the right hand, he would announce, "Sir, High Priest! Raise your right hand!" If it was in the left, he would say, "Sir, High Priest! Raise your left hand!"

The Two Goats

A priest brings the two identical goats to the *Azara*, before the altar, preceded by a priest carrying the two lots and the scarlet "sash" of material. The lots would determine which goat would be offered as a sacrifice and which would be sent to its death in the Azazel desert.

The High Priest would take of the blood of the sin-offering goat to the Holy of Holies, where he would sprinkle it opposite the curtain on top of the Ark of the Covenant. Its meat was not burnt on top of the altar like the other sacrifices, but was rather burnt in a designated place outside Jerusalem.

The High Priest would recite a confession upon the head of the other goat for the sins of all Israel He would do this while standing at the Gate of Nicanor, and the goat would then be taken to Azazel in the desert.

Placing the Lots ››

This illustration affords a close-up of the High Priest placing, the lot of the "Divine Name" that came up in the lottery, on top of the head of the goat to be offered as a sacrifice He thus fulfills the Biblical command, "He shall make it a sin-offering" (Leviticus 16:9). At the same time, the High Priest recites aloud the Ineffable Divine Name, and those hearing it prostrate themselves on the ground.

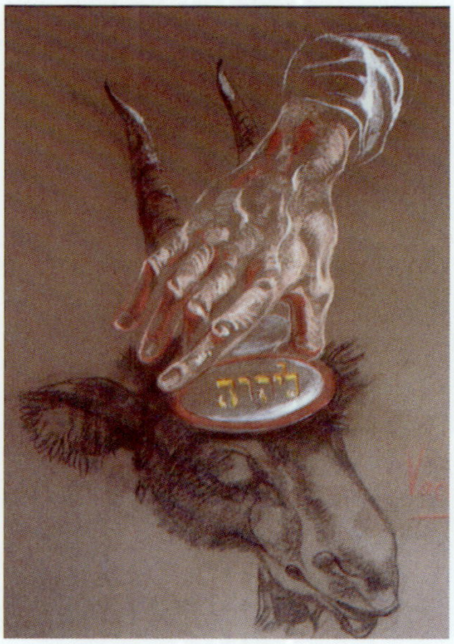

‹‹ Tying the Crimson Sash

This illustration shows the High Priest tying the scarlet-crimson sash on the head of the goat designated for Azazel. He would then point the goat towards the Gate of Nicanor in the east. The High Priest would tie another scarlet sash on the goat designated for the altar – not on its head, but rather around its throat, so that the two could not be confused for each other or for other sacrifices (Mishna, *Yoma* 2:2).

Semikha on the Bull How Is It Done?? ››

The High Priest would perform *semikha* – placing his two hands – on top of the bull's head, while reciting the confession. As the Torah states: "Aharon shall press his two hands on the live goat's head, and he shall confess upon it all the Israelites' sins. . ." (Leviticus 16:21). The Talmud adds (*Yoma* 36a) that he would place his hands between the horns of the sacrifice.

‹‹ *Semikha* on the Goat

The High Priest presses his hands on the goat differently than he did with the bull. Though the same words are written in the Torah – "he shall press his two hands" – it appears that since the goat's head was not big enough for both hands, the priest was to place one hand on top of the other, as in this illustration. *Targum Yonatan* in fact states: "Aharon pressed both hands in a specific order – the right hand on top of the left and the left hand on the goat's head."

The Lottery

Having concluded drawing the lots, the High Priest prepares to place them on the two goats before him. This took place in the east of the *Azara*, north of the altar, near Gate of Nicanor (seen behind the High Priest). Flanking the High Priest are the Deputy High Priest at his right and the head of the ministering family at his left. They all face west, towards the Sanctuary, and the wooden box of lots is on the table before them. If the lot with the Divine Name came up in the priest's right hand, the Deputy would say, "Sir, High Priest! Raise your right hand!" so that all would know that a sign of Divine blessing had occurred. If it came up in the left, he would say, "Sir, High Priest! Raise your left hand!" The priests on either side of the High Priest held crimson sashes, to tie on the goats – one around the throat, and one between the horns.

‹‹ Confession of the High Priest

The High Priest is seen here standing next to the east gate – the Gate of Nicanor – confessing the sins of Israel upon the head of the goat designated for Azazel. He performs *semikha* by placing the palm of his right hand over his left hand, and both above the head of the goat. He would begin with a prayer: "Please, God," pronouncing the Ineffable Name of God; when he did so, the priests and all those who heard would prostrate themselves on the floor, extending their arms and legs. This would occur three times, once during each confession.

According to the Jerusalem Talmud (*Yoma* 3:6), certain people began illicitly using and pronouncing the Ineffable Name outside of the Temple, and so the process changed: The High Priest would pronounce the Name in an undertone; those closest to him would hear it and bow down, while those further away (in the background) would see them and bow down themselves, while reciting *Barukh shem kevod malkhuto*.

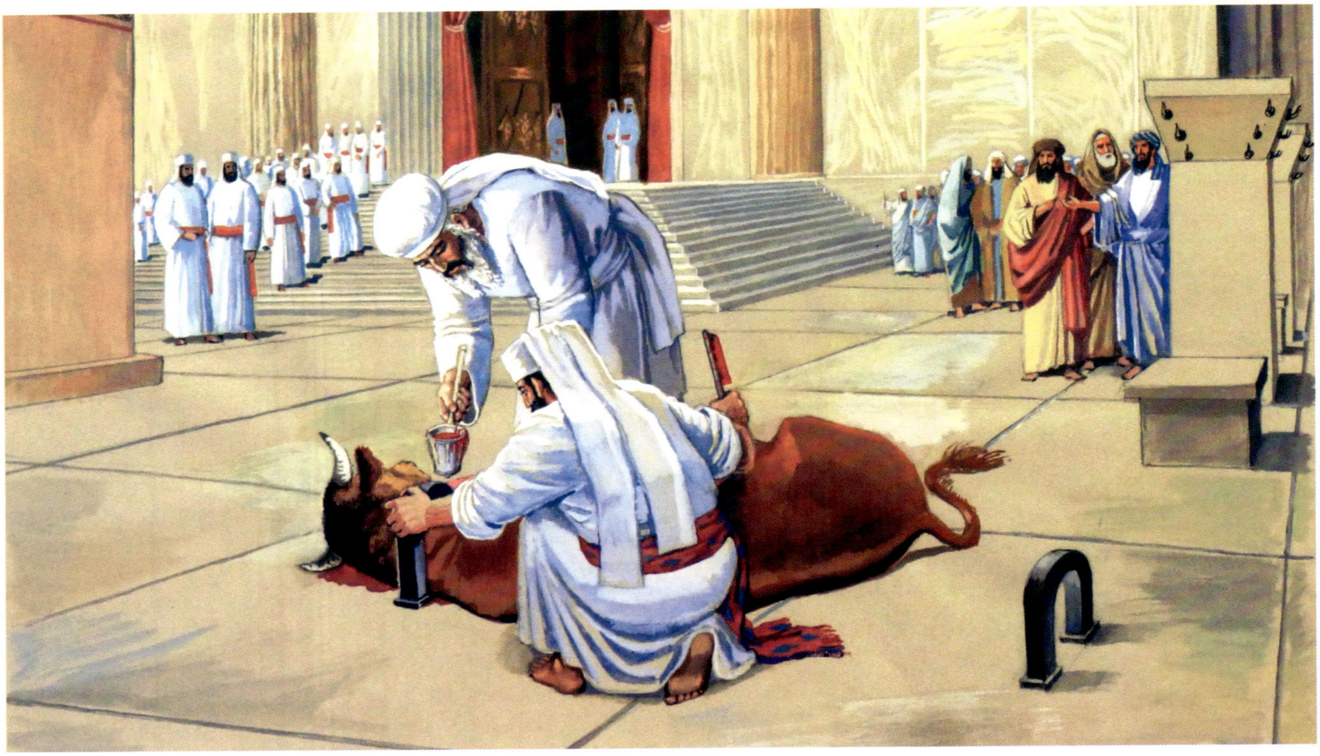

Slaughtering the Bull

After completing two confessions on the bull, the High Priest is seen here as he performs the ritual slaying of the bull, just north of the altar. This takes place near the 24 rings affixed to the floor (one ring for each priestly watch) meant to hold the animal's neck or limbs. The priest places the bull with its head to the south and its face to the west, and slays it. He then makes sure to "receive" the blood in a special utensil. A second priest is given the utensil to hold and stir, so that it does not congeal; he would stand on the fourth row of floor tiles in the *Azara*, stirring all the while. He would return it to the High Priest when the latter later makes his way to the Holy of Holies.

The *Mazrek*

This picture shows the *mazrek*, the utensil fashioned of seventy shekels of silver in which the blood of the sacrifice is received. The bottom is pointed so that the priest cannot lay it down on the floor and cause the blood to congeal. This *mazrek* holds some 15 liters, perfectly suited for the High Priest's *Yom Kippur* service, which includes receiving the blood not only of the *Musaf* bull, but also later of the goat that is not sent to Azazel. The blood in the *mazrek* is then sprinkled on the golden altar.

Bringing the Coals

The High Priest needed to bring coals from the altar into the Holy of Holies on which to offer the incense. He would ascend the altar [as seen here] and take from the pile of burning ash with a special pan. On *Yom Kippur*, this pan was made of gold – with a red hue, reminiscent of the blood of the bull. It also had an extra-long handle, so that it would not heat up too quickly. The priest would take three *kav*s of coal from the west side of the pile, in fulfillment of the verse "He shall take a pan full of coals from the altar [from the side that is] before God" (Leviticus 16:12), i.e., from the side closest to the Holy of Holies (Maimonides, *Avodat Yom HaKippurim* 4:1).

The High Priest would then descend from the altar and place the pan of coals on the fourth row of floor-tiles in the *Azara*. There it would remain until he was ready to take it, with the incense, into the Holy of Holies.

Preparing to Enter the Holy of Holies

The High Priest is seen here standing in the *Azara*, taking a double handful of incense to offer in the Holy of Holies. The Mishna states: "They brought him the *kaf* [a designated golden utensil, seen on the table at left] and the pan. He took his two hands full [of incense] from the pan and put it into the *kaf*" (*Yoma* 5:1).

Two items are waiting on the fourth row of floor-tiles (though there is another explanation as to what the "fourth level" means; *Yoma* 43b) to be taken into the Holy of Holies: The blood of the bull, which a priest is stirring so it will not congeal, and the pan with the coals. The High Priest takes the incense in the *kaf* in his left hand, and the pan with the coals in his right hand, climbs the steps, and enters the Sanctuary on his way to the Holy of Holies.

The High Priest Ascends the Stairs of the Sanctuary

This painting shows the High Priest climbing the steps to the Sanctuary on his way to burn the incense in the Holy of Holies. Mitzvot are generally carried out with one's right hand, but in this case, he carries the incense in his left hand because he needs his right hand to carry the heavy, burning coals all the way to the Holy Ark in the Holy of Holies. He enters the Holy of Holies all alone, of course, with the congregation waiting in the *Azara* in prayerful anticipation that the incense service will be accomplished without mishap.

Offering the Incense in the Holy of Holies

The picture shows the Holy of Holies (from the south) as the High Priest offers the incense atop the burning coals. The Ark is seen here on top of the *Even HaShtiya*, the Foundation Stone, raised three fingers above the ground. The rods of the Ark were long, "pushing into the curtain" (*Yoma* 54a). The priest would first place the pan of coals on top of the Foundation Stone, then take two handfuls of incense from the *kaf* and pile it carefully upon the coals so that its smoke would rise all at once (Maimonides, *Avodat Yom HaKippurim* 4:1). He would wait there until the room was filled with smoke, as it is written: "The cloud of incense covered the *kaporet*" (Leviticus 16:13).

« The High Priest Walks between the Two Curtains

Carrying the incense and burning coals to the Holy of Holies, the High Priest walks purposefully between the curtains dividing the Holy of Holies from the Sanctuary. He begins at the southern end of this cubit-wide path, walks to the north, then turns left and enters the Holy of Holies. Once there, he turns again and walks aside the curtain (on his left). He then turns right and faces the Holy Ark, standing between its two rods.

The cubit-wide path existed only in the Second Temple, and in fact was formed to symbolize the wall that stood there in the First Temple. Another difference between the two Temples was that the Holy Ark was present only in the First Temple; when King Solomon built the Second Temple, he hid the Ark deep underground, for fear that it might be desecrated by enemies (Maimonides, *Beit HaBechira* 4:1).

The First Handful of Incense »

The Talmud (*Yoma* 49b) teaches that Taking the two handfuls of incense was "among the most difficult of the Temple service activities," largely because whatever incense the High Priest first took in the *Azara* was exactly the amount he must take later in the Holy of Holies, without spilling a drop and under more difficult conditions. This picture shows the first "taking," while still in the *Azara*: he cups his hands, with his hands barely touching. A priest with larger hands would take more, and one with smaller hands would take less.

The Second Handful ››

Once in the Holy of Holies, the High Priest would have to transfer all of the incense from the *kaf* into his hands – a difficult feat. Maimonides explains (*Avodat Yom HaKippurim* 4:1): "Standing behind the curtain, between the rods of the Ark [or, during the Second Temple, opposite the Foundation Stone], he would hold the edge of the *kaf* with his fingertips, or with his teeth [dependent on the structure of the *kaf*], and pour the incense, using his thumbs, into his hands, until all of it is in his hands. This is a very difficult task [to ensure that not a crumb fell]." He would then place the utensil on the side and carefully place the incense on the burning coals in the pan.

Sprinkling the Blood

The High Priest, having gone to retrieve the blood of the slaughtered bull, returns to the Holy of Holies, and is seen here sprinkling the blood opposite the *kaporet* (Ark cover) and the cherubim. He again stands between the rods of the Ark, and begins to sprinkle the blood the prescribed number of times, counting out loud so as not to err. He says, "One," and sprinkles upwards towards the *kaporet* (seen here adorned with a golden decoration); the blood falls to the floor. He then takes some of the blood again, turns his hand over, and sprinkles seven times downward – each time lowering his hand further towards the floor (Rashi, *Yoma* 53b.)

Placing the Incense on the Foundation Stone ››

In the Second Temple, the incense was offered on the Foundation Stone; the Ark was buried deep below ground. The Talmud teaches (*Yoma* 53b): "After the Ark was removed, there was a stone from the days of the earlier prophets (Samuel and David), called *Even HaShtiya*, three fingers above the ground, on which the High Priest would place [the pan of burning coals and the incense]." This special *Yom Kippur* pan was equipped with legs and a stand, so that it would be stable.

‹‹ The Prayer of The High Priest Upon Leaving the Holy of Holies

This painting shows the High Priest engaged in prayer facing the parochet in the Sanctuary after completing his *Yom Kippur* service in the Holy of Holies.

The Talmud (*Yoma* 52b) states that he would make sure not to pray lengthily, "so as not to frighten" the Israelites waiting in the *Azara* for him to emerge safely. He prayed as follows: "May it be Your will, our God, that this year be one of plentiful rains. . . May there [always be] a ruler from the house of Judah, and may the Israelites not need to sustain one another, and may it not be necessary to permit travelers' prayers to find entrance before you [when the nation needs rain]."

It is further recounted there that it happened once that a High Priest prayed lengthily, and the other priests resolved to go in and see if he was still alive. As they began to enter, he came out. They asked him why he prayed so long, and he said, "Is it not acceptable to you that I prayed for Israel and asked that the Temple should not be destroyed?!" They said to him, "Do not accustom yourself to doing so, for we learned that the High Priest would not pray lengthily precisely so as not to frighten Israel."

Sprinkling the Blood on the *Parochet*

The High Priest is seen here in the Sanctuary sprinkling the blood towards the *parochet*– "once upwards and seven times downwards," the Mishna teaches (*Yoma* 53b). Standing precisely opposite the place of the Holy Ark in the Holy of Holies behind the curtain, he would not sprinkle directly onto the curtain, but merely in its direction. However, R. Eliezer son of R. Yossi related that in Rome, after the destruction, he saw the curtain stained with a few drops of blood that apparently hit it accidentally (*Yoma* 27a).

The painting shows the High Priest standing between the rods of the Holy Ark, which protruded slightly into the curtain. This was not the case in the Second Temple, when the Holy Ark was not in the Holy of Holies, but rather buried deep underground.

The curtain itself is known as the Tent of Meeting, as written: "And he shall do the same [sprinkle the blood] on the Tent of Meeting" (Leviticus 16:16), even though it was only a small part of the Sanctuary – because it was here that God would "meet" with Moses, who would hear the prophetic Voice through the *parochet* between the rods.

"Once Upwards and Seven Times Downwards" ››

These pictures show how the blood was sprinkled upwards and downwards during the *Yom Kippur* Avodah Service. The High Priest would first dip his finger into the blood in the utensil, then turn his hand so that his finger points upwards, and then flick the blood up one time. He would then turn his hand palm down, with the finger towards the floor, and flick the blood downward seven times.

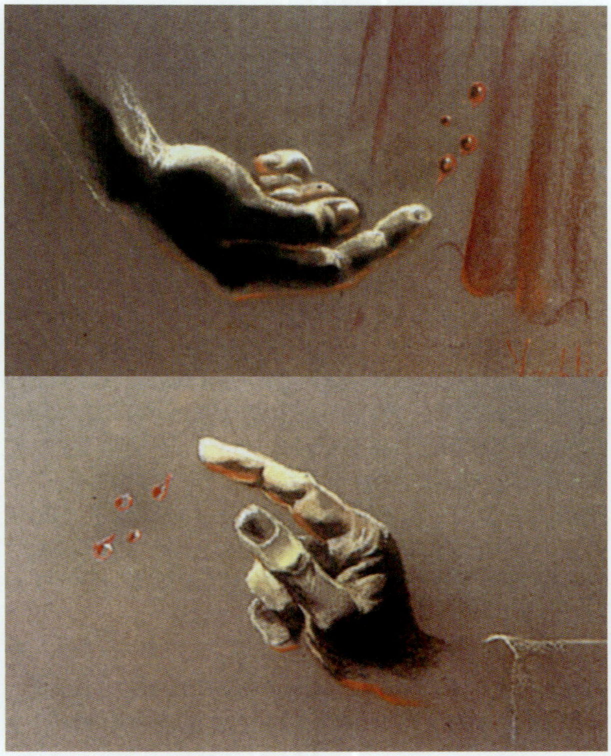

‹‹ Sprinkling the Blood on the Golden Altar

The High Priest stands in the Sanctuary, just south of the Golden Altar (diagonally between it and the Menorah), holding the utensil with blood from the slaughtered bull and goat. He then sprinkles the blood with his finger on the corners of the altar, in a counter-clockwise direction beginning with the northeast corner (to his far-right). As Maimonides explains (*Avodat Yom HaKippurim* 4:2), he would then "move aside the coals on the golden altar until the gold could be seen, and then sprinkle from the mixture of the blood on top of the altar seven times, beginning with the southeast corner."

The Remainder of the Blood

After the 43 sprinklings of blood that the High Priest did in the Holy of Holies and the Sanctuary, he would exit the Sanctuary, descend the steps of the *Ulam*, and make his way to the large altar. This picture shows the High Priest standing at the southwest corner of the altar, spilling the remainder of the blood on the corner. Two holes can be seen – one on the south side and one on the west; on *Yom Kippur*, the blood was spilled into the western hole, where it would drain into the Kidron Valley.

Temple Aqueduct Leading to the Kidron Valley

Seen here is the Kidron River, below and to the east of the city of Jerusalem and the Temple. During the rainy season the river is full (on the right). Also seen is the water draining from the Temple to the river (on the left). Farmers work the land (foreground) using the Kidron waters.

Holy Temple Waters: The Mishna (*Yoma* 5:6) explains that the blood from the sacrifices streamed through a Temple Mount aqueduct leading to the Kidron River base: "The High Priest would pour the remainder of the blood on the western base of the outer altar, and would pour the remainder of the blood of the outer altar at the southern base. Both mingled in the canal and flowed into the Kidron. The water/blood was sold to gardeners for fertilizer; if one uses it without purchasing it, he transgresses the law of *me'ila*."

The water flowing from the Temple is red in color (on the left), as it is mixed with the sacrificial blood. For this reason, it is considered sacred (Maimonides, *Me'ila* 2:11).

Oats for the Omer in the Kidron: The *Tosefta* (*Menachot* 10:21) teaches that the "*Omer* offering came from the Beit Makla Valley of the Kidron River. The grain would ripen there earlier than in other places... The sun would shine there in the morning as well as before sunset. The land-owner would plow half and plant half," so as to enhance the *Omer* crop.

The Goat is Sent to the Desert

The High Priest stands next to the goat designated to be sent off to Azazel, and gives it over to the *Ish Iti,* the man appointed to accompany it. Israelites are technically permitted to escort the goat, but the priests insisted on doing it. The appointed escort is seen (in the forefront) holding the crimson sash that had been tied around the goat's horns after the lottery. The handing-over of the goat took place at the Shushan Gate on the east side of the Temple Mount which looked out toward the desert. Leading Jerusalemites and others also accompanied the goat. Among those who came from all over to take part were residents of Babylon and Alexandria, noticeable by their special dress (*Yoma* 6:4).

"Take Our Sins and Leave!"

This picture shows what happened every *Yom Kippur* when the goat was sent to Azazel to "rid" Israel of its sins. The Talmud explains (*Yoma* 6:4) that Jews from Babylonia (or Alexandria) would follow the goat and pull out its hair, yelling at it, "Take [our sins] and go [to the desert]! Take and go!" To prevent this, a narrow bridge-like path was prepared, keeping most of the trouble-makers away. The Mishna in Tractate *Shekalim* indicates that this path was that which connected the Temple Mount and the Mt. of Olives in the east.

On the Way to the Desert

The priest escorting the goat is seen here on his way to the desert, passing by one of the food-and-water stations set up in case he should need it. "There were ten such stations," the Mishna teaches, "from Jerusalem to the cliff, a distance of 12 *mil* [approx. 12 kilometers]. At each station, he is told, 'Here is food and water'" – of which he would be permitted to partake, despite the fast, if needed. The Talmud notes that it never happened that the escort needed to eat.

The Way-Stations

This picture shows some of the booths set up by the priests, between Jerusalem and the cliff, for the *Ish Iti* (appointed man) escorting the goat to Azazel. These were way-stations with food and water, in case the man felt weak from the fast and needed to partake. Leading Jerusalemites would accompany him up to the first booth (*Yoma* 6:4). At each booth, a group of people would be waiting for him; they had arrived there the previous day. They would then walk with him to the next booth on the route, approximately a kilometer away. His arrival at each booth would be signaled by men waving cloths, and this was one of the ways by which the High Priest would learn that the goat had reached its destination.

The Barren Land

In the foreground the escorts are seen standing at a distance, in keeping with the words of Maimonides (*Avodat Yom HaKippurim* 3:7): "The men of the last booth stand and watch from afar how the priest fulfills the Torah commandment to hurl the goat off the cliff. The priest is seen at the top of the cliff as he brings the goat close to the edge, according to the Talmud's understanding of the words "barren land" (Leviticus 16:22). The Jerusalem Talmud relates (*Yoma* 6:3) that it occasionally happened, after the death of Simon the Just, that after the goat was hurled it would run off to the desert, where desert-dwellers would catch and eat it.

The Goat At the Top of the Cliff ››

The Mishna (*Yoma* 67a) describes the dramatic moment: "What would he then do? He would cut the crimson sash in two parts. One part he would tie onto a boulder (as seen at right)," and it would turn from red to white, symbolizing the whitening of Israel's sins. "The other part he would tie between the goat's two horns. He would then push the goat backwards over the cliff."

The Azazel Goat ››

The sending of the goat to Azazel is described in the *Rosh Hashanah* prayers: "He pushed it backwards with both hands, and it would tumble down. It would not reach half the way down the mountainside before it was dashed to pieces. The priest then says 'May the sins of Your people Israel be thus smashed.'" Maimonides adds (*Teshuva* 1:2): "The goat that is sent off to Azazel is an atonement for all of Israel."

‹‹ Public Reading of the Torah

The High Priest is seen here at the head of the 15 steps separating between the Women's Courtyard and the Israel Courtyard. The Gate of Nicanor is open behind him, enabling the altar and its fire to be seen. The Torah reading ceremony begins when the goat has reached the desert. The High Priest – wearing his own linen garments, if he wished, or his white priestly vestments – would then go out to the Women's Courtyard, where a large congregation had assembled for the occasion. The Mishna (*Yoma* 7:1) relates that the synagogue attendant would take a Torah Scroll and give it to the head of the synagogue, who gave it to the deputy, who gave it to the High Priest, who then stood and read aloud from *Parashat Acharei Mot* (Leviticus 16–18). The priest concludes his reading with a special set of *Yom Kippur* blessings.

The Talmud states that many in the congregation would bring their own Torah scrolls from their homes so that they could read together with the High Priest "and to show the beauty of the Torah in public" (*Yoma* 70a).

Disposal of the White Garments ››

At the completion of the service on *Yom Kippur*. the High Priest would hand in his used white garments to be disposed (*Yoma* 24a). In the picture, Pinchas the Valet is shown in his chamber, where the priests' clothing was placed. (*Middot* 1:4). At his side are priests with two sets of white garments, the ones the High Priest wore in the morning and the ones he wore in the afternoon (*Minchat Chinukh* 99 and 185), placing them there to be disposed.

Burning the Sacrificial Bull and Goat

This painting depicts the ceremony of burning the meat of the slaughtered bull and goat in the *Beit HaDeshen* (the place of the ashes, also known as the *Beit HaSreifa*) outside the Temple. Priests are seen carrying the remains of the two offerings, in fulfillment of the verse: "The bull and the goat representing the sins of Israel. He shall remove outside the encampment, and their hides shall be burnt on the fire" (Leviticus 16:26).

Where was the *Beit HaDeshen*? The Sages disputed (*Yoma* 68a) whether it was north of Jerusalem or in the east. According to the *Tosefta*, it was located north of the city, as in this painting, where the Temple is viewed from the north; at right is the northern gate of the wall, remnants of which still exist today at Damascus Gate.

The *Tosefta* adds that priests would stand round the fire to prevent the crowd from injury.

The fire was made on a high platform. The meat was woven and bound into braids, placed on poles, and brought to the *Beit HaDeshen*. Non-priests were also allowed to take part in this part of the service. Many people came just to watch; the Talmud says that those who did so, could not see the High Priest read from the Torah, "as the distance between them was far" (*Yoma* 68b).

He Would Make a Celebration for His Loved Ones When He Emerged in Peace from the Sanctuary,

Among the descriptions we have from the pilgrimage is that when the High Priest emerged from the Temple after performing the rigorous Temple service of *Yom Kippur*, his face was lit up. In addition, the Mishna (*Yoma* 70a) records that those gathered in the *Azara* would join him and escort him home. Even the heads of the Sanhedrin (seen at left), such as Shemaya and Avtalyon, came to greet him (*Yoma* 71b). After *Yom Kippur* the High Priest would make a "festival" for all his friends and partners who enabled and supported him to properly perform the service.

‹‹ The Closing of the Gates

The painting shows the Levites, the Temple gatekeepers, closing the gates of the *Azara* at the conclusion of the *Yom Kippur* service. The service ended just before sunset, followed by the closing of the gates of both the Sanctuary and the courtyards. At the same time, the last of those who came to watch the service left for their homes. The Jerusalem Talmud (*Berakhot* 4:1) teaches that the hour for closing the gate was the time at which the prayer of *Ne'ila* – Hebrew for "closing" – was recited.

›› The Daughters of Jerusalem Rejoicing in Dance.

The painting depicts a marvelous scene that typified the events occurring in the outskirts of Jerusalem every year on *Yom Kippur*. The Talmud states in Tractate *Ta'anit*: "There were no greater days for Israel than... *Yom Kippur*, on which the daughters of Jerusalem would go out in borrowed white clothing... and dance in the vineyards." Jerusalem is seen here from the east, and rings of girls can be seen on the hillsides, dancing in joy for Israel's atonement, purification from the sins of the year, and inscription in the Book of Life.

Declaring the Jubilee Year in the Sanhedrin

The elders of the Great Court are seen here in the Chamber of Hewn Stone – the seat of the Court – in the Holy Temple, declaring the onset of the Jubilee year. The head of the court (on the left) gives the order to sound nine shofar blasts, as on *Rosh Hashanah* (Maimonides, *Shemita VeYovel* 10:10). The sound of the Jubilee shofar is an especially happy sound for the slaves about to embark on a path of freedom (right).

The principle obligation of blowing the Jubilee shofar is incumbent upon the Sanhedrin in Jerusalem – but once it is sounded, the news of the declaration of the Jubilee is spread throughout the country by virtue of every individual blowing the shofar on his own. As is written: "You must pass on a shofar" (Leviticus 25:9) The shofar blast will publicize the news of the Jubilee Year throughout Israel.

With the onset of *Yom Kippur* and the blowing of the shofar, the slaves were freed to return to their homes and the fields were returned to their original owners.

Announcing the Jubilee Year

Every 50 years the Jubilee Year signaled the freeing of all slaves and the return of lands to their original owners. When the word comes from the Great Court in Jerusalem that the Jubilee has officially started and is sanctified, every person must blow a shofar on *Yom Kippur* and free his slaves.

The picture shows a family that employed a Jewish slave (who had sold himself as such) and his family. The master is seen at center-right, holding a shofar and waving to his former slaves as they leave for freedom; the ties of friendship that have developed over the years between the families are strong, as seen in their faces.

The Talmud (*Rosh Hashanah* 8:2) explains that during the period between *Rosh Hashanah* and the day of release, the slaves would "eat and drink and rejoice".

Sukkot in the Holy Temple

Introduction

The special joy that marks the celebration of the Festival of *Sukkot* in the Holy Temple renders *Sukkot* unique among the Three Festivals. One of the many reasons for the holiday's enthusiastic happiness is that *Sukkot* is the Festival of Harvest. The Jewish farmer, having gathered the fruits of his labor into his home and enjoying the abundance of God's blessing, comes to the Temple with his heart filled with exuberance and thanksgiving for all that God has given him.

A man of Israel comes to the Holy Temple to express his utmost joy. He takes in hand the four species, fresh and green, and arrives at the courtyards of the House of God to fulfill the Biblical commandment, "On the first day [of *Sukkot*], take the *etrog*, and *lulav*. . . and rejoice before Hashem your G-d for seven days" (Leviticus 23:40).

The mitzvah of the Four Species is fulfilled in its most perfect form with all of Israel gathered together as one in the Temple courtyard in Jerusalem, *lulavim* in hand, marching around the altar, singing the *Hallel* prayer and calling out, "*Ana Hashem Hoshia Na!*"

The "rejoicing before God" was manifest, as well, in the singing and music performed by the Levites in the Temple throughout the festival. Though the Levites sang and played every day of the year, on *Sukkot* it was especially felt – as the Mishna states (*Arakhin* 10a): "On twelve days each year the flute was played before the altar, [including] the eight days of *Sukkot*."

The streets of Jerusalem took on a holiday flavor during *Sukkot*, with many sukkahs standing proud on the roofs, in yards and on the streets, for the use of both residents and visitors from across the land. The streets were also filled with people carrying their four species wherever they went.

The uniqueness of the *Sukkot* festival is manifest as well in the many sacrificial offerings that are brought in the Temple during the holiday. Dozens of animals were offered as communal sacrifices, including 70 bulls corresponding to the 70 nations of the world. In addition, from all over the country came Jews with their many holiday offerings, as specified in the Torah. Many also brought first fruits of the season as well.

Several special joyous events are held on *Sukkot*. These include the Joy of the Water Drawing (*Simchat Beit HaShoeva*), the willow-branch beating in the Courtyard, the water libation, and the *Hak'hel* ceremony every seven years with the participation of all of Israel – men, women and children.

The days of *Sukkot* were long and very full. The Talmud quotes R. Yehoshua ben Chananya: "When we celebrated the *Simchat Beit HaShoeva*, we did not sleep at all. The first hour was the morning *Tamid* sacrifice, and from there we went to pray, and then to the *Musaf* offering, from there to the *Musaf* prayers, then to the Study Hall, and later to partake of the festival meal, continuing to the Mincha prayer, from there to the afternoon *Tamid* sacrifice, and finally– to the *Simchat Beit HaShoeva* festivities."

A summation of the great joy of these days is this famous phrase in the Mishna (*Sukkah* 5:1): "He who has not seen the *Simchat Beit HaShoeva*, has not seen joy in his life."

Sadly enough, the splendor of these days has been all but lost in the centuries following the destruction of the Temple and the ensuing Exile. What remains is only sitting in the sukkah and holding and raising the *lulav* on the first day, together with various rabbinic customs enacted to remember the original practices.

The chapter before us reveals a small part of the beauty and splendor of the *Sukkot* festival in the Holy Temple in Jerusalem. The paintings reflect just a portion of the special ambience of *Sukkot* during Temple times.

May God grant that the study of these pictures and the related laws of *Sukkot* in the Temple bring closer the rebuilding of the Beit HaMikdash and the renewal of our national life in their full beauty and completeness, as it was in days of yore.

A Jerusalem Street on *Sukkot*

The streets of Jerusalem in Holy Temple days took on a unique appearance during *Sukkot*. Jerusalemites would generally walk around carrying their *lulavim* and *etrogim* wherever they went, and sukkahs were erected all along the streets.

The Talmud teaches (*Sukkah* 41b): "Thus was the custom of the men of Jerusalem: A person leaves his house with his *lulav* in hand, goes to the synagogue with *lulav* in hand, prays with *lulav* in hand... goes to visit the sick or comfort mourners with *lulav* in hand..."

Another Jerusalem practice at this time was that of generous hospitality. The residents prepared sukkahs for the many pilgrims, such that people could both walk the streets during the day and sleep in sukkahs at night. The Sages stated: "The Jerusalemites would lower their beds down through the windows... and place *s'khakh* over them, and sleep under them" (Jerusalem Talmud, *Sukkah* 2:2).

This painting depicts an early evening scene, when sukkahs are being prepared for the night; the Temple can be seen at the end of the street.

Taking the *Lulav* on the Sabbath in the Holy Temple

On the Sabbath, too, the Temple worshipers would take the four species and walk around the altar, just as on every other day of *Sukkot*. However, carrying outside is forbidden on the Sabbath, and so the four species had to be left there on Friday and "picked up" on the Sabbath. The Mishna (*Sukkah* 42b) explains how this was done in the early Second Temple days: "They brought their *lulavim* to the Temple Mount [on Friday], and the attendants received them and arranged them upon the portico (the eastern portico is seen at right, with the Tadi Gate seen in the north; the Gemara explains that there was a double colonnade around the Temple Mount); the elders placed theirs separately in a chamber... The next morning they came early, and the attendants threw down their *lulavim* before them; the people grabbed at them, and it came to blows – so the Beit Din instituted that each man should wave his *lulav* in his own home."

Circling the Altar

The Mishna (*Sukkah* 4:5) describes the daily *Sukkot* practice of *hakafot*: walking around the altar while carrying the four species and reciting "*Ana Hashem Hoshia Na*."

The painting depicts the practice in accordance with the Jerusalem Talmud and Maimonides' ruling (*Lulav* 7:23): Everyone – Priests, Levites and Israelites – would walk once around the altar each day, and seven times on *Hoshana Rabba* (just as the Israelites marched seven times around Jericho, as described in the Book of Joshua). Though non-priests were generally not permitted between the altar and the Sanctuary (the entrance to which is seen at left, where the High Priest stands with his four species), this prohibition was suspended for the *hakafot*.

It is a matter of dispute whether only the four species were carried during the *hakafot*, or also an additional willow branch (*arava*), as Maimonides rules; there is even an opinion that only a willow branch was taken.

The Seventy Bulls ››

During the course of the seven days of *Sukkot*, the *Musaf* offerings included 70 bulls – beginning with 13 on the first day, 12 the next, and so on. This painting shows the animals that are to be offered as sacrifices on the first day. The Rambam writes (*Temidin UMusafin* 10:3): "On the first day of *Sukkot*, the *Musaf* sacrifice is brought as follows: Thirteen bulls, two rams, and 14 sheep – all burnt-offerings – and a goat as a sin-offering, to be eaten by the priests in the *Azara*." The *Musaf* offering on the rest of the days was the same, except for the decreasing number of bulls, which reached seven on the seventh day.

Beautifying the *Lulav* ››

In order to fulfill the commandment of the four species with extra splendor, some Jerusalemites would bind them together with gold bands, as seen here. The Mishna (*Sukkah* 3:8) stipulates that the willow and myrtle branches must be tied to the bottom half of the *lulav* with a *lulav* leaf, while on the top half, gold bands were allowed to be used as adornments. The Rambam, however, rules that the gold bands can be used anywhere on the *lulav*, because their purpose is to beautify it and are therefore not considered an invalid "obstruction." The man at right in the picture is holding invalid gold bands, as they do not unite the various species, but rather separate between them.

‹‹ The Seventh-Day Offering

The seventh day of *Sukkot* is known as *Hoshana Rabba*, and the bulls of its *Musaf* offering numbered only seven. The Sages of the Talmud (*Sukkah* 55b) liken the 70 bulls to the 70 nations of the world – and the daily decrease in the number of bulls symbolizes the weakening of those nations that harm Israel. Israel, on the other hand, "rises in sanctity" and adds holiness to the world.

Golden Vats for the Arava

This picture shows a Sabbath scene of men in the *Azara* choosing the willow branches, stored from the previous day in golden vats of water to keep them fresh. Newly cut branches were brought every day of *Sukkot* from Motza – except on the Sabbath. Early on Sabbath morning, the congregation would come to the Temple for the morning *Tamid* sacrifice, and would also choose willows with which to encircle the altar.

Beating the Willow Branches

We see here the Pilgrims beating the willow branches on the floor of the *Azara*. This custom dates back to the times of the Prophets. The Mishna states that it was done "on the ground aside the altar." Maimonides (*Lulav* 7:22) describes the contemporary custom as "in memory of the Temple," writing, "One would take a willow branch, or several of them – not the one in his *lulav* – and beat it on the ground two or three times. . . This was a custom of the Prophets."

The Willow Branch from Motza

The Mishna (*Sukkah* 4:5) describes how willow branches were brought to the Holy Temple, each day of *Sukkot*, for the fulfillment of the *Arava* commandment. The painting shows residents of Motza, a village near Jerusalem, and employees of the Beit Din cutting willow branches and loading them onto wagons bound for the Temple. (In the background can be seen the village of Motza, and Jerusalem to the west behind it.) As the Mishna states: "There was a place in the valley below Jerusalem, called Motza. The Beit Din would send people there to cut the long willow branches, known as *murbiyot*" – which were used to adorn the altar. A large quantity of branches was needed to supply the needs of the many visitors to the Holy Temple.

Filling the Jug from the Siloam Pool

Seen here are the Jewish people as they participated in the *Beit HaShoeva* celebrations during the night. At dawn, all those in attendance would descend, with torches in hand, to draw water from the Siloam Pool. The Mishna (*Sukkah* 5:4) indicates that three *terua* blasts were sounded on this occasion and the congregants would walk until the eastern exit of the Temple. When they reached that spot, they would turn and face west, and they would say, "Our ancestors who were in the place [during the First Temple period and did not conduct themselves properly] stood with their backs toward the *Azara*, but our eyes are to God." At the forefront of the picture the priest is drawing the water using a golden jug, which he gives to a different priest who will bring the spring water into the *Azara* and use it for the water libation on the altar.

A Golden Jug Filled from the Siloam Pool,

This picture depicts the people of Jerusalem and the pilgrims as they leave the Temple on their way to the Siloam Pool to perform the mitzva of *nisukh hamayim*.

At the end of the *Beit HaShoeva* celebrations which took place during the night in the Temple courtyards, the participants would walk in a large crowd through lower Jerusalem, known as *Ir David*, to the Siloam Pool. When they arrived, they drew the water to be poured on the altar. That was done at dawn, with singing and great joy, as it says "You shall draw water in joy from the springs of salvation" (Isaiah 12:3). From the Mishna (*Sukkah* 5:5) it seems that trumpet blasts accompanied three different drawings of water. This is also the view of Maimonides (*Kelei HaMikdash* 7:6).

Utensils for Pouring Water on *Sukkot* ››

The water (approximately a liter) that is drawn from the Siloam Pool is poured onto the altar from a special silver jug (seen at right). The chain attached to it facilitates its filling of water from the spring. Another larger utensil (at left) is used to pour wine on the altar for animal offerings throughout the year.

Utensils for Pouring Wine During the *Tamid* Offering ››

Two silver bowls were placed on top of the altar, into which were poured the water (on *Sukkot*) and wine. Pictured are a wide bowl for the wine, and a narrower bowl for the water.

The mitzvot of pouring the water and the wine on the altar were performed simultaneously, and the priests ensured that both liquids would completely drain out of their respective bowls at the same time. This was done, the Mishna tells us (Sukkah 4:9), by virtue of a wider spout in the wine bowl – for wine is denser than water. Both liquids would stream down from the top of the altar, through the special drain-holes, to the shittin, i.e., an underground reservoir.

At the Gate of the Water

The picture shows a view of the southern gates of the Temple Mount wall, including the Gate of the Water at right. This was the gate through which the golden pitcher of Siloam Pool water was brought on *Sukkot* for pouring on the altar. As explained in the Mishna (*Middot* 2:6), this gate was the easternmost of the southern *Azara* gates, and the closest to the altar ramp. It was called the Gate of the Water because through it was brought the pitcher of water for libation on *Sukkot*; R. Eliezer ben Yaakov says it was because there the water welled up and, in the future, will emerge there from under the Temple.

In the foreground a priest is seen holding the golden pitcher brought amidst joy and singing from the Siloam. The Mishna (*Sukkah* 4:6) states: "When they reached the Gate of the Water, they would blow *Tekia, Terua, Tekia*." The commentaries explain that these blasts of joy were for in fulfillment of the verse, "You shall draw water in joy from the springs of salvation" (Isaiah 12:3).

‹‹ Three Mitzvot

This painting depicts the simultaneous performance of three commandments, signaled by three trumpet blasts. The mitzvah of *Arava* was performed by placing long willow branches, known as *murbiyyot*, alongside the altar. These branches from the Motza Springs were some 11 cubits (over 5 meters) tall, rising just over the altar (*Sukkah* 45a). Two priests are seen here placing the branch in a rock base that was specially-designed for this purpose; it would thus not fall or lean on the altar. Maimonides writes that smaller branches from the *murbiyyot* would then be distributed to the people, and they would encircle the altar with them.

On top of the altar two priests are performing, the *Sukkot* commandment of pouring the water and the daily commandment of pouring the wine – at the same time as the placement of the willow branch. All three mitzvot were introduced with a triple trumpet blast: *Tekia*, *Terua*, *Tekia*. (This sequence is explained in *Sukkah* 5:5 and 4:9; Maimonides, *Lulav* 7:21; and Rashi to *Sukkah* 54a).

The trumpet-sounding is described in the Mishna (*Tamid* 7:3) as follows: "Two priests stood on the [marble] Table of the Fats with two trumpets in their hands, and blew *Tekia, Terua, Tekia*. . . One priest bent down to pour [the wine, while another poured the water, and others placed the willow branch], and the deputy waved a flag, and Ben Arza sounded the cymbals, and the Levites sang the Song of the Day."

The priest pouring the water was told to "Raise your hands!" when doing so. Why? The mitzvah to pour the water on *Sukkot* is not Biblical, but is rather a binding holy tradition transmitted orally from Moses on Sinai. It happened once that a priest of the Sadducee sect, which did not believe in the Oral Tradition and its laws, tried to deceive the public by pouring the water onto his feet instead of onto the altar. The people noticed, however, and threw their *etrogim* at him in protest. From then on, it was instituted that the priest must raise his hands when performing this mitzvah, so that all could see that he was doing it properly. This rule does not apply to the priest pouring the wine, who is seen bending down.

The Golden Vat ››

Seen here are two priests carrying a golden vat full of water to be used for the water-pouring mitzvah (*nisukh hamayim*) on the Sabbath. Carrying from one domain to another on the Sabbath is forbidden, which is why the water had to be drawn from the Siloam Pool and brought to the Temple before the Sabbath. The water was kept in the specially-prepared golden vat, in a chamber next to the *Azara* ready to be used for the water libation on the altar on the Sabbath.

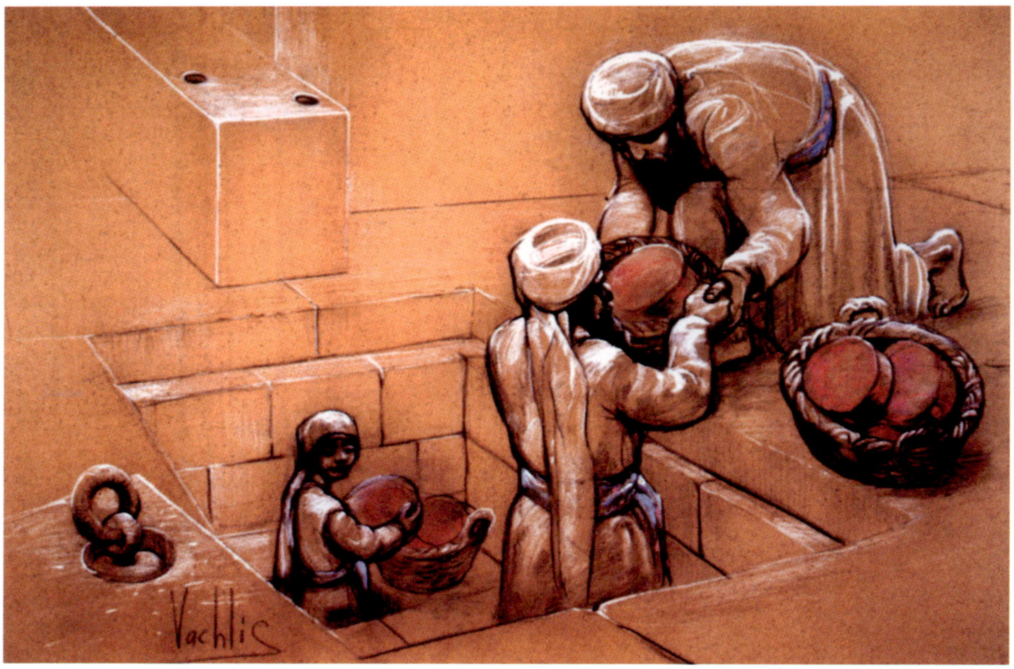

The Underground Hollow

This picture shows the entry to a small pool, at the foot of the southwest corner of the altar, used to store wine. The Mishna (*Middot* 3:3) states that the hollow was a square cubit in size, and was covered by a marble slab to which a handle-ring was attached (on the left). The Gemara (*Sota* 49a) adds that the wine that drained there would become solid after a while, and young priests would periodically bring up these pieces (as seen) via a narrow path between the altar and its ramp, and then clean the hollow. The holes seen at top left were used for the every-day sprinkling of the blood.

The Great Improvement

The Mishna (*Sukkah* 5:2) describes the preparations for the *Simchat Beit HaShoeva*. At one point, a great improvement or repair was made: the construction of balconies for the women. This prevented intermingling of the sexes during the festivities and the resulting frivolity that negated the required awe and respect for the Temple. Thus, this "great improvement" enabled the women to fulfill the Torah command to "rejoice on your holiday" in accordance with the letter and spirit of the law.

The picture shows workers holding boards to be used for building the new balconies and seats.

Young Priests Filling the Golden Menorahs

The painting shows a youthful priest climbing to the top of a tall pillar in the *Azara* and filling the gold candelabrum with oil thus increasing light for the *Simchat Beit HaShoeva*.

The Mishna (*Sukkah* 5:3) describes the process: "Each golden lamp had four golden bowls on top of it, with ladders leading up to them. Four young priests climbed up with jars of oil containing 30 *log* each [some 15 liters] that they poured into the bowls. They also brought up priestly garments that had become worn out, and these they used as wicks and kindling for the fires. There was not a courtyard in Jerusalem that was not illuminated by the light of the *Simchat Beit HaShoeva*."

« *Simchat Beit HaShoeva*

People from every sector of the nation participated in the *Simchat Beit HaShoeva* celebrations. The sages of the Sanhedrin, priests, Levites, women, youth, and the general population all participated. The illustration shows priests on the *Azara* steps; Levites and their musical instruments; Israelites and Torah scholars dancing in joy in the courtyard; and women on the balconies watching the *Sukkot* singing, dancing, music and all-encompassing joy.

The Mishna (*Sukkah* 5:4) describes the roles played by all: **The sages and "men of piety and good deeds"** would dance with lighted torches in their hands (at right) and sing songs and praises. **The Levites** "played their harps, lyres, cymbals and trumpets and countless other musical instruments standing on the 15 steps leading down from the *Ezrat Yisrael* (Courtyard of the Israelites) to the Women's Court (at left) and singing the Song of the Day. **Two priests** stood by the Gate of Nicanor (left) with trumpets in their hands. When the call came to begin the daily service, these priests would blow *Tekia*, *Terua*, *Tekia*, and repeat it several times as they proceeded to the eastern gate. On the steps a priest can be seen carrying the golden pitcher with water from the Siloam. **The young priests** took part by filling the golden candelabra (top right).

The rest of the nation took part, as Maimonides explains (*Lulav* 8:14) by "coming to watch and listen."

Singing, Praising and Juggling

The illustration shows sages dancing in utter joy before God in the Holy Temple. At the height of the happiness, the Sanhedrin members would juggle torches of fire, increasing the joy in the Divine service even more. Maimonides writes (*Lulav* 8:14): "The heads of the yeshivot, the judges of the Sanhedrin, the elders, and the men of piety and good deeds – they would dance and clap and play music and rejoice in the Temple on *Sukkot*." The Gemara (*Sukkah* 53a) relates that Rabban Shimon ben Gamliel would celebrate the Drawing of the Water as seen in the center of the painting, by juggling no fewer than eight flaming torches, without one touching another.

The Wooden Platform

In preparation for the *Hak'hel* ceremony, held every seven years, a raised platform was erected in the *Azara*. The king would stand at the top and read aloud from the Torah, and the entire congregation would be able to see and hear him, in fulfillment of Deuteronomy 31:11–12. The Mishna (*Sota* 7:8) teaches: "At the conclusion of the first day of *Sukkot* (following the *Shemitta* year), a wooden platform is made for the king in the *Azara*, and he sits there." The sukkah seen on the platform in the painting is not mentioned in the Sages' teachings, but it fits with Nehemiah 8:16, which states that sukkahs were built "in the courtyards of the House of God and on the street of the Gate of Water." It is therefore logical that a sukkah would be built for the king and the elders where they spend an extended amount of time.

"To God We Bow Down"

This picture depicts the final minutes of the nightly *Beit HaShoeva* celebration, as the sun rises in the east. The Talmud describes the scene: "The participants would reach the gate leading to the east, to the Women's Courtyard, and would then turn westward to the Sanctuary and would say: 'Our fathers who were here in this place [during the First Temple period] . . . would bow to the sun – but we bow to God'" (*Sukkah* 53b).

In the painting some of the participants are facing the Sanctuary and the altar. The priest carrying the jug of water from the Siloam for the libation stands on the steps of the Gate of Nicanor, also facing west. Some people prostrate themselves towards the Holy of Holies (foreground), according to the Rabbinic principle: "The Divine Presence is in the west" (*Bava Batra* 25a; and *Guide to the Perplexed* 3:45).

Announcing the *Hak'hel*

On the day of *Hak'hel*, priests would blow trumpets throughout Jerusalem in order to announce the event and gather everyone to the Temple for the royal Torah reading in the Women's Courtyard. The *Tosefta* says if people saw a priest without a trumpet to blow that day, they would think he was not a priest!

The painting shows the streets of Jerusalem on the day of *Hak'hel*. Priests stand on steps, at courtyard gates, and on street corners, sounding their trumpets and announcing the time of *Hak'hel*. The residents and pilgrims would stop their work and begin streaming to the Temple for the special event occurring only once in seven years.

The *Hak'hel* Ceremony

This classic illustration shows the throngs of pilgrims and Jerusalemites gathered in the Women's Courtyard for the Hak'hel Event. The king stands on the large wooden platform and reads the Torah aloud. On his right is the High Priest, wearing the *Choshen Mishpat* breastplate, holding the Torah scroll for the king to read. The Mishna teaches (*Sota* 7:8): "The Temple synagogue attendant takes a Torah scroll and hands it to the president of the assembly who hands it to the High Priest's deputy, who passes it to the High Priest, who gives it to the king. . . The king may read from a sitting position, but King Agrippas read it while standing and the Sages praised him."

Men stood in the *Azara* and women stood above in balconies specially prepared for them. Young children stood next to their parents; older ones can be seen in the picture climbing the ladders leading up to the golden lamps that illuminated the area of the *Beit HaShoeva* celebrations.

The Women's Courtyard During *Hak'hel*

Seen here is the dramatic, *Hak'hel* ceremony, as seen by the women standing above. The pilgrims are congregated below in the *Ezrat Nashim* as they hear the King of Israel read aloud from the Torah. The women stand above in the special balcony; they, too, are obligated to congregate in the Holy Temple for this special event.

The Last Day of the Four Species

On the last day of *Sukkot*, after the final Hakafot around the altar were completed, the children would grab the elders' *lulav* branches and eat their *etrogim* – another manifestation of holiday joy. The adults, in the spirit of the day, would be forbearing and allow them to eat the *etrogim*; so explains the Rambam, as depicted in the painting here. Others say that it was the adults who would snatch the *lulavim* from the young ones.

The *Musaf* Offering of *Shemini Atzeret*

Throughout the seven days of *Sukkot*, the number of bulls offered in the *Musaf* sacrifice was between 7 and 13. The eighth day, however, was the separate holiday of *Shemini Atzeret*, on which only one bull was offered for the *Musaf* sacrifice. This was in addition to a goat offered to atone for the sins of the people and a ram and seven lambs as burnt-offerings – as seen in the painting.

The Talmud (*Sukkah* 55b) states that the *Shemini Atzeret* offering is termed a "small feast," compared with the sacrifices of *Sukkot*. It is as if God is telling His beloved Israel, "Let us now celebrate. Prepare for Me a 'small feast' just for us so that I can enjoy you."

Watching the Smoke Rise at the end of *Shemini Atzeret*

This painting depicts that which is written in the Talmud (*Yoma* 21b) regarding the final *Shemini Atzeret* sacrifice: "At the conclusion of the final day of *Sukkot* (*Shemini Atzeret*), everyone would look towards the smoke emanating from the sacrifices burning on the altar. If the smoke wafted northward, the poor (on the right) would be happy, while the land-owners (on the left) would be sad – because it meant that the rains of the coming year would be plentiful and the fruits would rot. But if the smoke blew to the south, the farmers would rejoice, while the poor would be saddened, because it meant that rain would be sparse and the fruits would be better preserved. If the smoke went eastward, everyone would be happy, while if to the west, all would be sad."

Passover in the Temple

Introduction

Though pilgrims arrived en-masse for each of the Three Festivals, the largest number arrived on Passover. This was not only because of the importance of the Passover offering, but also due to the fact that while only men are obligated to visit the Temple on *Sukkot* and *Shavuot*, on Passover the mitzvah is incumbent upon women as well.

The entire nation took part in the Passover offering: men, women and children. A person who did not partake in the Passover offering, or have one brought for him, was liable for the grave punishment of *karet* for failing to fulfill this positive commandment. Even many Jews who resided in the Diaspora would make the long trip to the Holy Land to celebrate Passover with the Jewish Nation in Jerusalem.

The following story related in the Talmud (*Pesachim* 64b) provides a glimpse at the vast numbers of people who came to Jerusalem for Passover: "King Agrippa once wished to cast his eyes on the hosts of Israel [i.e., he wished to count them]. He told the High Priest, 'Cast your eyes upon the Passover sacrifices.' He thereupon took a kidney from each, and found 600,000 pairs of kidneys – twice as many as those who departed from Egypt... and at least ten people were counted for each Passover offering; and they called the festival that year, 'The Passover of the dense throngs.'"

One of the principal features of Passover in Jerusalem was the actual eating of the Passover lamb. Between 10 and 100 people would partake in each lamb – each eating at least an "olive's worth" – depending on the size of the animal and how many registered for it in advance. It followed, of course, that participating in large meals with many people made for an uplifting and joyous holiday atmosphere.

Families brought more sacrifices on Passover than on any other Festival. On the 14th of Nisan, the Passover lamb and the Chagiga were offered, eaten together with matza and bitter herbs during the course of the Passover seder, while telling of the story of the Exodus and the Redemption.

The seder would end at midnight (halfway between sundown and sunrise) with the eating of the Passover lamb. Everyone would then ascend to the roofs of Jerusalem to sing the *Hallel* in view of the Holy Temple. Myriads of Jews within the walls of the Holy City would thus break out in song celebrating Israel's redemption from Egyptian bondage. It is no wonder that the Sages said that this song caused not only hearts to tremble, but even the very walls of Jerusalem themselves.

Let us seek to comprehend even just a small part of the special aura and substance of the Passover holiday via the paintings and pictures, and their explanations, in the coming pages. Bringing the laws of Passover in the Temple to life, the illustrations will help us see a measure of how they left their imprint of sanctity and joy on the masses of people who entered the gates of Jerusalem at these joyous times.

Slaughtering the Passover Offering – During the Exodus

In this picture one can see a group sacrificing their Passover offering during the Exodus from Egypt. At left is a roasted Passover offering removed whole from the oven. In the foreground one sees a man kneading dough for the Seder night as well as food for their upcoming journey. There is also another man gathering silver and gold utensils, and placing them in a special sack as the Jews were commanded to take from the Egyptians. At the entrance to the home is the father of the household placing blood on the doorposts and lintel, as a sign. All the members of the group are seen preparing for the journey, fulfilling the night's special commandment "And thus shall you eat it: with your loins girded, your shoes on your feet, and your staff in your hand; and you shall eat it in haste – it is the Passover of the Lord" (Exodus 12:11).

The Preparations in Jerusalem for the Passover Sacrifices

Seen in this picture is the father of the household as he takes the Passover offering to the Temple. At the same time, the rest of the group is preparing the special Passover oven, to make sure it will be hot enough to roast the lamb quickly.

zSMEKHOV

The Pilgrims Arrive for Passover

Seen here are some of the masses of Jews on their way into the Holy Temple on Passover eve to slaughter the Passover offering.

The gate at left, in the northeast, is called the Gate of Song, and through it the Levites enter with their trumpets and other musical instruments. Above the gate is seen a pink colored structure: the *Lishkat HaGazit*, the Chamber of Hewn Stone where the Sanhedrin convened.

Entering the second gate from left is a long line of pilgrims – women who are obligated to bring a Passover sacrifice on their own, such as widows and single women. They enter the Women's Gate (*Middot* 2:3). Above this gate is seen the Chamber of the Exile (Maimonides, *Beit HaBechira* 5:16).

The third gate from left is the Gate of the Offering. Those entering are headed for the *Azara* where the Passover lambs and the Chagiga will be slaughtered. Above this gate is the domed *Beit HaMoked* (Hearth), sleeping quarters for the priests who performed the services.

The gate at right, on the northwest side, is the Gate of Jeconiah. Above it is the *Beit HaNitzotz*, the Chamber of the Spark, where the fire for the hearth was prepared.

Some of the doors of the gates are seen here as they are about to be closed by the Levite Temple guards. Some of the pilgrims wait outside for the "second group," i.e., the second cycle of Passover-lamb offering.

Changing of the Guard on Passover Eve

This painting shows those who have completed the Passover offering and those who are just beginning it. On the right are members of the first group carrying the permitted parts of the slaughtered lamb as they leave the Temple for the city, where they will roast it and eat it during the seder. On the left, members of the second group are entering the *Azara* with their lambs to be slaughtered for the same purpose.

The Mishna (*Pesachim* 5:5) teaches that the Passover lambs were slaughtered, and their blood "received" and sprinkled on the altar, in three groups: "The first group would enter, filling the Temple court, and the Levite doormen would close the doors. . . The Levite musicians (center) would sound *Tekia*, *Terua*, *Tekia*, and others would accompany them with the song of *Hallel*." The process would then repeat itself with the second and third groups.

Passover Eve on Sabbath

If the 14th of Nisan falls on the Sabbath, several changes are made in the Passover offering procedure due to the Sabbath prohibition on carrying from one domain to another. Generally, after the sacrifice was brought, the people would take home the permitted parts to roast and eat. On the Sabbath, however, this is not permitted, and so everyone would remain within the Temple area until the end of the Sabbath.

The picture shows the Temple scene on the Sabbath of Passover Eve (as described in Mishna *Pesachim* 5:10). The first group of those who came to bring their Paschal lamb has finished; they wait (at right) in the Temple Mount plaza for the end of Sabbath. Aside them can be seen one of their sacrifices, enwrapped in the lamb's skin, with the slaughtering knife leaning upon it. The second group waits in the *cheil* (rampart), on the steps (at left) behind the *soreg* (latticed gate) partition. The third group is seen still in the *Azara* (far left), waiting there until darkness falls. When three stars are seen, and the Sabbath is over, all depart to roast their Passover lambs in Passover ovens throughout Jerusalem.

Preparing the Passover Offering for Sacrifice ››

This picture shows a father and son arriving to sacrifice their Passover offering in the *Azara*. The son places the animal in one of the rings that are permanent fixtures in the *Azara*, in order to facilitate the slaughter. On the left we see the owner of the animal checking the slaughter knife for any nicks. If the knife is clean and declared fit, the owner may sacrifice it himself, as the halakhah says "slaughtering done by a non-priest is fit" (Maimonides, *Biat HaMikdash* 9:6).

Skinning the Passover Offering

These two pictures show two different methods of skinning the sacrifice. On the left, the animal is hung on *unkelayot*, iron hooks fastened to short stone pillars called *nanasim*. On the right is seen those who found all the *unkelayot* already in use; they would use specially-prepared sticks that they would place on their shoulders. The sheep were hung on the sticks, facilitating the skinning (Mishna, *Pesachim* 5:9).

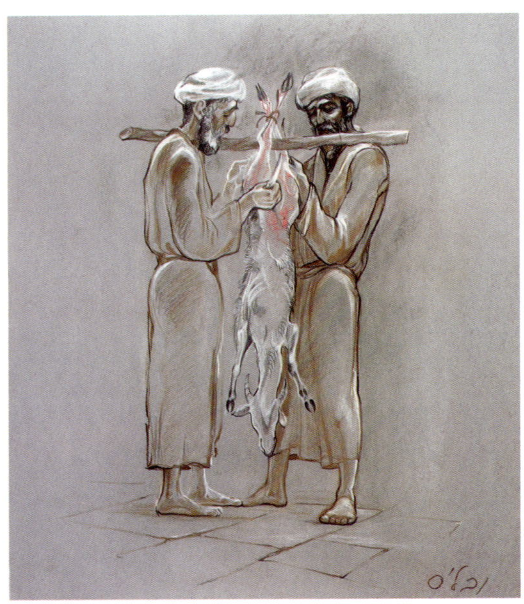

The Starting Time for the Passover Offering

The priestly watch responsible for the Passover offering is seen as they begin the process. The picture emphasizes that the sun shows it is after noon, with the *heikhal* in the shade, but the area of the altar is lit up with sunlight. This is the time they began to slaughter the Passover offering for the first group who brought their sacrifices to the *Azara*.

Slaying the Passover Offering

This painting depicts the ceremonious fulfillment of the cardinal Torah commandment, "The entire congregation of Israel shall slaughter it in the afternoon" (Exodus 12:6).

The Mishna (*Pesachim* 5:5) describes it: "The Paschal lambs were slaughtered in three groups. The first group would enter, filling the Temple court... The priests would stand in rows, and in their hands were basins [in which to receive the blood] – one row of silver basins and one of gold; they were not mixed." After the blood was received, each basin was passed quickly from one priest to the next, until it reached the one nearest the altar, who would pour the blood on the altar foundation, as required for every sacrifice. All this time the Levites would be singing the *Hallel*.

Closing the Gates of the *Azara*

The picture shows the gates of the *Azara* being closed to those coming to sacrifice their Passover offerings in order to allow 3 separate groups to bring their offerings.

The Passover Offering on the Altar

Parts of the Passover offering, known as *imurim*, were offered on the altar. Priests are seen here ascending the ramp to the altar with the *imurim*, carried on a special tray called a *magas*.

Leaving the Temple to Eat the Paschal Lamb

Calm and confident after the offering of the Passover sacrifice and the recitation of the *Hallel*, the people are ready to fulfill the commandment of eating it. This picture shows them as they leave, carrying their sacrifices with them.

There were times, however, when the scene was not as serene. The Talmud (*Pesachim* 64b) recounts that there were years of tremendous crowds – and that despite this, "No man was ever crushed there, except one elderly man on one Passover in the days of Hillel – and it was called 'The Passover of the *meukhin* (the crushed).'"

The Talmud also relates there: "King Agrippa once wished to count the number of Israelites. He told the High Priest, 'Cast your eyes upon the Passover sacrifices.' He thereupon took a kidney from each, and found 600,000 pairs of kidneys – twice as many as those who departed from Egypt... and at least ten people were counted for each Paschal lamb; and they called the festival that year, 'The Passover of *meubin* (crowded).'"

‹‹ The Passover Song of the Levites

This classic painting shows the Levites singing and playing musical instruments on the platform in the *Azara* as the Passover lambs are being offered. This day – the 14th of Nisan – is one of the 12 days of the year on which, in accordance with the Sages' decree, an extra instrument was added to the orchestra before the altar: the *chalil*, a type of flute. As Maimonides writes (*Kelei Hamikdash* 3:6): "Twelve days a year the flute would be sounded before the altar: The days of the regular and second Passover offering (the 14th of Nisan and Iyar, respectively); the first day of Passover; *Shavuot*; and the eight days of *Sukkot*."

The Levites' music was part of the sacrificial service, and took place when the wine was poured and the Passover offering was slaughtered. The music was performed by singers and musicians. The Levites stood in four levels on the platform in the eastern part of the *Azara*: the floor and three steps (Mishna, *Middot* 2:6; *Yoma* 16a).

Generally, four musical instruments were played, while the flute was added on the 12 above-mentioned days:

Trumpets – top row, being played by priests wearing priestly garments. Levites and Israelites also joined in.
Harps – on the first step, on the left
Lyres – on the first step, in the center.
Flutes – played only on 12 days. They are seen here in the center, played by the men in turquoise.
Cymbals – Only the Levite conductor plays the cymbals, and he is also the man responsible for the entire orchestra (Maimonides, *Kelei Hamikdash* 7:7).

On special days, especially Festivals, the number of musicians would increase to include Levites who came to the Temple from outside Jerusalem. On such days, the number of trumpeters could be as high as 120, while the number of lyres had no maximum (Maimonides, *Kelei Hamikdash* 3:4). On the first row of the choir, standing on the floor, were young children, whose sweet voices added beauty to the Holy Temple music. The Sages tell us (*Shekalim* 5:1) that Ben Arza played the cymbals, while Hugras ben Levi was responsible for the singing.

The Recitation of *Hallel* in the Temple ››

The picture depicts the members of a group who completed eating their Passover offering before midnight, as instructed in the Torah. They have ascended to the roof of the home in which they ate. This was at the same hour when all the other groups finished eating their Passover offerings as well. On the 15th of Nisan, a night with a full moon lighting the night, the members of a family – men, women, and children –sing the verses of *Hallel* with their eyes raised towards the Temple which has been lit up by the moon.

Cleaning the *Azara*

The picture shows priests engaged in washing the floor of the *Azara* after all the Passover offerings were sacrificed. This was permitted on the Sabbath as well, as Maimonides explains (*Korban Pesach* 1:16): "If the 14th of Nisan falls on the Sabbath, the same procedure is carried out – including the washing of the *Azara* floor, because Rabbinic prohibitions do not apply in the Temple, even regarding activities that are not needed for the Temple service."

For the cleaning, they stopped up the drain holes in the *Azara* floor; they would flood the floor with water, which would mix with the blood. The priests would then scrub the entire floor, open the drain holes, and the water and remaining blood would all drain out to the Kidron Valley.

The priests involved in other Temple activities would walk atop a stone platform raised above the floor, so as not to soil their priestly garments (*Pesachim* 5:8). The Sages of Israel describe these closing moments of the special Passover offerings by praising the priests: "It is to the great credit of the sons of Aharon, the priests, that they walk in the blood up to their ankles" (*Pesachim* 65b).

The Son Asks A Question on the Seder Night

The illustration depicts a family sitting down to its seder night meal in Jerusalem during the Second Temple period. On the table is the *chagiga* sacrifice, eaten as part of the meal. At right, the Passover offering is being brought in, having just been roasted in its entirety in a special Passover oven. Any group of ten, or even many more, can eat the Passover offering together.

The seder is designed so that children will ask questions and thus learn the story of the Exodus. When the second of four cups of wine is poured, "the son asks [among other questions]: Why is this night different? Every night we eat cooked meat and the like, yet tonight we are eating only roasted meat?" (*Pesachim* 116a).

The Passover offering is eaten at the end of the meal, for the law is that it must be consumed "when one is satiated" (*Tosefta Pesachim* 5:3).

The Group Members Bring the Passover Offering from the Temple ››

This picture depicts a courtyard in Jerusalem with an oven ready to roast the Passover offering. Also seen are the members of the group carrying the lamb on their shoulders while it is already on a spit ready to be roasted, after its skin has been removed.

«« Roasting the Passover Offering

The oven in the picture was designed especially for the Passover offering, which was roasted in its entirety. Many such ovens were built all around Jerusalem for the myriads of pilgrims who arrived in the city for Passover. The internal organs dangled outside the animal, so that they would not be "cooked" inside, but rather roasted as the Torah commands. Even the skewer stick on which it was roasted had to be of a pomegranate tree – dry enough so that it would not emit moisture that would "cook" the animal.

Eating the Passover Offering

This pictures show a typical family sitting down to partake of the Passover offering at the end of the seder meal in Jerusalem; the Holy Temple can be seen through the window. The participants recline and celebrate their freedom from Egyptian bondage. The father takes a piece of the roasted animal and asks, "This Passover offering – why are we eating it?" He does so in fulfillment of the educational nature of the event, as in the verse, "You shall tell your son that this is what God wrought for me when I left Egypt" (Exodus 13:8).

"You Shall Not Break A Bone"

The picture depicts the group after the lamb has been roasted, while they are preparing the meat to be eaten by those having their Seder together. While cutting the meat they remove the meat from the bone carefully, as one of the mitzvot of the Passover offering is a prohibition to not break its bones. The *Sefer HaChinukh* (16) explains that the prohibition of "neither shall you break a bone thereof" (Exodus 12:46) is due to the idea that we are comparable to the sons of kings who need not search for bones or break them like dogs and on Seder night it is unbecoming of us to do so, but rather is the norm for the hungry poor.

Eating the Passover Offering in a Group in Jerusalem

The Passover Offering is eaten in a "group," members of which "registered" to eat the sacrifice in a special house on Passover night. It often occurred that two or more groups would gather to eat in one place – and for such situations, special halakhic regulations applied to ensure that the groups did not mix and no one ate from the wrong sacrifice.

This picture shows two groups holding separate seder meals in one hall. Large jugs (center right) served as a partition between them. The Talmud states that the members of each group "focus on their respective sacrifices and seder leaders" (*Pesachim* 7:13). Two men carry in the Passover offering on their shoulders for their group (on the left). Another man is seen facing the same group and pouring wine for them from the vats – additional manifestations of the integrity of that group.

One person alone is allowed to face away from the group, and that is a new bride, still slightly uncomfortable before her new family. At right can be seen a young bride dressed in blue who is looking away from the others in her group (Maimonides, *Korban Pesach* 9:3–4).

Hallel on the Rooftops ››

"An olive's weight of the Passover offering, and *Hallel* that breaks through the roof." So did the Sages describe the happiness and joy that accompanied the *Hallel* prayers on the roofs of Jerusalem (*Pesachim* 85b), following the eating of the Passover lamb. The picture shows throngs of Jerusalemites and pilgrims climbing to their roofs in the middle of the night to celebrate the Passover joy.

Though Biblically the Passover lamb may be eaten until dawn, Maimonides rules that it must be consumed by midnight. This is because the Sages wished to ensure that it not be left over past morning, at which time it is forbidden to be eaten. It was around midnight, then, that everyone would come out and begin to sing the *Hallel* together. The full moon of the 15th of the month can be seen on top, illuminating the city and its Passover celebrations. The *Hallel* songs could be heard far and wide.

Jerusalem Bakeries on the Festivals

The illustration shows a baker selling bread in his store in Jerusalem. In stores like this, there is a suspicion that an *am haaretz* – one who is not punctilious regarding the laws of purity and impurity – touched the dough or bread and thus rendered them impure (though not forbidden). The Talmud discusses a baker "beginning his dough" on the Festival (left).

The matter of the purity or impurity of the foods touched by pilgrims during the Festival occupied the bakers in Jerusalem. It must be recalled that bread, whether made of wheat or oats, was a main staple for the visitors, yet the bakers could justifiably be worried that the pilgrims might refrain from buying, so as not to mistakenly eat impure food.

The Sages thus instituted the law that bread touched by customers during the Festival (center) was considered pure. However, bread that was touched by customers during the holiday was, on the very next day, no longer considered pure (Maimonides, *Metamei Mishkav UMoshav* 11:10).

Selling Wine to the Pilgrims

The picture shows a Jerusalem wine-seller in his store and a customer. The wine-seller often faced a problem trying to ascertain whether among his customers were some who were ritually impure and who would defile the wine when they invariably touched the wine barrels and jugs. However, on Festivals, the Sages stated that everyone is considered "pure," given the obligation to immerse in a ritual bath before entering the Temple. As a result, the wine on sale was also considered pure on the Festivals, even if the customers were people who throughout the year were not careful to remain pure.

However, this situation applied only on the Festival itself – on the very next day, any wine previously touched by someone suspected of being impure is considered impure (*Chagiga* 26a).

« Harvesting the *Omer*

The picture depicts the Harvesting of the First *Omer*, which took place the night after the seder. The barley grain that is cut is used for the communal *Omer* grain-offering, which is brought on the next day, the 16th of Nisan. It was carried out by emissaries of the Beit Din, and many of the pilgrims and Jerusalemites would come and watch the festive occasion.

The Mishna (*Menachot* 6:3) describes the event: "The messengers of the Beit Din would go out on the day before the Festival [to a place close to Jerusalem] and tie the unreaped grain in bunches, leaving them attached to the ground (on the left), making it easier to cut for the *Omer*. . . All the inhabitants of the nearby towns would come and take part, so that it might be reaped with much fanfare. . . After the harvest, they would place the grain in baskets and bring it to the *Azara* in the Holy Temple."

The Mishna records the dialogue between the harvester and those watching him, in which each question was asked and answered three times. The purpose was to strengthen the position of the Rabbis, who were challenged by the Boethusians and their anti-Oral Law approach. The latter felt that the *Omer* must be harvested every year on Sunday, in accordance with their understanding of the relevant verse – whereas the Rabbis ruled that it must be on the second day of Passover, no matter which day of the week it fell out. The dialogue was conducted as follows:

"When it became dark, the harvester would ask the assembled, 'Has the sun set?' And they would answer him, 'Yes!'
He would ask, 'Is this a scythe?' and they would answer, 'Yes!'
'Is this a basket?' And they would answer him, 'Yes!'
Each of these exchanges was repeated three times."

Sifting the *Omer* ››

The illustration depicts the *Azara* on the day of the sifting of the *Omer*, the 16th of Nisan. Some priests carry on their shoulders a pack of barley stalks (on the right), while others bang them on the ground with a stick to extract the seeds. The next stage is to roast the seeds: A priest waves the grains over the fire in a utensil called an *abouv* (left). The roasted seeds must then be ground into flour (center), and then sifted – in no fewer than 13 sifters (foreground). The priests then offer the finely-sifted *Omer* before God on the eastern side of the *Azara*, one priest burns a fistful over the altar, and the remainder of the flour may be eaten by the priests (*Menachot* 66b; Maimonides, *Temidin UMusafin* 7:12).

All of these steps are executed even if the 16th of Nisan falls on the Sabbath – teaching us how precious and beloved before God is the sanctity of the Land of Israel and its produce.

Berdichevsky

Reaping the *Omer* on the Night of the 16th of Nisan ››

The picture depicts the messengers of the court reaping the sheaves of barley with a scythe for the *omer* meal-offering. This took place by the light of a full moon, in the middle of the month of Nisan, in the presence of many pilgrims.

‹‹ Oil and Spice on the *Omer*

The priest pours a *log* of oil on the *Omer* of barley (on the right), while another priest places frankincense upon it (on the left). As is written: "You shall place upon it oil, and place upon it frankincense; a Mincha offering." Once the barley, grains and frankincense are mixed well, another priest takes a fistful and places it upon the fire of the altar (Leviticus 2:15; *Menachot* 67b; Maimonides, *Temidin UMusafin* 7:12).

The *Abouv* ››

A copper utensil, called an *abouv*, is used for the roasting of the barley grains. It is perforated on bottom. Beneath it can be seen a utensil with burning coals.

Waving the *Omer* ››

The Torah states that the priest "must wave the *Omer* before God" (Leviticus 23:11), after the oil and frankincense have been placed upon it. The priest stands on the east side of the altar, and raises and waves the *Omer* while facing west. The order of the waving is: forward, backward, up, down. He then walks to the southwestern corner of the altar, where he places the *Omer* offering precisely on the corner (Maimonides, *Temidin UMusafin* 7:12).

‹‹ The Fistful of the *Omer*

A priest is seen here taking a fistful of the *Omer* flour and placing it onto the altar fire as a *ketoret* (incense). This is done after the offering of the *Musaf* sacrifice (Maimonides, *Temidin UMusafin* 7:12). Following the waving of the *Omer* and its burning on the altar, the priests bring the "accompanying lamb" as a sacrifice (ibid. 9:9), and then conclude with the afternoon *Tamid* offering.

Placing the *Omer* on the Altar Corner ››

This drawing depicts the priest after he has come from the east side of the *Azara* to the west, where he now places the *Omer* offering "precisely on the southwestern corner" of the bottom of the altar (Maimonides, *Temidin UMusafin* 7:12).

Breaking the Clay Utensils

This picture shows priests, after having eaten the meat from the sin-offering inside the *Azara*, breaking the clay utensils that contained the sacred food.

Metal utensils used for sacrificial meat must be boiled and cleaned of all remnants of the food. Clay utensils, on the other hand, cannot be used again and must be broken, as is written: "An earthenware vessel in which it is cooked shall be broken, but if cooked in a copper vessel, it shall be purged and rinsed with water" (Leviticus 6:21). Maimonides rules (*Ma'aseh Hakorbanot* 8:11) that this applies to sin-offering sacrifices, eaten by priests in the *Azara* (as seen here in the background). Other early authorities hold that clay vessels must be broken after the eating of any sacrifice, including *shelamim* (peace offering) and the Passover offering. This explains why the pilgrims brought many such utensils with them from home.

The Golden Plaques on Display ››

The Temple's gold plaques were placed on display for the enjoyment of the pilgrims, to show them the splendor and beauty of the Temple.

The Talmud (*Pesachim* 57a) relates that the Sanctuary walls were covered with gold plaques, sized a cubit square and as thick as a golden coin. On Festivals, the priests would bring them, and other Temple ornaments, out to "a high place on the Temple Mount" in honor of the efforts made by the pilgrims to come to Jerusalem. Some of the beautiful Temple utensils and vessels were also put on display, for the same reason.

‹‹ "Paying" for the Hospitality

Seen here (on the left) is a family of pilgrims) taking leave of their hosts in Jerusalem following the Festival. The guests are holding a pitcher and a sheepskin with which they wish to show their appreciation and thanks to their hosts.

"Paying" for room and board in this manner was instituted by the Sages in light of the ban on paying money for Festival hospitality. As written in *Avot DeRabbi Natan* (35): "One may not rent out homes in Jerusalem on the Festival [for money], because they are not his... Nor may one rent out beds." The guests thus resorted to "paying" by "leaving behind" left-over goods from their Festival stay in Jerusalem. These included the skins of sacrifices brought as thanksgiving and peace offerings during the holiday, as well as clay jugs used for wine and oil used for the sacrifices (*Megilla* 26a).

Displaying The Menorah and Showbread Table

During the Festivals it was the custom to exhibit some of the beautiful Temple vessels for the holiday pilgrims who had come from far. In this picture we see the priests holding up the menorah and *shulchan* for the enjoyment of the visitors.

The Jerusalem Talmud (*Chagiga* 8:3) relates that 93 gold and silver vessels and utensils used in the Temple service were taken out to show the pilgrims. Among them was the menorah, which was once defiled by the visitors and required immersion in a *mikveh*. The Sadducees, who refused to accept the Oral Law, mocked those who immersed the radiant menorah, saying, "Look how the Pharisees immerse the sun!"

The Gemara (*Chagiga* 26b) teaches that the *shulchan* should be held up before the crowds of pilgrims: "The priests show the *shulchan* and the showbread, and say to the crowd: 'See how much God loves you and dwells amidst you, for the bread remains miraculously warm and fresh from one Sabbath to the next.'"

The picture is drawn in accordance with the ruling by Maimonides (*Metamei Mishkav UMoshav* 11:11), but Rashi and *Tosafot* are of the opinion that the vessels were shown only to the priests in the Sanctuary. The pilgrims were permitted, according to Maimonides, to enter the area between the Sanctuary (*Heikhal*) and the altar for this purpose – but special priests (seen standing on the steps) were appointed to warn the public not to come too close and possibly defile the *shulchan*.

The Jerusalem Market After the Offering of the *Omer*

Once the *Omer* sacrifice was offered, the new crop of wheat was permitted to be eaten. The picture shows the very busy Jerusalem market in the hours after the *Omer* was sacrificed. It was filled with people, especially visitors from afar who brought with them only small amounts of food and needed to replenish their supplies.

In order to meet the demand for wheat and bread immediately after the *Omer* sacrifice, many of the field owners would start harvesting before the *Omer* was offered. Some Sages (Mishna *Menachot* 10:5) felt that this was a bad practice, for it could lead to the eating of the grain before the permitted time. In any event, the Mishna tells us, "Once the Omer was brought, the pilgrims would leave the Holy Temple and find the Jerusalem markets full with flour and grain."

The picture, based on archaeological findings uncovered in recent years around the Temple Mount, shows the market place near the Temple Mount wall. Grinders can be seen preparing flour for baking, as well as peddlers selling sacks of grain and bakers offering freshly baked *matza*.

The Pilgrimage to Jerusalem

Introduction

One of the purposes for which the Holy Temple was built was for the three yearly pilgrimages to Jerusalem. Maimonides (*Beit HaBechira* 1:1) writes: "It is a positive Biblical commandment to build a house for God for the purpose of bringing sacrificial offerings, and [to] celebrating there three times a year." The commandment of *Aliya L'regel*, making the pilgrimage, unites the People of Israel around the Holy Temple, and distinguishes it as the nation that fulfills its mission as a "kingdom of priests and a holy nation" (Exodus 19:6).

Imagine the scene of *Aliya L'regel*: The people of an entire nation leave their homes, and make their way through the hills and plains to Jerusalem; entire villages and towns empty out of their inhabitants, other than the infirm and others who cannot make the trip. This is why the Torah makes sure to promise us that our property will be protected by the Creator of the World and Master of the Universe: "Three times a year all your males shall appear before the Master, the God of Israel. . . and no one will covet your land when you ascend to see Hashem your God three times a year" (Exodus 34:23). God is described here as the "Master," teaching us that there is a Lord over the Land of Israel guarding and protecting it when Israel ascends to Jerusalem.

The *Midrash* teaches:

"No man will covet your land" – The Torah here addresses itself to man's evil inclination: Israel should not say, "How can we leave behind our land, our homes, our fields and orchards and ascend to Jerusalem? Perhaps others will come and take everything!" God therefore gives His guarantee that this will not occur, nor will other forms of harm befall their property. There was once a Jew who left his produce and when he returned, he found lions protecting it. Another man left a chicken coop and found, upon his return, dead cats that had tried to attack the chickens. This is in fulfillment of "No man will covet your land" (*Mekhilta DeRabbi Shimon bar Yochai*, Exodus 34:24).

Similarly, those pilgrims who came with their entire families, including children, women, and elderly, were promised that they would complete the trip safely and without harm. The Talmud (*Pesachim* 8b) teaches: "Those who are sent to perform a mitzvah are not harmed, neither when they go nor when they return [as is written:] No man will covet your land, teaching that your cow will graze in the meadow and no [wild] beast will hurt it; your fowl will go scratching in the dungheap and no weasel will injure it. And if these will suffer no harm, though it is their nature to be hurt, how much more so for human beings, for whom it is not natural to be hurt!"

Hillel the Elder viewed this as compensation from God to the pilgrims, and would say (*Avot DeRabbi Natan* 12): "If you come to My house, I will come to your house – This refers to those who leave their silver and gold and go to Jerusalem to greet the Divine Presence in the Divine Temple; God watches over them in their camps, as is written, "No man will covet your land." Hillel would also sing in the joyous *Beit HaShoeva* celebrations in the Temple before the many pilgrims and participants (*Sukkah* 53a).

The beautiful paintings and drawings in the coming chapter show us what *Aliya L'regel* looked like when the Holy Temple was standing. Making the Pilgrimages in modern times will be much easier due to modern methods of transportation and new technological developments. More than ever, it will soon be possible for everyone to reach Jerusalem easily and quickly, find spacious lodgings, and observe the Festival joy in sanctity and purity in rebuilt Yerushalayim.

The *Aliya L'regel* Map ››

The accompanying illustration is a modern copy of an ancient map depicting several routes for the pilgrimages to the Second Temple in Jerusalem. Of the two principle routes, one was via the Mediterranean coast, passing through locations such as Caesarea, Lod, and Modi'in. The second went through the Jordan Valley in the east, from Tiberias and Jericho. Both these routes were not only easily walked, as they detoured the mountains of Samaria, but were also considered ritually pure. This enabled priests, who tended to make sure to remain pure all year, as well as others bringing pure wine and oil for the sacrifices, to arrive in Jerusalem in the same state of purity. Samaria, on the other hand, the "Land of the Cutheans," was rabbinically decreed "impure" (*Chagiga* 25a).

Wells and Ritual Baths Along the Way ››

This illustration depicts employees of the Beit Din, sent from the Holy Temple to prepare the way for the expected throngs of pilgrims. One particular Temple officer was responsible for digging wells for water for the pilgrims; Masechet *Shekalim* (5:1) tells of an appointee by the name of Nechunya, Digger of Ditches. His job included digging wells and cisterns for drinking water, building ritual baths for purification, and preparing the roads – particularly necessary for the Passover pilgrimage, because the winter rains had ruined roads and washed away small bridges. Work would begin on the 15th of Adar (*Shekalim* 1:1) for the benefit and purification of the pilgrims on their way to Jerusalem to celebrate the Passover Festival.

‹‹ "Let's Go to Zion!"

In every district there was a town or village in which convoys on their way to Jerusalem would gather for the night. The pilgrims would sleep outside, in the town square; they would not enter houses, so as not to become impure. Every morning, Beit Din emissaries would awaken the pilgrims and call, "Arise and let us go up to Zion!" (*Bikkurim* 3:2). The convoys would thus continue from town to town, gathering more pilgrims along the way, until they arrived at the gates of Jerusalem in large numbers.

Sabbath in the Fields

This painting shows a group of pilgrims on their way to Jerusalem resting for the Sabbath in a field, near a well that had been specially prepared for them. In the lower-right corner can be seen one of four *pasei biraot* – L-shaped corners that the Sages instructed to be built to allow the drawing of water on the Sabbath. The corners marked out a "private domain" in which water could be drawn without "carrying" from one domain to another (*Eiruvin* 17b). Maimonides stipulates (*Shabbat* 17:27–30): "This dispensation was allowed only in the Land of Israel, and only for the [sake of the] animals of the pilgrims to the Temple."

Rest Station for the Pilgrims On Their Way to Jerusalem

The picture depicts the pilgrims at one of the rest stations on the way to Jerusalem. Messengers of the court would prepare places in the shade to rest or to pitch a tent. They also dug wells that would serve the pilgrims and their animals, both on their journey to Jerusalem and on their return home.

The Talmud (*Bava Kamma* 50a) relates a story about an incident in which the daughter of Nechunya the ditch-digger fell into a large well and no one could extricate her from it. They came and informed Rabbi Chanina ben Dosa to pray on her behalf. An hour went by and he told them that she is at peace and unharmed. He said the same thing after the second hour. After the third hour he informed them that she had ascended from the well [and indeed this was the case]. They said to her: Who brought you up [out of the well]? She said to them: An old man leading a ram walked by and he pulled me out. They said to Rabbi Chanina ben Dosa: Are you a prophet? [How did you know?] He said to them: "I am no prophet, neither am I a prophet's son" (Amos 7:14), but this is what I said [to myself]: Shall the offspring of Nechunya stumble by means of the very matter that distressed that righteous man?

Modi'in: The "Central Rest Station"

The city of Modi'in was an important stop for many of the pilgrims arriving from the north via the coastal plain (the *Shefeila*). The relative proximity of Modi'in to Jerusalem, and the fact that many priests lived there (such as Mattathias and his sons) made it an important city for the pilgrims.

An interesting halakhic issue arose regarding Modi'in. It is known that one who found himself a "long way" from Jerusalem on the 14th of Nisan and could not arrive in time to bring the Passover offering, is exempt from bringing it on that day. Instead, he must bring it a month later, on the 14th of Iyar. The Sages determined that one who was in Modi'in on the morning of the 14th of Nisan was not considered to be a "long way," because from that distance, "he could reach Jerusalem after midday while walking comfortably by foot" (Maimonides, *Korban Pesach* 5:9). The Talmud (*Pesachim* 94a) states that if one arrives in Modi'in on the morning of the 14th, but is delayed by the large numbers of camels and other animals in the convoy and cannot arrive on time, he should instead observe *Pesach Sheni*.

The Mishna (*Chagiga* 3:5) states that a potter's testimony regarding the purity of his pottery is accepted: "From Modi'in and on [towards Jerusalem], potters are trusted to say that clay utensils are pure for the eating of the sacrifices in Jerusalem; before Modi'in, they are not trusted." A pilgrim is seen here (on the right) negotiating with a local potter in Modi'in, regarding both the price and purity-status of his wares. The potter's word is trusted even if it is known that he came with his pottery from outside the city.

The Journey of the Pilgrims via Modi'in on the 14th of Nisan

The picture depicts the journey of the pilgrims from the center of the land of Israel to Jerusalem. Their route passed through Modi'in, and sometimes the route became unusable due crowding by pilgrims, animals, wagons, and caravans. In light of this blockage, the family is making an effort to circumvent the crowd in order to arrive in Jerusalem on time, so that they will not need to observe a *Pesach Sheni*, on the 14th of Iyar. In Maimonides Commentary on the Mishna (*Pesachim* 9b) he explains that the distance between Modi'in and Jerusalem is 15 *mil*. Maimonides says that this is the distance that a person walking at an average pace can walk in a day, if he walks from sunrise until the afternoon. Therefore, if someone slept in Modi'in and left in the morning to Jerusalem, he would arrive in time to be able to slaughter his Passover offering at the proper time. However, if on the 14th of Nisan he sleeps further from Jerusalem than Modi'in, he is considered to be "far away", and needs to observe *Pesach Sheni*. This leaves many questions for the Talmud to discuss, such as whether someone further than Modi'in, but with horses to carry him rather than walking, should he also observe *Pesach Sheni*? Alternatively, someone closer than Modi'in, but blocked due to the masses of camels and caravans blocking his way, should he also observe *Pesach Sheni*?

Marking Graves

An emissary of the Beit Din is seen here (on the left) putting white paint on a grave found in a field on the way to Jerusalem. This was to ensure that pilgrims on their way to the Holy Temple would not accidentally walk too close to it and become ritually defiled. Starting from a month before Passover, the Beit Din would send its men to find and mark the graves. This would enable priests and others to walk freely without concern that they or their sacrificial oil and wine would become impure.

A Procession of Pilgrims at the Gates of Jerusalem

This picture shows a procession of pilgrims as they approach Jerusalem. Many of the pilgrims came from the east, some from across the Jordan River, and some from the Galilee. They entered Jerusalem from the area of Mt. Scopus and Mt. Olives. The Mishna (*Bikkurim* 3:2) describes the procession of pilgrims on their way to Jerusalem: "On the way they would recite: 'I rejoiced when they said to me 'Let us go to the house of the Lord" (Psalms 122:1). In Jerusalem they would recite 'Our feet are standing within your gates, O Jerusalem' (Psalms 122:2). On the Temple Mount they would say: 'Let every soul praise the Lord, Hallelujah'" (Psalms 150:6).

Beit Haperas – Walking in an Area of Uncertain Purity ››

It sometimes happened that pilgrims would come upon a field in which a grave had been plowed, and the bones of the deceased were spread throughout the field. Such a field is called *beit haperas*, and its status is of assumed ritual impurity. On the right side of the field we see a man telling the pilgrims to stop, for they have entered the boundaries of the *beit haperas*. For the benefit of the pilgrims the Sages decreed that one can clear a path out of the *beit haperas* by blowing along the dirt in order to reveal any bones that may be hidden on the ground. The Talmud records (*Eiruvin* 30b): "A person who passes through a *beit haperas* may blow on the dust before taking each step, so that if there is a bone beneath the dust he will expose it, avoid it, and proceed." According to Rashi (*Chagiga* 25b), this method of purification was permitted only for those proceeding to sacrifice the Passover offering, for one who does not fulfill the commandment of Pesach is liable for excision, and that is the view of Maimonides (*Korban Pesach* 6:8).

‹‹ A Place of Purification in the Marketplace

The picture depicts pilgrims planning to enter the *beit hatahara* (place of purification). The purification of the community before a festival was a necessary process for many thousands of people. Some needed to merely immerse themselves in a mikveh, for example those rendered impure by a crawling animal, therefore many *mikva'ot* were established in Jerusalem. In addition, many become impure due to contact with a corpse, and they needed a special type of *beit hatahara*. A person needing this type of purification would come there on his third day of impurity to be sprinkled with the ash of a red heifer. He would do the same on the seventh day and then immerse in a mikveh. Many of these mikva'ot were also scattered around Jerusalem. The picture depicts one such house of purification, located in the marketplace.

Greeting the Pilgrims

The picture depicts a family of pilgrims in the streets of Jerusalem. The citizens of Jerusalem would go outside to greet the new arrivals. The Talmud (*Kiddushin* 33a) relates: "When farmers bring their first fruits to Jerusalem, all craftsmen stand before them, and greet them, and say to them: Our brothers from wherever you have come, you are welcome!"

To the Holy Temple

This dramatic painting shows the masses of pilgrims having just arrived at the outskirts of the Holy Temple. Some of them, especially women and the elderly, arrived on camels or horses (on the right), while others can be seen having brought their first fruits (in the center). Shepherds can also be seen (center-right) bringing their flock for sale for sacrificial offerings. Among the pilgrims are also musicians, who would perform and gladden the pilgrims (center-left); the others would join in, and the joyous song would intensify as they neared the Holy Temple.

Around the Temple can be seen numerous bridges and entrances, facilitating a quick entry to the courtyards.

The Pilgrimage to Jerusalem [364-365]

Pilgrims at their Inn in Jerusalem ››

The picture depicts a homeowner in Jerusalem who is greeting the pilgrims who would like to lodge in his home during the festival. The guests are greeted with smiles and are invited in rent-free, as the Talmud (*Yoma* 12a) states: Homeowners did not charge rent for their houses in Jerusalem because the houses were not actually theirs. Residents of Jerusalem did not own their residences, as the city belonged to the entire Jewish people.

The Red Heifer ››

One of the prerequisites for entry to the Temple was purification, even from "light" forms of impurity, and all the more so for those who had become defiled by coming in contact with death, such as touching or being in the same house as a corpse. This would require the ashes of a red heifer for purification. Such ashes would be prepared periodically on the Mt. of Olives (*Har Hamishcha*), opposite the Beit Hamikdash.

The process of preparing the red heifer ashes is described by Maimonides (*Para Aduma* 3:2): "The elders of Israel would walk to the Mount of Olives first. There was a mikveh there. The priest, the assistants, and the heifer would go out on the ramp and come to the Mount of Olives... Wood was arranged there: cedar, oak, pine, and smooth fig wood, arranged like a tower for the fire... [After the heifer is slaughtered and burnt,] the priest takes a branch of cedar and a handbreadth of hyssop, and wool dyed crimson, and asks the people standing there: 'Is this cedar? Is this cedar? Is this cedar?" and then similarly three times each for the hyssop and the crimson thread [because there are several types of each], and the people answer "Yes!" three times for each set of questions. The priest then binds the hyssop with the cedar branch and the crimson thread and throws them into the belly of the heifer, as written in Numbers 19:6."

The platform on which the red heifer was burnt was elevated on arches, with an empty space underneath to halakhically dissipate the impurity (Maimonides, *Para Aduma* 3,1). The ramp/bridge leading from the Temple Mount to the Mt. of Olives was built atop arches for the same purpose, as written in the Mishna (*Para* 3:6).

The ramp/bridge led from the eastern gate of the Temple Mount to the Mt. of Olives. Over the eastern gate was a representation of the palace of Shushan, in commemoration of the permission to rebuild the Temple given by Cyrus of Persia, and "through it the High Priest who burnt the red heifer, and all who assisted with it, would go forth to the Mount of Olives" (Mishna, *Middot* 1:3).

Drawing Water from the Siloam

Ritually pure water for the red heifer purification mixture must be drawn from the Siloam Pool by someone who is ritually pure. To this end, young children who were specially raised in a completely pure environment are taken to the Siloam. They are seated on boards which have been placed on the backs of cattle, blocking any impurity from reaching them from the ground. Other measures taken to ensure that nothing defiles the process include special stone utensils for drawing the water; stone cannot become defiled. In addition, the water itself was transferred to the Temple on top of the wooden boards which protected both the children and the utensils in their hands from impurity.

Maimonides writes (*Para Aduma* 3:2): "When they wanted to sprinkle ashes on the priest who burns the red heifer, they would bring oxen with fat bellies and place boards on their backs. [Both of these measures are for the purpose of blocking impurity.] The children held cups of stone in their hands and went to the Siloam Pool. Once there, they would descend and fill the cups... They would then ascend, sit on the boards, and proceed back up until they reach the Temple Mount."

Seen here are young priests, seated on boards on the backs of the oxen. One child draws water from the spring, while adults supervise the process. The children wear priestly garments (*Targum Yonatan,* Numbers 19:18, 21). In the final analysis, Maimonides rules (*Para Aduma* 6:2) that the water may be drawn even by a non-priest.

A Courtyard in Jerusalem Where Children Were Raised in Purity

The picture depicts a courtyard carved into a Jerusalem rock, with a large area underneath it. This courtyard is clean and ritually pure, despite the risk that in Jerusalem there may be a grave hidden in the ground. This situation is to ensure that there will always be people who are ritually pure. Since they live in an area carved into a rock, with space beneath it, any impurity will find its way out of the courtyard. This courtyard was used to raise the children of priests in purity, allowing them to go draw water from the Siloam Pool in purity, in order to prepare the ash of the red heifer. The Mishna (*Para* 3:2) states: "Courtyards were built in Jerusalem on top of the rock, and beneath [these courtyards there was a] space [of at least a handbreadth] due to [the concern lest there is] a grave in the depths. [In that case, the space served as a barrier preventing the impurity from reaching the courtyards above.] Pregnant women would be brought there and they would give birth there [in those courtyards] and they would raise their children there as well.

Beating the Ashes into Dust

This picture shows the priests grinding the ashes of the burnt red heifer into dust. The dust was then sifted and turned into a fine powder. It was then mixed with water and sprinkled on those in a state of defilement from having come in contact with a corpse.

Maimonides (*Para Aduma* 3:3) adds that the wood on which the heifer was burnt was not separated from the remains of the heifer, but was rather beaten and became part of the powder mixture.

Preparing the Water and the Ashes

This picture shows a priest pouring fresh water, brought from the Siloam Pool, into a stone bowl. This mixture would then be sprinkled on the impure, to purify them. Stone utensils were used for the ash of the red heifer, because stone utensils cannot become impure.

The Purity of the Pilgrims

As seen in this painting, special arrangements were made in the streets of Jerusalem during the Festivals to ensure cleanliness and purity. The Talmud (*Pesachim* 7a) relates that the streets were swept every day (see at right).

The Sages instructed that once the Festival began, all impurity and defilement in Jerusalem was suspended. However, before the onset of the Festival, in order to ensure maximum purity, the practice was that those who were pure would walk in the middle of the street – to their homes, on errands, or to the Temple – while those who were impure would move to the sides. Some commentaries say that "monitors" were stationed at various places in the city to remind the impure to remain on the sides of the street; one such monitor can be seen at the top of the picture.

This was a season of buying animals for sacrifices. To the right is seen a man checking a potential purchase for possible blemishes on its eyes and ears. Many of the pilgrims bought animals from *Ma'aser Sheni* money they brought with them from home, i.e., money on which they redeemed their Second Tithe produce and that had to be spent in Jerusalem. According to Jewish Law, coins that were found next to the animal sellers were to be considered sacred as *Ma'aser Sheni*. A man is seen here (bottom right) picking up a purse of money found near the merchants selling the animals.

Ritual Baths in Jerusalem

This picture shows the immersion of utensils in a mikveh, and the special layout of the entrance and exit paths to the mikveh. The entrance is down the steps, on the right, and the exit is upwards, on the left. The entrances must be separated so that those entering in an impure state do not defile those who have just immersed and are leaving. The same arrangement was made for those who wished to purify their clothing or utensils. Many Jerusalem ritual baths were designed in this manner because of the many people who wished to enter the Holy Temple.

The Sages decreed that any utensil or article of clothing found on the ground or elsewhere in Jerusalem during a Festival is to be considered pure – even, something found on the steps leading down to a mikveh (Maimonides, *She'ar Avot HaTumot* 13:5).

Purifying the Pilgrims

This picture shows a family that has arrived in the Holy Temple's Purification Room to become purified from the contact they had with a corpse. The priests sprinkle several drops of the red heifer ash mix upon them, using three clusters of hyssop for the purpose. Their clothing, the utensils they hold in their hands, and they themselves thus become ritually pure.

Even 100 people at once can become purified in this manner (Maimonides, *Para Aduma* 10:9), for only a few drops need be sprinkled on a person to purify him. The purification is done both on the third day and the seventh day of the seven-day process. To complete the purification, the people immerse in a mikveh on the seventh day. They must also immerse their utensils and clothing in order to purify them.

Preparing Pure Utensils for the Pilgrims

This painting depicts the manufacture of pottery in Modi'in, where many pilgrims would stock up on their way to Jerusalem for Passover. The Sages decreed that all utensils made in Modi'in are pure and acceptable for Festival use in the Temple. Thus, the pilgrims could safely stop in Modi'in along their way and purchase the pottery and utensils they needed for the Festivals in the Beit Hamikdash.

According to Jewish Law, a clay utensil that was defiled (by the presence of a dead reptile inside it, for instance) cannot be purified; it must be broken. The manufacture of such pottery, therefore, required extraordinary caution, so that they could be used by the pilgrims on the Festivals. The Mishna states (*Chagiga 3:5*): "Within Modi'in and on [towards Jerusalem], the potters were relied upon to say that a given utensil was pure, but in the areas before Modi'in [further from Jerusalem], the potters are not relied upon." This is because Modi'in was a city of priests and the potters were expert in the relevant laws.

The Half-Shekel

Seen here is a man contributing his annual half-shekel Temple tax, collected annually from every Jewish male above the age of 20. The funds were used towards the purchase of public sacrifices and other Temple needs.

The man sitting at the table is the *shulchani*, charged with exchanging coins and collecting the tax, beginning on the first day of Adar. According to Maimonides, one could find a *shulchani* stationed not only in the Temple and in Jerusalem, but also in cities throughout the country, and would then bring the collected funds to the treasurers in the Temple.

A Half-Shekel Coin ››

Seen here is a half-shekel coin that was minted towards the end of the Second Temple, during the great revolt against the Romans. On the coin is written "Jerusalem the Holy" and "half-shekel." In addition, the coin depicts one of the incense ingredients and shows the bowl used for the incense in the Temple. Coins like these were found throughout the land of Israel. Even recently coins were found by archaeologists in the piles of dirt that were removed from the Temple Mount.

The Half-Shekel Chamber

The half-shekels collected from around the country were brought to a special chamber designated for this purpose in the Holy Temple. They were stored there together with the other contributions that had been deposited there directly. The picture shows one of the special deposit windows, through which a man is making a contribution.

The Temple treasurers would fill the coffers with the collected half-shekels, and purchase animals for the *Tamid* sacrifices, *Musaf* offerings, and other public sacrifices. The Mishna (*Shekalim* 3:1) teaches: "Three times a year they would fill the coffers with half-shekels: Before Passover, before *Shavuot*, and before *Sukkot*."

The Mishna continues to describe how the treasurer would enter the chamber and fill three vats with coins for the purchase of animals for the coming weeks leading up to the next Festival. The vats would be marked *aleph*, *bet*, and *gimmel* (or with Greek letters, according to R. Yishmael), so that the first-contributed coins would be used first. In addition, special precautions would be taken to prevent any suspicion of wrong doing connected to the treasurer: He would not wear a robe with folds, so that no one would think that he had hidden some coins there, nor would he wear any article of clothing that might lead to similar suspicions.

The Chamber of the Shekels and the Chamber of the Sacrifices

Seen here are two offices designated for the half-shekel coins. The offices were located, according to Maimonides, in the north of the *Azara*. On the left is the *Lishkat Hashekalim* (Chamber of the Shekels), where all the half-shekel coins were brought from all of Israel and the Diaspora. In the foreground we see people escorting the delivery of the coins from foreign lands.

On the right we see the *Lishkat Hakorban* (Chamber of the Sacrifices), where some of the half-shekels were later brought to purchase animals for the *tamid* and *Musaf* sacrifices. At the entrance we can see the collectors bringing the half-shekels in 3 boxes, ensuring the ability to purchase animals for the sacrifices throughout the year.

The Festival Sacrifices

In this picture we see the shepherd bringing his herd to be offered as public sacrifices on one of the days of Passover: Two bulls, one ram, seven year-old lambs, and one goat for a sin-offering.

On *Sukkot*, the amount of animals sacrificed for the public offerings differed from day to day, while on Passover the amount remained the same – except for the second day of the Festival, when an additional lamb was added as a burnt-offering for the *Omer* waving. On the left, a man is seen carrying a scythe and a sheaf of barley for the *Omer* offering, and leading a lamb for the burnt-offering.

Preparing to Enter the Temple Mount

A family is seen here preparing to enter the gates of the Temple Mount. The entry requires preparation, so that the commandment of "Awe of the Temple" can be properly fulfilled. Specifically here, the pilgrims are removing their shoes, as Joshua bin Nun was told by the angel: "Remove your shoes from your feet, for the place on which you stand is holy earth" (Joshua 5:15). The family members deposit their shoes with the guards responsible for watching the property and enter the Temple to bring the Passover offering.

Welcoming the Pilgrims

The Jerusalemites had a very pleasant custom of welcoming the Festival pilgrims arriving from all around the country. In this painting we see leading city residents and Temple officials coming to greet their brothers upon their arrival. The Mishna describes the scene as follows: "When they neared Jerusalem, they would send messengers ahead to inform of their arrival... The deputies and treasurers and officials come out to greet them. All the skilled artisans of Jerusalem would stand and greet them: 'Brethren, people of such-and-such a place, we are delighted to welcome you'" (*Bikkurim* 3:3).

Signaling the Time to Burn The Hametz

A priest is seen here signaling that the Passover prohibition on eating Hametz has begun and the obligatory time to burn it has arrived.

The public at large did not generally know when precisely the prohibition on eating Hametz on Passover Eve began, nor did they know when the obligation to burn all Hametz in one's possession began (one hour later). Without clocks, the people relied on the Temple officers to inform them that the time had come. The signal is described in the Mishna (*Pesachim* 1:5): "Two [unfit] loaves of the thanks-offering would be placed on the roof of the Temple portico... When one was removed, Hametz would be neither eaten nor burnt; when both were removed, the people would commence burning their Hametz."

« Jerusalem Hospitality

"There was a great custom in Jerusalem," the Sages teach, "People would spread a cloth over the entrance of their house to signal that guests are invited to enter and join the diners in the house and in the courtyard. If the cloth was removed, guests could not enter" (*Tosefta, Berakhot* 4:8). This picture shows such a cloth over the entrance, would-be guests pointing at it, and other guests enjoying a meal.

Hospitality was a well-known attribute of the people of Jerusalem, and especially on the Three Festivals. Even pilgrims to Jerusalem sought to host others at their meals, paying special attention to those in need. As the Torah commands (Deuteronomy 16:14): "Rejoice in your festival – you, and your son and daughter and servant and maidservant and the Levite and foreigner and orphan and widow at your gates."

The Family and the Sacrificial Offerings for the Festival »

This painting depicts a family on its joyous way to Jerusalem, bringing animals to be offered as sacrifices. On each of the Festivals sheep and lambs are brought for the *Olat Re'iya*, *Shalmei Chagiga*, and *Shalmei Simcha* offerings. (Occasionally, doves or young birds – carried on the woman's head, on the right, would be brought for the *Olat Re'iya*.) On Passover, two extra sacrifices were offered: a Passover lamb offering, carried by the man on the left and a lamb or ox (on the left, for the Passover Eve *Chagiga*.

The *Shavuot* Holiday in the Holy Temple

Introduction

Shavuot – The Festival of Weeks – is the name of the holiday that comes seven weeks after Passover. This name was given following the Destruction and Exile, and the holiday has several other names as well. It is known as the Day of the Giving of the Torah; the Sages refer to it as *Atzeret;* and its less well-known names are Harvest Festival and Festival of the First Fruits. These last in fact characterize the main aspects of the holiday as it was celebrated at the time of the Beit Hamikdash.

The main aspect of the Festival of the First Fruits in the Holy Temple was the bringing of the *Shtei HaLechem* – two large loaves made of the first wheat grains of the new harvest. In addition, every Jewish farmer brought the first fruits of the Seven Species growing in his fields. These Seven Species were: Wheat, barley, grapes, figs, pomegranates, olives and dates. The farmers would bring this produce, known as *bikkurim*, to the priest in the *Azara* (courtyard) of the Holy Temple.

The *bikkurim* brought on *Shavuot* were, to be sure, just a partial gift – for only the wheat and barley were ready for harvest by this time of year. The other fruits would totally ripen only later on in the summer.

The Mishna describes in a very picturesque manner how the first fruits were chosen: "A man goes into his field and sees the first ripe fig or the first ripe cluster of grapes or the first pomegranate to ripen. He ties that fruit with a reed and says, "These are *Bikkurim*" (*Bikkurim* 3:1). The three fruits mentioned here grow and ripen in mid-summer. As such, we can assume that the main bringing of *bikkurim* took place on the joyous day of Tu B'Av, the 15th of Av – for this is the time when a person can go to his field and find all three of the above fruits ready at the same time! (Olives and dates still need a few more weeks to ripen.)

Evidence that Tu B'Av was in fact a day when many Jews brought their *bikkurim* to the Temple can be found in this account related in Tractate *Ta'anit*:

"...On the 15th of Av the families of *Gonvei Eli* and *Kotzei Ketziot* brought their wood donations and accompanying sacrifices... It happened once that an evil government made a decree against Israel... forbidding them from bringing wood to the altar or the first-fruit offerings to the Temple. The government stationed guards along the roads, in the manner of Jeroboam ben Nevat, to prevent Israel from making the pilgrimage. What did the upstanding and God-fearing people of that generation do? They brought baskets of first-fruits and covered them with dried figs (*ketziot*), and carried them on their shoulders along with a pestle. When they reached the roadblocks, the guards asked them: 'Where are you going?' The people would answer: 'To prepare two rounds cakes of pressed figs with the mortar that is down the road before us and with the pestle that we are carrying on our shoulders.' Once they had safely passed the guards, they decorated their baskets and brought the first-fruits to Jerusalem. Thus these families were known as *Gonvei Eli* and *Kotzei Ketziot*."

This shows that the 15th of Av, when the grapes ripened and when these families went to Jerusalem, was a time of bringing *bikkurim*.

We have learned that *Shavuot* is when the first *Bikkurim* were brought to the Temple. But even more *bikkurim* were brought on Tu B'Av – an extra date of pilgrimage to Jerusalem, mainly for the purpose of bringing first fruits. In Tractate *Bikkurim*, too, we see that the bringing of the first fruits was a ceremony not directly connected with *Shavuot*.

The paintings on the following pages will teach us much about these and other topics having to do with *Shavuot* in the Holy Temple. We pray that these illustrations speedily become reality in the courtyards of the Temple Mount, as we recite in our prayers: "May our eyes behold Your return to Zion with mercy."

BARANOVSKY

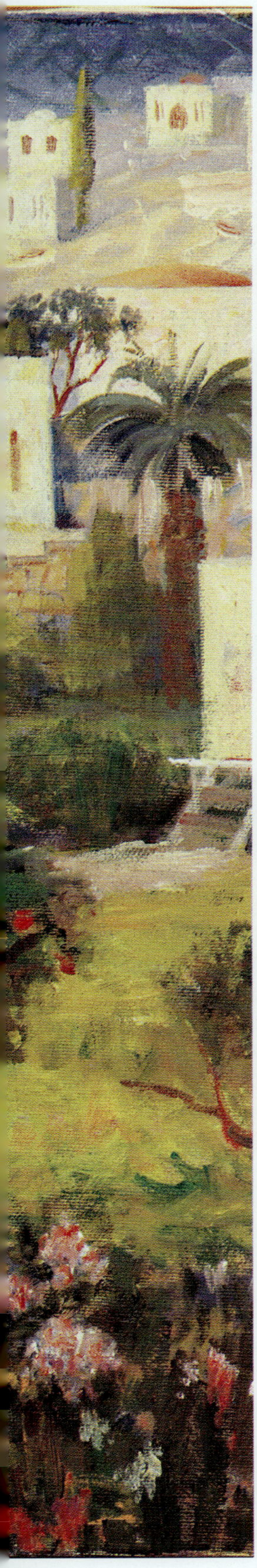

« Tying the Reed

Preparations to bring first fruits (*bikkurim*) to Jerusalem begin well before the actual journey. This picture shows a man designating a ripe fig for *bikkurim*: As is customary, he ties it with a reed and thus designates it as a *bikkurim* fruit to be brought to the priests in the Holy Temple.

« Preparing to Bring the First Fruits

This picture shows a home in a small village in the Land of Israel, as the family makes its preparations for the *Shavuot* Festival pilgrimage. The master of the household ties a reed around the very first fruits of the tree to ripen, and prepares to take them as *bikkurim*. Pomegranates and grapes are also being picked for the same purpose. On the top step of the house at left, a man takes young pigeons from their coops, to offer them as sacrifices in Jerusalem. In the center foreground can be seen a goat, designated to become a "*Shelamim* (peace-offering) of happiness." Food and water are also being prepared for nourishment during the journey to Jerusalem.

On the Way to Jerusalem

Pilgrims from cities and villages all over the Land of Israel come to Jerusalem during the harvest season. Individuals and small groups would set out on their own, soon joining up with others and arriving at an "interim station" – one of the cities known as *arei ma'amad* (*Bikkurim* 3:2). From there, they would form large convoys of people on their way to celebrate the Festival in the Holy City – some walking, others riding on animals or traveling in wagons.

The picture shows many people carrying their first fruits to the Holy Temple. The convoy also includes lambs, goats and oxen to be offered up as sacrifices for the Festival. Also seen is a farmer who has not yet completed his work in the field; planning to join the next convoy, he waves in greeting to those who are already on their way.

First Fruits from The Vine

How should one separate the first fruits? He should go into his field and see... a cluster that is the first to have ripened... tie it with a string and say "these are first fruits" (Mishna *Bikkurim* 3:1).

Pomegranates, Figs, and Grapes

The pomegranates are listed with the figs and grapes, as it says: "And they... cut down from there a branch with one cluster of grapes, and they bore it upon a pole between two; they took also of the pomegranates, and of the figs" (Numbers 13:23). Rav Zemba, the former rabbi of Warsaw, Poland, may the Lord avenge his murder, explains that the figs and grapes we bring as first fruits are a way to amend the wrong the spies did when they brought back those fruits for nefarious purposes. Instead we bring these fruits in praise of the land of Israel.

Large Gathering in the *Ma'amad* City ››

The pilgrims bearing *bikkurim* are seen here gathering together – having come from all corners of the Land – in a local *ma'amad* city (so called because of the priestly shifts, *ma'amadot*). From here, they would all ascend together to Jerusalem, thus fulfilling the Biblical command of *Aliya L'regel* – pilgrimage to Jerusalem – in a festive and resplendent manner, as is written: "In a multitude of people is a king's glory" (Proverbs 14:28).

Ascending en-masse also had practical benefits, in the help that people could give each other, and the joyous atmosphere created by the large crowds.

The custom was that the pilgrims would bed down for the night outside, in the city square. This would help them avoid the problems of possible impurity inside the residents' homes (*Bikkurim* 3:2).

They would be awoken at dawn with the cry, "Arise and let us ascend to Zion, to the house of Hashem our God!" The picture here depicts the scene just after the morning wake-up with the sun's first rays. People can be seen on the rooftops encouraging the pilgrims to awaken – which they eagerly do, making haste to load their animals and finalize other preparations for the remainder of the journey. Shepherds are seen leading their flocks of sheep and herds of cattle to Jerusalem for the sacrifices. Jerusalem is visible in the horizon.

The Shavuot Holiday in the Holy Temple [390-391]

The Procession of the *Bikkurim*

This picture provides a view of a small procession of pilgrims singing and playing music on their way to the Holy Temple. "The ox leads the way, its horns plated with gold and a crown of olives on its head. The flute plays before them until they near Jerusalem" (*Bikkurim* 3:3).

A Basket of First Fruits

A preferred manner of bringing the *bikkurim* to the Temple was by placing the basket on one's head. This prevented jostling and crushing of the fruits. Accompanying this man and his son is a goat brought for a sacrifice, its horns plated with silver – in accordance with the custom of those who did not arrive together with the larger convoys of pilgrims (Jerusalem Talmud, *Bikkurim* 3:3).

Nearing Jerusalem

The convoy of the pilgrims bearing *bikkurim is* seen on the Mt. of Olives as it approaches Jerusalem. The longed-for destination – the Holy City and the Beit Hamikdash – is close at hand. On the left can be seen an ox with horns painted gold, preceded by flute-players dressed in the traditional special white clothing for the joyous ascent to Jerusalem for the Festival.

Accompanying the sacrificial ox were singers and dancers, chanting from Psalms: "I was joyous when I was told, let's go up to the House of the Lord" (*Bikkurim* 3, Mishna and Jerusalem Talmud). As the pilgrims neared the Holy City, an advance delegation would go ahead to inform the residents that a convoy was about to enter. The residents would wait to greet and welcome the pilgrims at the city gate; in the picture on the right people are seen on top of the gate, welcoming the visitors.

In the foreground we see pilgrims arranging and adorning their first fruits as they await the signal that the Jerusalemites have arrived to welcome them. They place the dried fruits on the bottom of their baskets, and the fresher ones atop them (Maimonides, *Bikkurim* 4:16).

Once the visitors entered the city gates, all would continue the above Psalm and sing together: "Our feet were standing within your gates, O Jerusalem."

Fulfilling the Commandment

The painting shows a father and his sons bringing the family's first fruits to the Temple. They climb the 15 steps up to the Gate of Nicanor. The Seven Species of the Land of Israel are brought in seven different utensils, with each fruit carried individually by one of the children. One of them is also carrying a jug on his shoulder, in order to add wine and oil to the *Bikkurim* (*Yalkut Shimoni*, *Mishpatim* 23).

When bringing the first fruits in this manner on *Shavuot* and *Sukkot*, the father fulfills the commandment most perfectly, as is written: "All your males shall be seen." The father even made an effort to bring a young child with him to the Temple, even a child who is not completely independent and sometimes needs his father's help (*Chagiga* 1:1).

The Seven Species, The Baskets, and the Sacrificial Doves

This painting shows a special *bikkurim* basket in which each of the Seven Species of the Land of Israel is in a separate receptacle. The Sages ruled as follows: "The commandment is performed most worthily and beautifully when the Seven Species are brought separately in seven receptacles... He should not bring them all mixed together; rather, the barley should be on bottom, and the wheat above it; olives above that, then dates, then pomegranates, and the figs above them all" (*Tosefta*, *Bikkurim* 2:8).

The Sages also tell us that doves brought with the baskets of first fruits are to be offered on the altar as burnt-offerings (*Bikkurim* 3:5). Some opinions are that the doves were placed on top of the figs, while others hold that they were placed aside the baskets so that the fruits would not be ruined. There are similarly various opinions regarding how to adorn the first fruits with grapes.

The picture shows, the principles of bringing the *bikkurim.* A separate basket for each fruit; the doves are separate, either on top or on the side; palm leaves and others are placed between the fruits; grapes adorn the figs and other fruits.

The King, the Rich, and the Poor ››

This illustration shows the King of Israel during the Second Temple period, bearing a basket of first fruits on his shoulder. As is written in the Mishna: "Even King Aggripa brought a basket on his shoulder and entered, until he reached the *Azara*" (*Bikkurim* 3:4). Representatives of the general population are also seen here bringing their *bikkurim* and animals for sacrifices.

The background of the picture is the entrance to the Temple Mount – remnants of which have been uncovered in recent archaeological excavations at the Huldah Gate of the Mount's southern wall.

The king's *bikkurim* basket is made of gold, in keeping with the custom of the wealthy men, who thus wished to "beautify" the commandment. Others brought their first fruits in baskets made of silver (on the right) or wicker reeds (left). Afterwards, the rich would take their baskets home, while the poorer people would leave their wicker baskets for the priests (Maimonides, *Bikkurim* 3:8).

Khvedantsevich Dmitry

« Entering the Temple in Awe and Joy

This painting shows the pilgrims with their *bikkurim*, singing with joy and thanksgiving as they approach the courtyards of the House of God. Notable Jerusalem residents and Temple priests are on hand to welcome the visitors at the entrance to the Temple Mount. All sing and make music together, celebrating the joy of the mitzvah. The visitors bring baskets of fruits and doves for sacrifices, together with the ox adorned with gilded horns and olive branches.

The Torah tells us in the passage of the *bikkurim*: "You shall rejoice in all the good that God has given you and your household" (Deuteronomy 26:11). The *Midrash Sifrei* adds that this joy was expressed in singing. And indeed, the entire process of bringing the *bikkurim* was replete with sanctity and happiness, as their song attested (Psalms 122:1): "I rejoiced when I was told that we were on our way to the house of God" (Maimonides, *Bikkurim* 4:16).

Bringing *Bikkurim* to the Sanctuary Gate

The first fruits are brought to a very special part of the Temple: the place known as "between the *Ulam* and the altar." It has a special holiness for being adjacent to the Sanctuary, and regular Israelites – and even priests who are unfit for service – are forbidden from entering it (Maimonides, *Beit HaBechira* 7:20). However, the *bikkurim* are more beloved than the other sacrifices, and those who bring them are not only permitted, but are obligated to fulfill this mitzvah specifically in this part of the Temple (*Midrash Sifrei*, Deuteronomy 26:4, and see Malbim's commentary). So precious is the mitzvah of bringing *bikkurim*!

A pilgrim is seen (in the center) fulfilling the mitzvah of waving his first fruits before God together with the priest. According to *Tosafot* (*Menachot* 81b), the pilgrim bringing the *bikkurim* places his hands under the basket, and the priest places his hands beneath the pilgrim's hands and the two of them wave it together. The Israelite then places his *bikkurim* near the southwest corner of the altar (bottom right).

An integral part of the mitzvah is to recite the required verses (Deuteronomy 26). Standing before the Sanctuary gate, the farmer

‹‹ The *Bikkurim* Reading Passage

The priest (on the left) is seen here helping the farmer recite the *bikkurim* passage, reciting it with him verse by verse. It must be said out loud and in the original Hebrew (*Sota* 32a). It was done in this manner for all, in order not to shame those who were truly unable to recite the verses by heart.

recites aloud, "My forefather was a wandering Aramean..." The *Midrash Tanchuma* (*Ki Tavo*) expounds:

Come and see how fulfilling a mitzvah gives us access to Hashem. If a man has an issue with the government, he is likely to have to pay much money in order to get to meet with the king – and then once he meets him, it is not certain whether the king will fulfill his desire. But with the Holy One, Blessed be He, the situation is different: A man goes into his field, sees the first ripened fruits, and places them in his basket and takes them to Jerusalem. He then comes to the Temple courtyard (see men at left-center with their hands raised) and prays for himself, his family, his people and the entire Land of Israel, as is written: "Gaze from Your holy abode, from the Heavens..." Not only that, but he would also say, "I will not move from here until You fulfill my needs this day..." and a Heavenly voice would announce and say to him, "You will merit the next year!"

Following the recital of the *bikkurim* passage, the pilgrim would prostrate himself on the special *Even Maskit* stone (foreground) and thank God for His kindness.

Waving the *Bikkurim* ››

This picture depicts Maimonides' method of waving the *bikkurim*. The farmer removes the basket from his shoulder and then holds it at its sides or with its handles. The priest places his hands under the basket, and together the priest and the farmer wave the *bikkurim* in accordance with the customary Temple waving practice: "Front, back, up and down" (Maimonides, *Bikkurim* 3:12).

‹‹ Placing the *Bikkurim*

The farmer places his first fruits near the southwest corner of the altar, after having recited the first verses of the *bikkurim* passage, as the Torah states: "Place it down before Hashem your God" (Deuteronomy 26:11). He would then prostrate himself and leave the area. (Maimonides, *Bikkurim* 3:12).

Prostration Before God ››

Bringing the *bikkurim* ends with an act that expresses one's thanks to God and acceptance of His yoke. He bows down totally, with outstretched arms and legs, on the ground "before God," opposite the Sanctuary and the Holy of Holies. This act of submission and humility marks the end of the process that began weeks before with the harvest of the fruits in his field in the Land of Israel, and the ending of this joyous and uplifting moment before the Sanctuary of God.

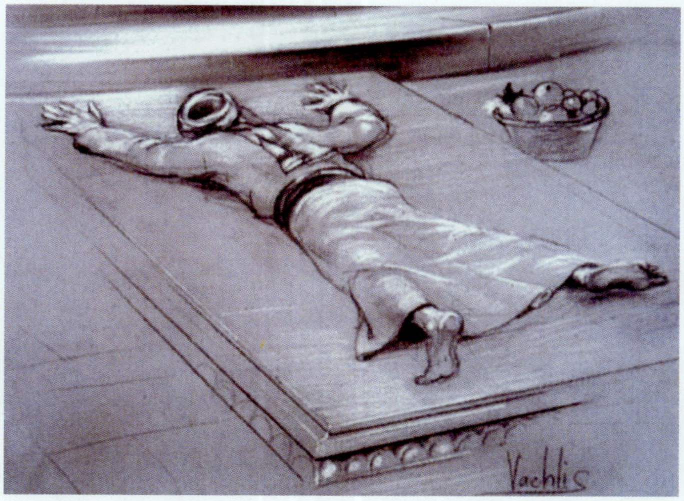

‹‹ The *Shavuot* Offerings

This picture depicts the public sacrifices brought to the Temple on *Chag HaShavuot*:

Two lambs brought with the showbread, known as *Kivsei Atzeret* (foreground).

An ox, two rams, seven lambs, and a goat as a sin-offering.

For the *Musaf* offering, the following are brought: Two oxen, a ram, seven one year old lambs, and a goat for atonement.

At the head of the procession are two lambs brought as the daily morning and late-afternoon *Tamid* public offerings.

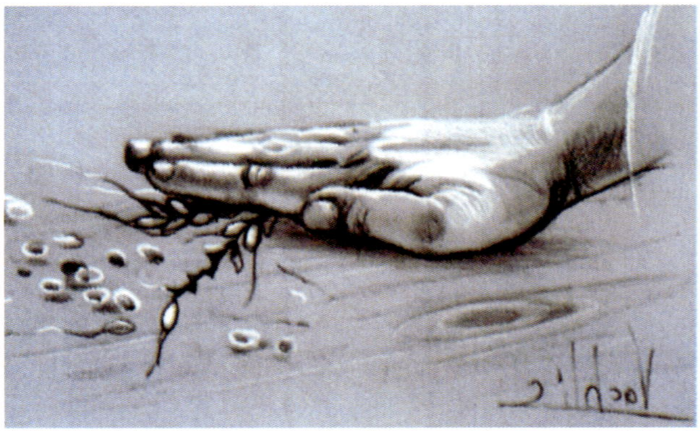

The Music Accompanying the Offering of the Twin Loaves

This picture portrays the offering of the Twin Loaves to God on *Shavuot*. When it is time for the Wine Libation the Levites who are magicians, poets, flutists and trumpet blowers join in with music and song. The wine libation is poured (far left, on the altar), the Twin Loaves are presented, together with the two lambs for peace offerings – and at the same time, the Levite choir performs (right). *Shavuot* is one of the 12 days of the year on which flutes are added to the Levites singing – even if it falls on the Sabbath. The flutists are seen here on the second step.

The schedule for the day is as follows (Maimonides, *Kelei HaMikdash* 3:2–6):

Two priests bring the Twin Loaves to the *Azara*, followed by two priests bringing the two *Atzeret* lambs to be waved, and they are given to the officiating priest.

The officiating priest comes towards them, east of the altar, and receives the loaves, as well as the lambs.

As the lambs are being slaughtered, a priest pours the wine into the silver cup – and then onto the corner of the altar.

Priests then begin sounding the trumpets. They cannot be seen here, because they stand on one of the tables west of the ramp leading up to the altar.

The priest leading the singing then waves with a white cloth as he stands on top of corner of the altar (left of center) This serves as a signal that the singers should begin chanting the Song of the Day. Thus, the singers sing, the trumpeters blast, and the musicians play their instruments. On this day, the flutes were heard the loudest (*Tamid* 7:3; Maimonides, *Temidin UMusafin* 6:6–8).

Preparing the Offering of the Twin Loaves

These two illustrations show two stages in preparing the kernels of newly-harvested wheat for flour for the Twin Loaves brought on *Shavuot*. Instead of utilizing the usual methods of threshing and winnowing, two steps known as rubbing and beating were used for this Mincha offering.

Maimonides explains (*Issurei Mizbe'ach* 7:5): "All the wheat of the *Menachot* (meal-offerings) must be rubbed 300 times and beaten [with the hand] 500 times. He must rub once, beat twice, rub twice and beat three times – and then repeat this process 100 times. This assures the removal of the husk... The grains are then ground and sifted very well."

Some commentaries say that the beating is done not with the hand, as seen here at right, but with the foot (Maimonides' Commentary to the Mishna, *Menachot* 6:5).

Preparing the Flour for the Twin Loaves

One sees here the Chamber where the Bakers of the Showbread prepare the meal offering of Twin Loaves for *Shavuot*. A priest brings freshly-harvested wheat stalks from the new crop on the (left) – a quantity of three *se'a*, about 24 liters. Another priest pours the coarse flour into a large grinder (on the right), where it is ground very finely. Only the finest milled flour will be used.

The law is that the loaves must be baked "inside," that is, inside the holy area of the *Azara* (*Temidin UMusafin* 8:7). In Tractate *Middot* (1:6) we learn that this chamber, with its special oven for both the showbread and the Twin Loaves, was located in the southeast corner of the Chamber of the Hearth.

After the grinding, the flour is sifted in 12 different sifters, one after the other. Each sifter was more finely-meshed than the one before it, in order to produce two *esronim* worth of the finest ground flour – one for each loaf. Each *isaron* is equivalent to about 2.5 liters (*Menachot* 6:7).

Kneading and Baking

Each of the Twin Loaves was kneaded separately (on the left) Unlike every other grain product in the Holy Temple, leaven is added to these loaves, so that the dough will rise; the other meal-offerings are not permitted to become *chametz*. The priests responsible for the baking form the loaves into precise, unique shapes: rectangles seven *tefachim* long and four *tefachim* wide, and four fingers thick, with (according to Rashi), raised corners, as seen on the right.

The dough is placed in its precise form into the tray, and each of the two loaves is then baked separately in the special oven (in the center). When the loaves are removed from the oven, they are again placed in special trays (*Menachot* 11:1).

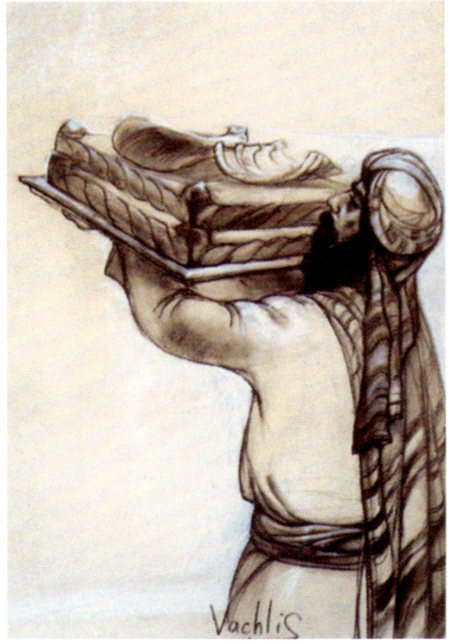

Waving the Lambs

This illustration depicts the waving of the two *Atzeret* sacrificial lambs, as Maimonides explains: "How are the Twin Loaves waved with the two lambs? He brings the two lambs, and waves them while they are still alive," (*Temidin UMusafin* 8:11). Some commentaries explain that the intention is that the lambs are waved together with the Twin Loaves. However, this would seem to be a difficult feat for most people, because of both the quantity of items and their combined weight – up to 100 kilograms and more! For this reason, the picture illustrates the words of Maimonides according to their plain meaning, meaning that the lambs are waved alone. Even if each sheep is waved individually, it is acceptable.

Waving the Loaves

The Twin Loaves are waved after the lambs are slaughtered. In the words of Maimonides (*Temidin UMusafin* 8:11): "[A priest] takes the breast and the thigh from each [of the slaughtered lambs] and places them aside the two loaves. He then places both of his hands below them and waves them all as one, in the eastern side of the Temple Courtyard."

The utensil seen here, on which the loaves and the meat of the lambs are placed is not mentioned by Maimonides or other commentaries. However, it appears logical that such a large, wide tray would be used, especially if the lambs and the loaves were to be waved together. The priest places his hands beneath the tray and waves it forward and then back, up and down (*Menachot* 62a).

« Waving the Loaves After the Slaughter of the Lambs

The Mishna (*Menachot* 61a) teaches that the loaves must be waved a second time, together with meat (the breast and thigh) from the slaughtered lambs. This picture illustrates the straightforward meaning of the verse, "The priest shall wave them [the breast and thigh] on the *bikkurim* bread" (Leviticus 23:20). There are other opinions as to how this waving was carried out. Maimonides rules (*Temidin UMusafin* 8:11) that even if he waved the meat and bread separately, he fulfilled his obligation.

The Loaves are Eaten By the Priests

The priests are seen here sitting down to eat the loaves in the Chamber of the Hearth. Two priests are seen (in the center) entering from the *Azara* with the bread, which must be eaten in sanctity. The meal is taking place in the sanctified area of the chamber, facing the *Azara*.

After the waving, the Twin Loaves and the remaining meat of the communal peace-offerings are eaten by priests of all shifts. It must be eaten as other "Holy of Holies" meat, i.e., in the *Azara* (*Temidin UMusafin* 8:11). Generally, no one is permitted to sit in the *Azara* except for those from the royal Davidic dynasty; however, in this case, eating the Twin Loaves is considered part of the Temple service and an honor thereof, and the priests may "sit and eat like kings" when partaking of this meal (*Tosafot* to *Yoma* 25a; *Zevachim* 91a).

Actually, each priest received only very small amount of the Twin Loaves and of the meat. He was allowed, however, to eat his portion together with other foods (*Temura* 23a) – again, so that the meal would be honorable, dignified, and satisfying.

It appears that the meal that was eaten in the Chamber of the Hearth because everywhere else in the *Azara* on *Shavuot* was likely to be filled with pilgrims from around the country.

From Destruction to Rebuilding

Chronicles of the Holy Temple During the Exile and Destruction

Introduction

Our period of Exile, since the destruction of the Second Temple, has lasted some two millennia – nearly 30 times longer than the 70-year exile following the destruction of the First Temple. Despite the many centuries that have passed, the Nation of Israel has never ceased cleaving to the Temple – in prayer, in fasting, in mourning, and in many laws and customs that were enacted "in memory" of the Temple and its destruction.

Many Jews over the years have expended great efforts to ascend to Jerusalem, despite the destruction and hazardous roads and major hardships simply to see the site of the Holy Temple. A description of one of these visits, by pilgrims from North Africa and other lands during the 14th century C.E., is cited in the responsa of the Tashbetz (Rabbi Shimon ben Tzemach Duran). Part of it reads as follows:

"The pilgrims say they still experience some of the miracles that took place in Jerusalem while the Temple still was standing. No man has ever said that the synagogue in Jerusalem was too crowded. On the *Shavuot* holiday, the worshipers number more than 300, and they all fit in the synagogue and sit in comfort. For Jerusalem's sanctity is still extant – and this is a sign of the upcoming third Redemption."

Attempts were also made to rebuild the Holy Temple throughout the long centuries of destruction. One of these attempts is described in the *Midrash* (*Bereshit Rabba* 64), which recounts that during the days of R. Yehoshua ben Chananya, the Roman regime granted permission to rebuild the Beit Hamikdash. Amid the general enthusiasm, generous donors immediately rose to the occasion, opening their storehouses and contributing gold and silver to the Jews who began streaming to the Holy Land to rebuild the Temple in Jerusalem.

The Gentiles of the Land were alarmed by this sudden activity, and sent a delegation to Rome warning that the rebuilding of the Holy Temple would foment rebellion against the rulers. The Roman rulers dispatched a royal decree, ordering the Jews to significantly reduce the size of the Temple they intended to build. A large crowd of Jewish pilgrims that had gathered in Beit Rimon in the Galilee received the decree with rage, and a new rebellion appeared on the brink, endangering the remaining Jews then living in the Land. The scholars there called upon R. Yehoshua ben Chananya to attempt to mollify the crowd. He did so by comparing the Jewish community to a bone caught in the throat of a lion: "We have entered the lion's cage and we are in national danger. It is enough that we entered this nation [the Romans] safely and have departed it safely. Let us disperse now, and wait for a better opportunity."

The crowd indeed dispersed, but its wrath did not actually die down. In fact, it reignited after the Romans began building a city of idol-worship in Jerusalem, setting off the Bar Kokhba rebellion. With the help of several Sages, most notably Rabbi Akiva, Bar Kokhba attempted to block the construction of a pagan temple on the site of the Beit Hamikdash, and even sought to rebuild the Holy Temple itself. The utter dedication that he and others exhibited showed the extent of the nation's longing to rebuild the House of God.

This is but one of many examples of the strong bond between the Nation of Israel and the holy site of the Beit Hamikdash, manifest in the many attempts throughout the generations to rebuild it.

The paintings and illustrations in this chapter tell the story of various milestones throughout the generations signifying the attempts of the People of Israel to rebuild the Holy Temple.

Titus and His Army at the Gates of Jerusalem

This painting depicts Jerusalem as it looked in the last days of the Second Temple, according to the detailed accounts provided by Josephus in his book *The Jewish War.* Titus is seen (in the foreground) at the head of the Roman legionnaires, overlooking Jerusalem and the Temple from the Mt. of Olives. He is carefully calculating whether he and his soldiers can conquer and occupy the large, well-fortified and populous city with its thousands of fighters. Facing Titus and his men are the steep slopes of the Kidron Valley, and the various sections of the walled city. In the center is the Temple, and to its left is the City of David, the Lower City. Behind the Temple is the Upper City, with Herod's palace at its summit.

Roman Soldiers Break into the *Azara*

Seen here are the Roman soldiers breaking into the *azara* while the priests were performing their service at the altar.

The Destruction of the Second Temple ››

This painting depicts the Holy Temple in flames, as Roman soldiers storm it with their weaponry. The priests stand on top of the altar (in the center) continuing the Temple service as long as they can, even as they lift their arms in prayer Roman soldiers are seen here looting the various golden utensils from the Sanctuary – specifically, the Menorah, the showbread table and the golden altar. Titus transported the sacred items by ship to Rome, where they were paraded before throngs of Romans celebrating their victory over Judea (*Gittin* 56a). The Temple utensils were kept on permanent display in Rome, and the Sages even visited there in later years (*Sukkah* 5:1)to learn more about them.

The Menorah on the Arch of Titus ››

This is a rendition of the Menorah from the destroyed Temple, borne on the shoulders of the captive Jews being exiled to Rome. The engraving on the famous arch in Rome has lasted nearly 2,000 years, though there has been some damage from wind, rain and drilling on the arch stones. It teaches us some important facts about the Menorah, such the shape of the base, the style of its decorations, and the fact that its branches were round, not straight.

The Sages Visiting the Destroyed Temple

After the destruction of the Second Temple, Jews from all over the Land of Israel would come to the site and mourn, despite the fact that the Romans forbade the Jews from living in Jerusalem. A famous passage at the end of Tractate *Makkot* depicts a scene in which R. Akiva and other Sages journeyed to Mt. Scopus in Jerusalem and observed the Temple Mount in ruins. They then walked to the Temple Mount, and saw a fox walking out of the Holy of Holies. This brought most of them to tears, though R. Akiva comforted them with words of encouragement.

In the foreground can be seen the Foundation Stone, upon which stood the Holy Ark in the Holy of Holies. Sages can be seen at the top left looking down upon the ruins, praying for the speedy rebuilding of the Beit Hamikdash.

Rending Garments on Mt. Scopus »

This painting depicts a Jew (bottom left) who has arrived in Jerusalem during the period of the Exile. As he sees the city unfold before him from Mt. Scopus, he rends his garments in mourning. This is a fulfillment of Jewish Law, as cited in a prayerbook found in the Cairo *geniza*:

"If you merit ascending to Jerusalem, tear your clothes in mourning for the destruction. When you look [at the city] from the mountain called *Tzofim* (Scopus), and you see the entire city, then: if you are riding a donkey, get off; if you are wearing shoes, remove them; tear your clothes and recite, 'Your holy cities have become a desert... Jerusalem is desolate... He ignited a fire in Zion and it consumed its foundations.'"

After ripping the garments for the destruction of Jerusalem, another tear must be made in memory of the Temple.

« The Building of the Dome of the Rock by Moslem Invaders

The Dome of the Rock was erected on the holy Temple Mount site some 1,300 years ago. It was built by Muslims who had set out from Mecca and Medina in Saudi Arabia on a campaign of conquest of the Middle East. When they arrived in Jerusalem, they learned from the Jews there that this was the site of the Holy Temple, and that the sanctity of the Temple Mount still existed. The Jews further told the invaders that the large rock in the center of the Mount is the holy Foundation Stone – the site of the Holy of Holies. The Arabs thereupon announced that the site was "holy to Islam," rivaling the city of Mecca, and built a monument – the Dome of the Rock – around the Foundation Stone.

Rending Garments a Second Time

This picture shows pilgrims to Jerusalem during the period of the Exile, fulfilling the obligation to rend their garments in memory of the destruction of the Temple. This is the second rending of their garments; they tore their clothes when they first saw the city from afar. The practice, as recorded in a Cairo *geniza* prayerbook, was as follows: "If you merit ascending to Jerusalem, first tear your clothing for the destruction of Jerusalem, then walk through the city gates as a mourner, with your head bowed. When you reach the site of the Temple and you see the Mount in its destruction, tear your garments again, and recite: 'Our house of sanctity and glory, where our forefathers sang praise to You, has been burnt down; our ultimate pleasure has been reduced to ruins. . .' And then recite this blessing: 'Blessed art Thou. . . the True Judge.'"

Negotiating the Purchase of the Temple Mount

The 18th century saw a reawakening of the drive to rebuild the Holy Temple and renew the sacrificial service. Rabbi Tzvi Hirsch Kalischer corresponded on this topic with the leading Torah scholars of his day, and explained in his book *Derishat Zion* why renewing the sacrificial services was viable and permitted. At one point, Rabbi Kalischer even turned to Baron Rothschild and suggested that he purchase the site of the Temple from Ibrahim Feha, who ruled the Land of Israel during that period. He wrote as follows:

"We have been fortunate to live during a period when God has sent to the Jewish people a great man like yourself, who stands before kings... At this time, when the Land of Israel is under the rule of the Feha regime... if my lord [Baron Rothschild] would purchase this area that is small in quantity but large in quality... When the leaders of Israel will gather on the holy land, a government of Israel will arise... And if the Feha does not wish to sell the entire land, let him sell just the site of the Temple and its environs, so that we can bring sacrifices to Hashem our God."

Rabbi Kalischer summed up his opinion on the renewal of sacrifices: "I have shown that the Halakha is clear on the matter of sacrifices during our times... when we receive permission to build an altar and bring sacrifices... It is clear that the Torah's commandment of offering sacrifices will never be nullified! For our holy Torah will never change and will never be replaced."

Maimonides in Jerusalem

Depicted here is the Temple Mount and surrounding buildings as they looked during Maimonides' lifetime, in the 12th century. The renowned scholar and leader wrote about his visit to the site in his commentary to Tractate *Rosh Hashanah*:

"On Saturday night, the 4th day of Iyar, I set off by ship [from North Africa]. . . and on Sunday night, the 3rd of Sivan, we arrived safely at the port city of Akko (Acre); I was saved from religious persecution and we arrived in the Land of Israel. I vowed that this date would henceforth be a day of joy, happiness, festivities and gifts to the poor, for me and my family for all generations. And on Tuesday, the 4th day of MarCheshvan 4926, we set off on the dangerous route from Akko to Jerusalem, and I entered the 'Great and Holy House' and prayed there on Thursday, the 6th day of MarCheshvan. And on Sunday, the 9th of the month, I left Jerusalem for Hebron, to kiss the graves of my forefathers in the cave. And on that day – great praise to God for everything! – I arrived at the cave and prayed. And these two days – the 6th and 9th of MarCheshvan – I vowed would be as a festival for me, with prayer and joy unto God, eating and drinking. May God help me in everything, and enable me to 'fulfill my vows to God' (Psalms 116:18), Amen."

Rabbi Binyamin of Tudela's Visit

This picture portrays the Dome of the Rock, with an entrance to the Foundation Stone. Rabbi Binyamin MiTudela describes his 12th century visit to Jerusalem in his book of travels. This visit was made subsequent to Maimonides' visit. MiTudela describes the side of the Dome of the Rock seen in this picture as the "western wall of the Holy of Holies," and this is apparently how it was known by the Jews of Jerusalem at that time. In his words:

"The Jehoshaphat Gate [in the eastern side of the Mount] before the ancient Temple... and on the site of the Temple, Omar bin al-Qattab built a large and very beautiful dome, where the Gentiles do not allow any picture or idol, but they only allow prayer there. And in front of it is the Western Wall, one of the walls that were in the Holy of Holies, and it is called Gate of Mercy. It is there that all the Jews come to pray before the wall in the *Azara* [courtyard]."

The western wall of the Dome of the Rock, the Sages teach, is the western wall of the Sanctuary: "'Behold, He stands behind our wall' (Song of Songs 2:9) – this is the Western Wall of the Holy Temple" (*Midrash Bemidbar Rabba* 11).

The Sages also stated (*Shemot Rabba* 2) that the Divine Presence never left the Holy of Holies: "The Divine Presence never moved from within the Sanctuary, as is written, 'My eyes and heart will be there all the days.'"

The Gate of the Cotton

This painting depicts Jews coming to pray at the Gate of the Cotton in the center of the Western Wall of the Temple Mount. From this entrance one can look inside and see the "western wall" of the Dome of the Rock, which the halakha refers to as the "western wall" of the Sanctuary, and in practice was a wall of the Holy of Holies. Behind this wall stood the Ark of the Covenant and on it the cherubim, and therefore our Sages said that the Divine presence did not leave the western wall (*Shemot Rabba* 2:2). Rabbi David ben Zimra, among the exiles from Spain and a respected Halachic expert of Jewish law, wrote a responsum regarding entering the boundaries of the Temple Mount, and in order to write it he stood at this spot with the experts from Jerusalem in order to render an informed decision.

Rabbi Ishtori HaParchi Prays at the Mercy Gate

One observes in this picture a congregation of Jews praying at the Eastern Gate, opposite the Holy of Holies. The 13th century scholar Rabbi Ishtori HaParchi, in his classic work on the Land of Israel *Kaftor VaFerach*, explains the custom of his day:

"The wall [of the eastern Temple Mount] has two towering gates, oval at the top, with doors of metal that are perpetually closed. They are popularly called the Gates of Mercy (*Sha'ar HaRachamim*), and the Ishmaelites similarly call them Bab al-Rahma. It is likely that these are the two gates that King Solomon built for the purpose of doing kindness, one for bridegrooms and one for mourners, as taught in Tr. *Soferim* 19:12 . . . The general practice is that people come to these walls and pray to God, may He be exalted before these two gates. King Solomon requested of God that prayers offered in this spot be accepted (Kings I 8:9)."

R. Ishtori HaParchi corresponded with the great Torah scholars of his generation (in the 13th century) regarding the renewal of the Temple service on the Temple Mount. He wrote:

"Rabbi Baruch of Jerusalem told me, when I showed him my book so that he could review and correct it, that Rabbeinu Yechiel of Paris said to come [from Akko] to Jerusalem, in the 17th year of the 6th millennium (1257 C.E.) and offer sacrifices [though the Temple was not built]. And because of my rush to complete the work with him, I did not ask him what must be done about our impure state, nor how could we find a priest of pure lineage. Before I reached Shiloh, I turned back, and then I remembered the Law that the impurity was not a concern . . . because public sacrifices are offered even on the Sabbath and even in an impure state."

The Holy of Holies and the Radbaz

This illustration shows the Dome of the Rock from the inside. Tradition tells us that this rock is the Foundation Stone, from where the world was created, and the site of the Holy of Holies. The stone is seen in the center, raised above the floor, and Muslims are pictured here bowing down before it.

The Radbaz, R. David ben Zimra, of 16th-century Egypt, was a leading Jewish scholar and author of a commentary to Maimonides' Yad Hazakah. Among the many thousands of halakhic questions he was asked over the years, several of them dealt with the sanctity of the Temple Mount when the Temple is in ruins. He wrote a long responsum regarding where exactly on the Mount one is permitted to enter, which states in part:

"You asked for my opinion as to whether it is permitted to enter the structures built around and into the area of the Holy Temple, where they overhang on various protrusions. You note that this is the unprotested common custom. My answer is as follows:

"This question requires careful consideration, for it is evident that under the dome lies, most undoubtedly, the Foundation Stone, which they call Al-Sakra... We have now asked them and they said that it is higher than the ground by three times the height of a man [approx. 5.5 meters], and we see from outside that they in fact climb up many steps to the dome ... The Gentiles also said that under the dome is a cave, and that when the early kings wanted to know what was there, they sent people down there – where they met their death, and so they closed up the cave and filled it with earth... Perhaps they heard that the Holy Ark was hidden there... Most certainly the rock under the dome is the Foundation Stone on which was placed the Ark in the western part of the Holy of Holies. Therefore, one who ascends the upper structures in the west, or who enters to see from the western [Temple Mount] entrance – must make sure that he remains more than 11 cubits from the dome... And I estimated that between this wall on the south up until the structures built on the north, there are more than 135 cubits, and they are not inside the holy area, and it is permitted to enter them... And all the structures and the like on the east are permitted for entry... And in general I say that the structures and the like on the north and east are most definitely permitted for entry... I have thus explained to you the reason for the custom, but you should be among the cautious, and do not enter anywhere and stay far away from the dome.

‹‹ Exposing the Western Wall

The Western Wall of the Temple Mount is first mentioned in a classic commentary to the Mishna by R. Ovadia of Bartenura, who arrived in Jerusalem in the 15th century. From there, he wrote to his family in Italy: "The Western Wall still exists – that is, part of it. Its stones are very large and thick; I never saw such large stones in any other ancient building, not in Rome nor anywhere else." Over the course of the centuries, the narrow street in front of the Western Wall has become a site for prayer.

Tisha B'Av Prayers at the Wall ››

This illustration shows the Western Wall and the area in front of it on a typical Tisha B'Av fast day, during the period of the Exile. The worshipers sit on the ground in mourning for the Temple, reciting the Book of Lamentations and Tisha B'Av lamentation *(kinot)*.

Rav Hai Gaon's Tradition ››

This is a depiction of Jews gathered on Mt. of Olives for prayer opposite the Temple Mt. as was the tradition of the 10th-century Jewish leader Rav Hai Gaon, the last of the *Ge'onim* of Babylon. Dean of the famed Pumbedita Yeshiva, Rav Hai responded to thousands of halakhic questions from all over the Jewish world in Asia, Europe and North Africa.

He and others would gather every year on *Sukkot* to recite prayers on the Mt. of Olives, overlooking the Temple Mount. His custom on the 7th day of *Sukkot*, *Hoshana Rabba*, was to circle part of Mt. of Olives seven times, in memory of the seven circuits the Israelites would make in the Temple on *Sukkot*. Tradition tells that "they would recite Psalms arranged by Rav Hai, and priests would walk before him dressed in silk, and behind him followed the rest of the congregation."

A letter sent from the leaders of Jerusalem around that time encouraged the Jews of the Diaspora to continue this practice: "Mt. of Olives is the place in which he prayed on holidays and on Hoshana Rabba, and there they would bless the entire House of Israel in every country, all its communities, elders, patrons, and all who remember Jerusalem and place it upon their heart – they will all be remembered there in prayers and blessings."

The Struggle for the Right to Pray at the Western Wall ››

Shown here is a typical Western Wall scene witnessed over the course of many centuries: A handful of worshipers at the holy site...

Over time, the Arabs tried to oust the Jews not only from the Temple Mount, where they absolutely forbade Jewish entry, but also from the Western Wall. A notable struggle for the right to pray at the Wall took place between 1929 and 1932, during the period of British mandatory rule. The British established a special commission of inquiry to determine the respective prayer rights of the Jews and Moslems. The main responsibility for presenting the Jewish position fell on the shoulders of Rabbi Abraham Isaac Kook, the chief rabbi of the Holy Land. Among other restrictions, the Muslims wished to ban benches for sitting, a partition between men's and women's sections, and shofar-blowing on *Rosh Hashanah* and the end of *Yom Kippur*. These baseless demands instigated the riots of 1929 in which hundreds of Jews were killed across the country, and which led to the destruction of the Jewish community in Hebron.

While other public officials succumbed to the heavy international pressure and agreed to compromise on Jews' rights to pray at the Western Wall, Rabbi Kook insisted on the eternal Jewish rights to the remnants of their Holy Temple, and indeed, this ultimately safeguarded the rights of Jews there for many years.

Introduction

Our generation has merited something that countless generations before were not privileged to see: After nearly two millennia the Temple Mount is once again under the control of the Jewish People. The question of renewing the service in the Temple has become a very practical question and a topic for discourse in many sectors of the public. Young and old debate the issue in Torah study halls, scholars write about it in Israel and abroad, and the question of the Holy Temple in contemporary life has once again become a focal point in the public arena.

The classic halakhic literature on Temple matters is far-ranging and vast, and perhaps the most significant contributor to it is Maimonides – the greatest Posek (adjudicator) of Jewish Law since the redacting of the Talmud. Maimonides is the central pillar on which stands the entire structure of Jewish Law of the priestly service in the Temple. No other authority in history has shown such prowess in maneuvering among the complexities of these halakhic issues and determining the final law.

The pictures and paintings in this work essentially reflect Maimonides' halakhic positions, integrating other sources when necessary. The following chapter, which deals with the Temple in modern times, focuses on the Rambam's opinion on the question of building the Holy Temple today.

In his classic work on the 613 Commandments, Maimonides lists as #20 that of building the Holy Temple – which he describes as a mitzvah that is "binding for all generations." He further writes that we are "commanded to build a Sanctuary to serve [God], in which we are to offer sacrifices, burn the eternal flame, offer our prayers, and congregate for the festivals each year, as is written, "Make a sanctuary for Me" (Exodus 25:8) . . . We thus see that building the Sanctuary is counted as a distinct mitzvah, [though] it includes many parts: the Menorah, the Table, the Altar, and others are all parts of [this commandment]."

Maimonides further wrote (*Beit HaBechira* 6:15) that even when the Temple has not yet been built, it is still incumbent upon us to offer sacrifices on the altar there: "Thus, all the sacrifices are offered even if the Temple is not built."

The following chapter illustrates and brings to life various aspects of the Temple, based on the work and projects of The Temple Institute. The objective is to prepare the priests, and all of Israel, to begin performing the Temple service as soon as it becomes possible.

A team of scholars in the Temple Institute deals with clarifying the practical questions of building the Temple, how to execute the Torah's commandments regarding Temple activities, and how to carry out Maimonides' rulings in practice.

The reader of this book will be able to learn, in a concise manner, the practical aspects of building the Temple in our generation. These include: How to fashion the Menorah, table, and basin; how to make the garments for a simple priest, and the special ones for the High Priest, and how to use new technologies for this purpose; and more.

The reader will also learn of the plans and designs, compiled by Torah scholars and architects of the Temple Institute, for the construction of the various wings and sections of the Temple, using state-of-the-art planning and construction methods.

This chapter also includes details of the altar built in the Institute, and how it can be dismantled and rebuilt easily and quickly. This will enable its quick delivery and assembly in the Holy Temple so that the sacrificial service can be performed as promptly as possible.

Some of the pictures in the upcoming chapter focus on the Temple Institute's "School for Priests," where priests who are Torah scholars train for the various Temple services: the Passover offering, the wine and water libations, and more. The priests wear vestments woven and sewn especially for them, and they in general prepare themselves in practical ways for the renewal of the full Temple service.

Readers who wish to delve deeper into these subjects can enjoy the wide range of Temple Institute literature, where many concepts and topics covered here in brief are dealt with more extensively. The Institute is also preparing an encyclopedia of 1,000 entries on an exhaustive array of Temple topics. The "Holy Temple Scroll" will cover in depth the range of issues associated with the Beit Hamikdash, with the addition of many Rabbinic sources from the period of the Mishna and later.

One of the halakhic foundations on which Maimonides relies for his rulings regarding the Temple is that which he wrote in *Iggeret HaShemad*: "The performance of the commandments is not dependent on the coming of the Messiah. Rather, we must perform them to the best of our ability [under all conditions]. Once we fulfill our obligations, then if God grants us or our descendants the right to see the Messiah – that will be even better, but if not, we have not lost anything, but have rather profited by fulfilling our obligations."

That is to say, Jews are always obligated to carry out the Torah's commandments, even if the Messiah does not come in a given generation. How fortunate will be the generation that will be allowed to welcome the Messiah, but this is not a factor in our timeless commitment to fulfill the commandments in the Torah.

In the Temple Institute, we attempt to hang onto the coat tails of Maimonides' cloak, we do what we can to prepare for the onset of the Temple service. He Who brought the People of Israel to the Land of Israel and to the sacred courtyards, He will bring about – today, or tomorrow, or the next day – the restoration of the priestly service in the Holy Temple, and we will soon see priests and Levites and Israelites fulfilling their various functions in the Temple. Amen.

The Menorah Today: One Piece of Pure Gold

This the Menorah fashioned in the Temple Institute, plated with a *kikar* (a talent, 43 kilograms) of pure gold. The gold underwent a process known as electrolysis, in which it is broken down into its basic elements, and can thus uniformly plate the structure of the Menorah and fulfill the requirement of "one piece." The process was overseen by the artist Chaim Odem, and completed with the help of other artists and workshops.

The preparations for forming the Menorah involved vast research and study of the many details of the Menorah, such as the branches and their shape; the base and its form; the lamps and holders and their special shapes; the various adornments mentioned in the Torah, including the cups, buttons and flowers; and of course the process of "one-piece" assembly.

Making the Menorah is a positive commandment of the Torah. This Menorah, kosher for use, is publicly displayed by the Temple Institute, ready to be lit as soon as the Holy Temple is rebuilt.

‹‹ Liberating the Temple Mount

Rabbi Shlomo Goren, together with other top Israel Defence Force commanders, is seen here arriving at the Temple Mount on the day Jerusalem was liberated, the 28th of Iyar 5727 (June 8, 1967). The IDF Chief Rabbi Shlomo Goren is carrying a Torah scroll and blowing a shofar, in fulfillment of the Torah command to sound the trumpet during wartime. This blast echoed throughout the Jewish world, heralding the approaching footsteps of the Messiah.

When the first IDF soldiers set foot on the Temple Mount, this was an act with profound halakhic significance for coming generations. As of that moment, the People of Israel had an obligation to fulfill all the commandments concerning the Temple. Some 22 centuries earlier, the Hasmoneans faced the same situation: As soon as they returned to the Temple that had been desecrated by the Syrian Greeks, they began fulfilling all of the commandments practiced on the Temple Mount, such as building the altar, lighting the Menorah, and restoring the routine of Temple service as it had been carried out in days of yore.

‹‹ Fashioning the Menorah

This picture illustrates one of the possibilities for fashioning the Menorah, as the Torah commands, out of a single piece of gold. Two identical 4-meter molds are prepared, one for each half of the Menorah, into which molten gold is poured. The two halves are then brought together, and the gold hardens into the required one piece. (Proposed by the artist Chaim Odem.)

The Music of the Levites in the Temple ››

This is one of the young Levites wearing the garments of the Levites. In the school for priests and Levites "Nezer Hakodesh" there are classes for both priests and Levites, teaching singing and playing musical instruments.

The Altar for the Burnt Offering

Seen here is the large altar as built by the Temple Institute, where it is currently on display. The bricks for the altar are made of clay heated to a temperature of nearly 1,000 degrees Centigrade, strengthening them to withstand the altar's intense heat. At the foot of the ramp are whole rocks brought from Bik'at Beit HaKerem – the place cited by the Mishna (*Middot* 3:4) as the source for the altar's rocks.

Clearly seen in back of the ramp are the corners and foundation of the altar. The entire altar is to be plastered; the altar is seen partially plastered in a light color.

The altar is five cubits square, the same size as the altar built by Moshe in the desert, and the required size for the offering of sacrifices (*Zevachim* 62a; Maimonides, *Beit HaBechira* 2:17). On the ramp are two of the altar tools: a three-pronged fork, and the *pesakhter* for removing the ashes from the altar. On top of the altar is seen the silver cup used for the wine libations.

Building the altar is a positive commandment of the Torah. This altar, kosher for use and easily disassembled and reassembled, is being stored at the Temple Institute, ready to be transported and assembled for use when the Holy Temple is rebuilt.

The Priestly Headband ››

This is the sacred golden *tzitz*, worn by the High Priest upon his forehead. It is two fingers (some five centimeters) wide, and the words *Kodesh LaHashem*, Holy unto God [the Tetragrammaton is written out], are inscribed upon it. A flower adornment is seen on top at the right, as described by Josephus. The front is called the *tzitz* (Exodus 28:36), while the back is known as the *nezer hakodesh* (29:6), the sacred plate; the latter is attached to the *tzitz* and helps secure it in place on the forehead.

‹‹ Learning to Light the Menorah in the Temple

Yehoyada is a priest practicing the removal of the ashes and the lighting of the candles on the Menorah with seven branches. At the time of the lighting the blessing is: "who blessed us with the sanctity of Aaron and commanded us to light the Menorah."

Blasting the Trumpets for the *Tamid* Offering ››

Young priests from the division known as the "Mikdash Youth" of the Temple Institute are blowing trumpets as part of training for the *Tamid* offering and the candle lighting in the Temple.

Modern Planning for the Sanctuary

This is a modern architectural design of the Sanctuary, prepared for the Temple Institute by the architect Rabbi Shmuel Balsam. The Sanctuary Gate can be seen at right-center, opposite the Large Gate with its golden doors. On the right is a marble table, on which the showbread will be placed when it is brought into the Sanctuary. In the foreground on the right appears the northern "narrow" entrance, through which the priests enter the Sanctuary each morning. Also seen is the chain in the Sanctuary, upon which the young priests would climb to see the adornments on the Sanctuary wall.

Towards the back, further inside the Sanctuary, can be seen the golden table on which the showbread is placed on its way out. The southern "narrow" entrance and windows in the southern wall can also be seen; here knives that have become unfit for use are placed.

The plan shown here is precise and practical – one of several commissioned by the Temple Institute for various parts of the future Holy Temple. Plans have been drawn up for the various chambers, gates, and courtyards – all for immediate implementation when the time arrives for the Jewish People to build the Beit Hamikdash.

The Priestly Blessing ››

Students from the school for priests "Nezer Hakodesh" established by the Temple Institute, are performing the priestly benediction raising their hands according to the special laws for doing so in the Temple.

Training to Prepare the Candles ››

A student from the school for priests "Nezer Hakodesh" practices removing the ashes. The priest then pours olive oil into the candles and puts in fresh wicks for the afternoon *tamid*.

The Chamber of Hewn Stone ››

Seen here is a three-dimensional portrayal of the *Lishkat HaGazit*, the seat of the Sanhedrin, planned by the architect Rabbi Shmuel Balsam. Seats for the 71 judges are arranged in a semicircle, with a "cathedra of gold" before them, as stated in the Talmud (*Sukkah* 51b). Special seats are reserved for the President and Head of the Court, while in the galleries are seats for students and others who wish to hear and study the halakhic rulings of the Sanhedrin.

Making the Priestly Vestments

This workshop is where the priestly garments are woven. The owner is learning the relevant laws from a team of Temple Institute scholars. He was also trained to weave the garments in a criss-cross fashion, and of course to have constantly in mind that his work is in fulfillment of the command to fashion priestly garments.

Specifically, here is where the fabrics are made for the young priests from the Institute's School for Priests, where young men of priestly descent study the laws and prepare to carry out the Temple service when the time comes. Dozens of priests have purchased these clothes, tailor-made to fit them; these garments are kept in their homes, ready for immediate use.

The Ordinary Priest's Garments ››

This is a photo of one of the Temple Institute exhibits, showing a priest wearing the four "ordinary" priestly garments. (The High Priest wears a total of eight garments: the four "ordinary" ones, and four others.) The weaving is done here on a special machine; the spinning and interweaving were carried out earlier in designated workshops. All activities are carried out expressly for the sake of the Torah's commandment and the Holy Temple.

Dozens of sets of priestly vestments have been made in this manner, for the dozens of priests around the country who have purchased them and keep them ready and waiting for the day when they will be necessary. As the Talmudic Sage Rabban Yochanan ben Zakkai taught, "The Temple will speedily be rebuilt" – and we must be prepared!

‹‹ The New Copper Laver

This laver, on display in the Temple Institute, enables 12 priests to wash their hands and feet simultaneously. It was hand-fashioned by Moshe Buchbut and his son Eyal, who then donated it to the Temple Institute.

The 12 faucets are based on the Mishna in *Yoma* (3:10), which says that a High Priest named Ben-Katin enlarged the laver and installed 12 faucets.

The laver has three parts. The bottom one is the stand, known as the *ken,* and on top of it is the receptacle for the water, with the faucets. The upper level is the *mukheni* (machine), which held water that, unlike the water in the more sacred receptacle, would not become impure merely by remaining there overnight. Water would drip into the laver from the *mukheni.*

The laver was adorned with many decorations. At the top is a crown fashioned by the artist Chaim Odem.

Musical Instruments on Display

This is the Temple Institute's display of musical instruments that are used in the Beit Hamikdash. The Levites would sing on the *dukhan* (platform) and play trumpets, harps, and lyres. In the center of the picture is a large lyre, with chords that sound unique tones.

Raising a Red Heifer

In this photograph there is a picture of the late Rabbi Mordechai Eliyahu and other rabbis during a visit to a farm in Mazkeret Batya where red heifers are raised. In the course of his visit, Rabbi Eliyahu – Chief Sephardic Rabbi of the State of Israel – reviewed various options for raising a special species of red heifers, so that red heifers would again be raised naturally in the Land of Israel. One possibility that he discussed was the import of frozen embryos of red heifers from abroad.

The overall objective is to fulfill the commandment of burning the red heifer on the Mt. of Olives, and of preparing the special ash mixture mandated by the Torah to purify those who have come in contact with a corpse.

The Menorah at the Temple Gates ››

The "Menorah of pure gold" that was taken into Roman captivity many centuries ago is now on proud display in rebuilt Jerusalem. It was ceremoniously installed to the sounds of silver trumpet blasts, just as those sounded during the times of the Torah and the Holy Temple.

The Menorah stands in what is known as the Jewish Quarter of the Old City of Jerusalem, opposite the site of the Holy Temple, waiting for the day that the People of Israel renew the Temple service and the priests of God will once again light its lamps, "as in the days of old and as in former years."

›› "Make a Sanctuary for Me" – in Modern Times

This painting shows the Third Temple as perceived by a contemporary artist using state-of-the-art tools. Cranes rise very high in the distance, and a train carries workers, boulders, and other materials to the construction site. On the right are engineers and contractors consulting with Torah scholars as to how to proceed with the work.

Ascending to the Temple ››

This futuristic picture shows visitors to the Holy Temple from all over the world, as prophesied by Isaiah (2:2): "The mountain of God's house shall be established atop the mountains . . . all the nations shall flow unto it." The visitors carry flags of their countries; some arrive by train, others by cable car – but all have the same goal: to worship God in His Temple and to study His Word, as the Prophet continues: "Many shall go and say, 'Let us go up to God's mountain . . . and He will teach of His ways and we will walk in His paths – for from Zion the Torah will go forth, and God's word from Jerusalem."

Isaiah (66:23) states: "It shall come to pass that on every new moon and every Sabbath, all flesh shall come to bow down before me, says God." The *Midrash* (*Yalkut Shimoni* 503) asks how it can be that everyone will come every month and every week? R. Levi answers: "In the future, Jerusalem will be like the Land of Israel, and the Land of Israel will be like the entire world. And how will people be able to come to the Temple from the ends of the world? The clouds will come and take them . . . The clouds will take them early in the morning to Jerusalem, where they will pray in the morning, and they will then return them to their homes. As is written (Isaiah 60:8): 'Who are these that fly like a cloud' – these are the morning clouds; 'and like doves to their cotes?' – these are those of the afternoon."

בית
המקדש

Glossary

Adam HaRishon – Adam, the first man created at the end of Genesis, Chapter 1.

Aliya L'regel – The Festival pilgrimage. Jewish people ascended to Jerusalem's Temple Mount 3 times annually for the major festivals – Passover, *Sukkot*, and *Shavuot*.

Amud HaAnan – A pillar of cloud that protected the Israelites during their desert journey (Exodus 13:22)

Amida – The standing prayer, known as the Shemoneh Esrei (lit. 18, for the 18 blessings it traditionally contained), recited thrice daily.

Avot DeRabbi Natan – contains ethical teachings that expound upon those found in tractate Avot.

Azara – Courtyard of the Temple

Bama (pl. *bamot*) – A private altar or extra-Temple altar. At various points of Jewish history these were allowed and encouraged, banned, or frowned upon.

Bazakh – A bowl.

Beit Avtinas – House of Avtinas, one of the chambers in the Temple, named for a family of priests who were experts at preparing the incense.

Beit Din – A Jewish court.

Beit HaChalifot – Chamber of Knives

Beit HaDeshen – the place of the ashes

Beit HaKaporet – Hall of the Ark Cover

Beit HaMikdash – The Holy Temple

Beit HaMoked – Chamber of the Hearth, where the priests would gather in preparation for their daily work.

Beit HaNitzotz – Chamber of the Flame, one of three central chambers in the Temple.

Beit HaSreifa – place of burning, a designated place outside the Temple where items to be burnt were brought.

Beit HaTekiya – the spot from which trumpet blasts were sounded each Friday to warn of the onset of Shabbat.

Bikkurim – first fruits, which were brought to the Temple as described in Deuteronomy, Chapter 26.

Chagiga – a Festival peace-offering

Chatat – A sin-offering

Cheil – rampart, a demarcation in the Temple beyond which certain people could not cross.

Cheshev – A band worn by the High Priest, described in Exodus 28.

Dukhan – platform

Ephod – An apron-like vestment worn by the High Priest, as described in Exodus, Chapter 28.

Eretz Yisrael – The Land of Israel

Etrog – A citron, one of the four species waved on the festival of *Sukkot*, as described in Leviticus, Chapter 23:40.

Even HaShtiya – The Foundation Stone, upon which the Ark in the Temple sat.

Ezrat Nashim – Women's courtyard

Geniza – Internment or repository for disposal of sacred items

Hakafa (pl. *hakafot*) – A circular procession that was part of the Simchat Torah or Hoshana festivities.

Hallel – Joyous singing of Psalms 113–118 on festivals.

Hak'hel – During *Sukkot* of the year following the Sabbatical Year, all of the Jews, including little children, gather in the Temple to hear the Torah read, as described in Deuteronomy 31:10–13.

Hatavat Hanerot – Removal of ashes from the lamps of the Menorah.

Heikhal – Sanctuary of the Temple

Hoshana – A willow branch, used on *Sukkot* either in place of the 4 species or in tandem with the 4 species. Also refers to the ceremony performed with that branch.

Hoshana Rabba – The seventh day of *Sukkot*.

Isaron (pl. *esronim*) – A measurement of about 2.5–4 liters

Kav – A measurement of volume of about 2.2 liters

Ketoret – incense

Kemitza – A handful, or the removal of a handful.

Kikar – a talent (43 kilograms) of pure gold

Kiyor – Basin

Korban Pesach – The Passover lamb offering.

Lechem hapanim – The showbread

Lishkat HaGazit – Chamber of Hewn Stone, where the Sanhedrin sat in the Temple.

Lishkat HaGolah – Chamber of the Exile, one of the water sources in the Temple.

Lishkat HaKorban – Chamber of the Offering, used to store the shekel coins donated and designated to purchase offerings.

Lishkat HaShekalim – Chamber of the Shekels, used to store the donated shekel coins.

Log – A measurement of about .5 liters.

Luchot – The tablets upon which the Ten Commandments were inscribed.

Lulav (pl. *Lulavim*) – The palm frond used as part of the 4 species on *Sukkot*, as described in Leviticus 23:40.

Ma Nishtana – The 4 Questions asked as part of the Passover seder.

Machtah – Coal pan used in the Temple

Maneh – one hundred dinars (an ancient currency)

Marcheshvan – The 8th Hebrew month, which follows the holiday-filled month of Tishrei (*Rosh Hashanah*, *Sukkot*).

Melkachayim – tongs

Menachot – Meal-offerings (see Leviticus, Chapter 2).

Midrash – a collection of rabbinic teachings that offer complementary and supplementary interpretations of the Biblical text.

Mikveh – ritual bath

Mincha – A meal-offering (Leviticus, Chapter 2), or the afternoon prayer.

Minchat Chinukh – written by Rabbi Yosef Babad (1800-1874), as a commentary on a book of unknown authorship called Sefer HaChinukh, it offers the background explanations of the Talmud and its commentaries for each of the 613 Mitzvot.

Mishkan – The Tabernacle.

Mishmar (pl. *mishmarot*) – A priestly watch, or the members of a priestly watch.

Mishna (pl. *mishnayot*) – The first recorded version of the Oral Law, compiled around the 3rd century CE, which served as the foundation of the Talmud. It is split up into multiple different tractates on different topics.

Mishneh Torah –Code of Law of Maimonides (c. 1135-1204), carefully organized into different topics.

M'nakiyot – rods of gold

Moshe Rabbeinu – Hebrew for Moses, our teacher. The leader of the Jewish People who led the Jews out of Egypt through the desert to the edge of the Land of Israel and brought the Torah down from Mt. Sinai.

Mukheni – A mechanism or machine in the Temple, with differing views as to how it worked.

Murbiyyot – long willow branches.

Musaf – An additional offering, offered on various Jewish holidays.

Nesakhim – Libations (on the altar).

Nazir – A nazirite (Numbers 6:1–21).

Ne'ila – The closing prayer of the *Yom Kippur* service.

Nisan – The first month of the Hebrew calender, the month of Passover.

Nisukh hamayim – the water libation on *Sukkot*, as a water libation was poured onto the altar in addition to the wine libation that accompanied sacrifices throughout the year.

Olat Re'iya – burnt-offering of appearance in the Temple brought on the 3 Pilgrim Festivals.

Omer – the measure of barley brought as a communal offering on the 16th of Nisan.

Para Aduma – The red heifer, as described in Numbers, Chapter 19.

Parokhet – Curtain, separating the sanctuary from the Holy of Holies.

Pesach – Passover

Pesach Sheni – Second Pesach, takes place a month after Passover, allowing those who were ritually impure or too far from the Temple during Passover a second opportunity to participate.

Pesakhter – a bowl or device used to remove the ash from the Temple altar.

Rosh beit av – The head of a family of priests who are part of the same mishmar.

Rosh Chodesh – The new moon, or first of the new month.

Rosh Hashanah – The celebration of the Hebrew new year that takes place on the first of Tishrei.

Sanhedrin – The Jewish high court, which met in the Temple, comprised of 70 sages.

Se'a – a measurement of about 8 liters

Sefer HaMitzvot – The first section of Maimonides Mishneh Torah, which lists all 613 Mitzvot, split up into 365 negative commandments and 248 positive commandments.

Semikha – 1. Ordination, the transfer of rabbinic leadership and scholarship. 2. Placing hands on the head of an offering.

Shalmei Chagiga – a peace-offering of the festival

Shalmei Simcha – a peace-offering of rejoicing

Shabbat – Saturday, the Jewish day of rest.

Shavuot – Pentecost, or the feast of weeks, which takes place during the month of Sivan, exactly 7 weeks after the start of Passover.

Shelamim – peace-offerings (Leviticus, Chapter 3).

Shekel (pl. *Shekalim*) – coins collected in the Temple to purchase communal offerings and other causes.

Shekhina – The Divine Presence.

Shema – An important prayer recited multiple times a day, mentioning the acceptance of the yoke of heaven, many commandments, including the requirement to remember the exodus from Egypt. Consists of verses from Deuteronomy, Chapters 6 and 11 and Numbers, Chapter 15.

Shemini Atzeret – The holiday that immediately succeeds the festival of *Sukkot*, a day of great joy and festivities in the Temple.

Shir Shel Yom – Song of the Day, the song the Levites sang in the Temple for each day of the week.

Shofar – A ram's horn, blown on various occasions in the Temple, such as on *Rosh Hashanah* or to announce the onset of Shabbat.

Shtei HaLechem – the two loaves, i.e., the public offering on *Shavuot* of two loaves from the new wheat crop.

Shulchan – The table in the Temple on which the showbread sat.

Shulchani – A money-changer.

Simchat Beit HaShoeva – Celebration of the Drawing of Water

Sivan – The third Jewish month, the month of the festival of *Shavuot*.

Soreg – the latticed gate of the Temple Mount.

Sota – A woman suspected by her husband of having been unfaithful. A ceremony to prove her innocence was performed in the Temple and is described in Numbers 5:11-31.

Sukkah (pl. *Sukkot*) – The temporary dwelling during the festival of *Sukkot*.

Sukkot – A festival taking place from 15–21 Tishrei, named for the temporary dwellings used during the festival.

Talmud – The oral law containing elucidation of the Mishnah, biblical verses, ethics, philosophy, history and customs, completed around the 6th century CE.

Tamid – daily offering

Tapuach – the pile of coals in the center of the altar.

Targum Yonatan – An Aramaic translation of the Prophets attributed to Jonathan ben Uzziel, a scholar from the time of King Herod.

Tekia – a shofar blast, especial a long continuous shofar blast.

Terua – a staccato series of shofar blasts.

Terumat HaDeshen – removal of the ashes from altar.
Tisha B'av – The 9th day of Av, a day of sadness on the Jewish calendar, commemorating many historic events including the destruction of the Temple.
Tishrei – The 7th Hebrew month, containing the holidays of *Rosh Hashanah* and *Sukkot*.
Tosefta – A collection of Oral Jewish law, often seen as supplemental to the Mishna.
Tzitz – The frontplate, one of the garments worn by the High Priest.
Ulam – Entrance Hall of the Temple.
Urim VeTummim – The Urim VeTummim (described in Numbers 28:27-30) was a breastplate and served as a medium through which the High Priest could communicate with God about important matters and receive guidance about the proper course of action. When a question was asked, certain letters on the breastplate became illuminated, providing the answer (*Yoma* 73a-b).
Yalkut Shimoni – An aggadic compilation on the books of the Bible.
Yom Kippur – The 10th of Tishrei, the Jewish day of atonement.

Tractates

Arakhin – primarily deals with the laws of valuations, based on the verses of Leviticus 27:1-8
Avoda Zara – primary deals with the laws of idol worship
Avot – contains ethical teachings from our Sages
Bava Kama – deals with the laws of damages
Bava Metzia – deals with the laws of property, especially lost and found property
Bava Batra – deals with the laws of contracts
Berakhot – deals with the laws of blessings and prayer
Bikkurim – deals with the laws of the first fruits, as described in Deuteronomy, Chapter 26.
Chagiga – deals with the laws of the Festivals, especially the Festival peace-offering.
Ketubot – deals with the laws of the marriage contract, but is a tractate known for having a little bit on many different topics.
Kiddushin – deals with the laws of marriage.
Ma'aser Sheni – deals with the laws of the second tithe.
Megilla – deals with the laws of the holiday of Purim as well as the laws of the Torah readings for different occasions.
Menachot - deals with the laws of the meal-offerings.
Middot – describes the measurements and provides descriptions of the various parts of the Temple.
Nazir – deals with the laws of the nazirite (Numbers 6:1-21).
Para – deals with the laws of the red heifer (Numbers 19).
Pesachim – deals with the laws of Passover.
Sanhedrin – deals with the laws and makeup of Jewish courts and rendering legal decisions.
Semachot – deals with the laws of mourning, eulogies, and burial.
Shabbat – deals with the laws of the Sabbath.
Shekalim – deals with the laws of the collection of shekel coins for the purchase of communal offerings and other details of daily Temple life.
Sota – the laws dealing with the ceremony of a wife suspected of having been unfaithful, as described in Numbers 5:11-31.
Sukkah – deals with the laws of the holiday of *Sukkot*.
Ta'anit – deals with the laws of fast days.
Tamid – deals with the laws of the daily offering.
Temura – deals with the laws of replacing an animal designated for an offering.
Yoma – deals with the laws of *Yom Kippur*.
Zevachim – deals with the laws of offerings.

Sections of Maimonides

Avodat Yom HaKippurim – deals with the laws of the *Yom Kippur* service
Berakhot – deals with the laws of blessings and prayer
Biat HaMikdash – deals with the laws of entering the Temple
Beit HaBechira – deals with the laws of the Temple

Bikkurim – deals with the laws of the first fruits, as described in Deuteronomy, Chapter 26
Issurei Mizbeach – deals with the laws of invalid offerings for the Temple altar
Kelei Hamikdash – deals with the various vessels and utensils in the Temple
Keriat Shema – deals with the recitation of the Shema prayer
Korban Pesach – deals with the laws of the Passover lamb offering
Lulav – The laws of the 4 species on *Sukkot*, as described in Leviticus 23:40.
Mamrim – deals with the laws of those who violate the Torah and/or disagree with the authority of the Sanhedrin and the Rabbis.
Ma'aseh Hakorbanot – deals with the laws of how to offer the various Temple sacrifices.
Mechusrei Kappara – deals with those whose actions rendered them liable to bring certain offerings to the Temple as a way of rectifying their sins.
Metamei Mishkav UMoshav – deals with the laws of those who are ritually impure and render other items ritually impure by sitting on them.
Nezirut – deals with the laws of the nazirite (Numbers 6:1-21).
Para Aduma – the laws of the red heifer (Numbers, Chapter 19).
Shabbat – deals with the laws of the Sabbath.
She'ar Avot HaTumot – deals with the laws of ritual impurity.
Shegagot – deals with the laws of the offering after an unwilling or unintentional sin.
Shemita VeYovel – deals with the laws of the Sabbatical Year and the Jubilee Year.
Sota – the laws dealing with the ceremony of a wife suspected of having been unfaithful, as described in Numbers 5:11-31.
Ta'anit – deals with the laws of fast days.
Temidin UMusafin – deals with the laws of the daily and additional offerings in the Temple.
Teshuva – deals with the laws of repentance.

Personalities

Gra – Rav Eliyahu ben Shlomo Zalman (1720-1797), also known as the Vilna Gaon, was an expert in Gemara, Halakha, and Kabbala. His rulings are incorporated in the standard practices and customs of many Jewish communities today. He also wrote a commentary on the Mishna and on the Torah. It is also believed that he translated math books into Hebrew or Yiddish.

Rosh – Rabbi Asher ben Yechiel (1250–1327) was born in Germany and died in Spain. His commentary on the Talmud is known for being systematic, being able to parse long talmudic passages, and being averse to unjustified leniency. His commentary appears in the back of most standard printings of the Talmud.

Rashi – Rav Solomon Ben Isaac (1040–1105) lived in France. He is considered the greatest commentary on the Bible and the Talmud, with his commentary serving as the basis for any serious study of either, and serving as the foundation for any subsequent commentary.

Maimonides – Rav Moshe Ben Maimon (1135–1204), also known as Rambam, lived in Spain and later Egypt, serving in the latter location as the royal doctor. He dealt with every area of Torah and organized it very methodically in his magnum opus, the Mishneh Torah. He also authored a commentary on the Mishna and The Guide for the Perplexed, a philosophic work.

Nachmanides – Rav Moshe Ben Nachman (1194–1270), also known as Ramban, lived in Spain, fleeing in his final days to the Land of Israel as the result of a religious disputation with a Christian scholar. He published a commentary on the Bible and on the Talmud.

Meiri – Rabbi Menachem Meiri (1249–c. 1310), was born in Perpignan (Catalonia/Barcelona). His commentary on the Talmud discusses each Mishna and the various discussions that are raised concerning each one, citing many other commentaries.

Lubavitcher Rebbe – Rabbi Menachem Mendel Schneerson (1902–1994), the leader of the Lubavitch sect of Jewry, was born in Russia but lived the majority of his life in Brooklyn. With over 300 books of published teachings and disciples in countries across the globe, his work continues to exhibit vast influence on the Jewish world.

Rabbi Meir Simcha HaCohen (1843–1926) – was born in Lithuania and later served as the rabbi in Dvinsk. He served in that position for 39 years until his death. He is best known for writing Or Sameach, a commentary on Maimondies' Mishneh Torah, as well as Meshech Chochma, a commentary on the Torah.

Rabbeinu Bechayei – Rabbi Bahya ben Asher ibn Halawa (1255–1340) lived in Spain and wrote a commentary on the Bible.

Rabbi Yosef Kapach – Rabbi Kapach (1917–2000) was a Yemenite-Israeli authority on Jewish law known for his editions and translations of the works of Maimonides.

Rabbi Menachem Zemba – Rabbi Zemba (1883–1943) was a distinguished rabbi in Warsaw whose life was tragically cut short when he was killed by the Nazis.

Rabbi Tzvi Hirsch Kalischer – Rabbi Kalischer (1975–1874) lived in Prussia and was very active in the Jewish community there. His book Drishat Tzion espoused his views about the need to buy and cultivate land in the Land of Israel.

Baron Rothschild – Baron Rothschild was a well-known Jewish financier who lived in the United Kingdom in the 18th century. He was the first Jewish member of the House of Lords to not have previously converted to Christianity.

Radbaz – Rabbi David ben Zimra (1479–1573) lived in Egypt, and he is the author of a commentary to Maimonides' Mishneh Torah.

Rabbi Ovadia of Bartenura – Rabbi Ovadia of Bartenura (c.1445–c.1515) lived in Italy and later Jerusalem, and is known for his commentary on the Mishna, often referred to in shorthand as "The Bartenura."

Rav Hai Gaon – Rav Hai Gaon (939–1038) was the leader of a Talmudic academy in Pumbedita.

Rabbi Abraham Isaac Kook – Rabbi Kook (1865–1935) was the first Chief Rabbi of British Mandatory Palestine, and he wrote and spoke about the importance of the Western Wall and Temple Mount as holy sites of the Jewish people.

Rabbi Shlomo Goren – Rabbi Goren (1917–1994) lived in Israel and served as the first Chief Rabbi of the Israel Defense Forces and the third Chief Rabbi of Israel. Due to his role with the IDF, he was able to be present to blow a shofar on the Temple Mount when Israel reunited Jerusalem in 1967.

Rabbi Mordechai Eliyahu – Rabbi Eliyahu (1929–2010) was the Sephardi Chief Rabbi of Israel from 1983-1993.